T0301346

Housing Wealth and Welfare

NEW HORIZONS IN SOCIAL POLICY

Series Editors: Patricia Kennett and Misa Izuhara, *University of Bristol, UK*

The *New Horizons in Social Policy* series captures contemporary issues and debates in social policy and encourages critical, innovative and thought-provoking approaches to understanding and explaining current trends and developments in the field. With its emphasis on original contributions from established and emerging researchers on a diverse range of topics, books in the series are essential reading for keeping up to date with the latest research and developments in the area.

Housing Wealth and Welfare

Edited by

Caroline Dewilde

Department of Sociology, Tilburg University, the Netherlands

Richard Ronald

Centre for Urban Studies, University of Amsterdam, the Netherlands

NEW HORIZONS IN SOCIAL POLICY

Edward Elgar
PUBLISHING

Cheltenham, UK • Northampton, MA, USA

Published by
Edward Elgar Publishing Limited
The Lypiatts
15 Lansdown Road
Cheltenham
Glos GL50 2JA
UK

Edward Elgar Publishing, Inc.
William Pratt House
9 Dewey Court
Northampton
Massachusetts 01060
USA

A catalogue record for this book
is available from the British Library

Library of Congress Control Number: 2016953919

This book is available electronically in the **Elgar**online
Social and Political Science subject collection
DOI 10.4337/9781785360961

ISBN 978 1 78536 095 4 (cased)
ISBN 978 1 78536 096 1 (eBook)

Typeset by Servis Filmsetting Ltd, Stockport, Cheshire
Printed and bound by CPI Group (UK) Ltd, Croydon, CR0 4YY

Contents

Figures

Tables

Contributors

Bo Bengtsson is Professor of Political Science at the Institute for Housing and Urban Research, Uppsala University (Sweden) and the Department of Urban Studies, Malmö University (Sweden). Starting with his PhD thesis *Housing: Market Commodity of the Welfare State* (1995), he has published a large number of books and articles on Swedish and comparative housing policy and politics, on integration policy and politics, on the role of civil society organizations in housing and integration and on case study methodology. He is a member of the editorial board of *Housing, Theory and Society* and an honorary professor at Heriot-Watt University in Edinburgh (Scotland, UK).

Sandra Buchholz is Professor of Sociology at the Otto Friedrich University Bamberg (Germany). Before, she served as a research scientist in various international comparative research projects. Her research focuses especially on how national institutions and cultures influence the structure and development of social inequalities and individual life courses. She has published several articles and books on this topic.

Caroline Dewilde is Associate Professor at the Department of Sociology, Tilburg University (the Netherlands). Her main research interests concern the dynamics of inequality and poverty at different levels of analysis, from the individual life course to the welfare state, from a cross-national perspective. She has published in a range of (inter)national journals and books across the social sciences. In 2011, Caroline received a European Research Council (ERC) Starting Grant for the HOWCOME project (www.tilburguniversity.edu/howcome). The project analyses changes in economic and social inequalities and housing regimes and the interplay between these, in particular the increase in owner-occupation, during the postwar period.

John Doling is Emeritus Professor at the University of Birmingham (UK). He has researched and published widely in a number of related fields, principally housing markets and housing policy, in addition to population change and welfare systems. His main focus of attention has been on Britain and other advanced industrialized countries in Europe, North America and the Asia Pacific Region. He has undertaken research and consultancy funded by a variety of organizations including the United Nations (UN), the European Union (EU), the UK Government, research councils and foundations.

Theodore P. Gerber is Professor of Sociology and Director of the Center for Russia, East Europe, and Central Asia, University of Wisconsin–Madison (US). He conducts research on social stratification, demography, public opinion and related topics in Russia and other former Soviet countries.

Kathrin Kolb is Research Scientist at the Otto Friedrich University Bamberg (Germany), where she is engaged in various international comparative research projects. Her main research interests lie in the areas of life courses, education, housing, social inequality and wealth inequality.

Stephan Köppe is Lecturer in Social Policy at the School of Social Policy, Social Work and Social Justice, University College Dublin (Ireland). His research focuses on the public–private nexus of welfare finance and provision. He has published on welfare markets in the areas of private pensions, school choice and welfare users, as well as on housing wealth and intergenerational transfers.

Christian Lennartz is a postdoctoral fellow at the Amsterdam Institute for Social Science Research (AISSR), University of Amsterdam (the Netherlands). His main research interests and areas of publication are housing systems and welfare states, the political economy of housing, housing and family relations, housing careers of younger adults, and comparative social research.

Srna Mandič is Associate Professor at the Faculty of Social Sciences and Head of the Centre for Welfare Studies, University of Ljubljana (Slovenia). She has served as a member of the Group of Experts on access to housing at the Council of Europe, as member of the Coordination Committee of the European Network for Housing Research (ENHR) and as Chair of the Council for the Protection of Tenants' Rights of the City Council of the City of Ljubljana. Her research interests include housing, quality of life, demography and welfare. Recent publications are 'Decisions to renovate: identifying key determinants in Central and Eastern European post-socialist countries' (2013, *Urban Studies*) and 'Housing conditions and their structural determinants: comparisons within the enlarged EU' (2012, *Urban Studies*).

Maja Mrzel is a researcher at the Faculty of Social Sciences, University of Ljubljana (Slovenia). Her field of research primarily focuses on social networks and social support. Since 2009 she has been a member of different national projects and research groups covering quality of life, intergenerational solidarity, care for the elderly, sexuality and intimate lifestyles of the young. Her main focus remains on social science methodology.

Michelle Norris is Head of the School of Social Policy, Social Work and Social Justice, University College Dublin (Ireland). She has researched and published widely on social housing management and finance, as well as urban regeneration in Ireland and Europe. Her latest book, *Social Housing, Disadvantage and Neighbourhood Liveability*, was published by Routledge in 2014. She is co-conveyor of the European Network for Housing Research working group on comparative housing policy. She advises the Irish Government on housing policy issues and is a member of the National Economic and Social Council, which advises the Irish Government on social and economic policy. She also chairs the Housing Finance Agency, which finances housing for low-income households in Ireland.

Richard Ronald is a professor at the Centre for Urban Studies, University of Amsterdam (the Netherlands) and in the School of Social Policy at the University of Birmingham (UK). His research focuses on housing in relation to social, economic and urban transformations in Europe and Pacific Asia. He has held Japan Foundation as well as Japan Society for the Promotion of Science Fellowships at Kobe University (Japan) and has been a Visiting Professor at Kyung Hee University (Seoul, South Korea) as well as at the Asia Research Institute, National University of Singapore. He is currently Editor-in-Chief of the *International Journal of Housing Policy*. In 2011, Richard received an ERC grant in support of the HOUWEL project (www.houwel.uva.nl), investigating the role of family-held housing property wealth in shaping welfare relations and regimes.

Hannu Ruonavaara is Professor of Sociology and Head of the Department of Social Research, University of Turku (Finland). In recent years his research has focused on the retrenchment of Finnish housing policies, methodology of comparative–historical social and political research, neighbour relations and actor-centred social theory. He has published English-language articles on housing tenure, owner-occupation, home ideology, self-building, process tracing, housing equity and other topics in major housing studies journals as well as in edited books. He is the present editor of *Housing, Theory and Society*.

Beverley A. Searle is Senior Lecturer and Head of Geography at the University of Dundee (Scotland, UK). Her research interests combine long-term trends in subjective wellbeing and social welfare with concerns around housing inequalities and intergenerational transfers. A particular focus has been on the changing role of housing wealth as a substitute for publicly provided welfare.

Adriana Mihaela Soaita is a Romanian chartered architect and planner with a prolific portfolio of residential and commercial projects undertaken over two decades. Her postgraduate academic inquiry has been inspired by the encounters with the people for whom she designed; their narratives aroused her fascination with the multiplicity of meanings attached to housing. This lead her to undertaking a PhD in Housing Studies at King's College, London (UK) (awarded in 2011) and a period of postdoctoral research at the University of St Andrews (Scotland, UK) and Tilburg University (the Netherlands). As an interdisciplinary social scientist, Adriana is interested in research receptive to cultural patterns and social stratification in the fields of human geography, housing and urban studies, the built environment and post-communist change.

Jardar Sørvoll is a Senior Housing Researcher at NOVA, Oslo and Akershus University College of the Applied Sciences (Norway). His main research interests include housing policy in the Nordic countries, housing in the ageing society and comparative history. Sørvoll's PhD dissertation is an analysis of the politics of cooperative housing in Norway and Sweden between 1945 and 2013. His research has also appeared in the journals *Housing, Theory and Society* and *The International Journal of Housing Policy*.

Alison Wallace has been a research fellow with the Centre for Housing Policy, University of York (UK) since 2001 and a Churchill Fellow since 2016. She has undertaken a range of projects for various UK government, third-sector and private funders, including the Department of Communities and Local Government, the Joseph Rowntree Foundation, Office of the First Minister and Deputy First Minister Northern Ireland and Lloyds Banking Group. These projects concern new housing supply, poverty and home ownership, sustainability of residential and buy-to-let markets, the limits and potential of shared ownership and self-build housing. Previously a social housing practitioner for many years, she completed her doctoral research into the cultural economy of local housing markets in 2007.

Jane R. Zavisca is Associate Professor of Sociology and Associate Dean for Research in the College of Social and Behavioral Sciences, University of Arizona (US). Her areas of expertise include housing stratification, policy and politics in the former Soviet region, as well as the cultural meaning of mortgages in the United States.

Preface

Despite its obviousness, or maybe exactly because of it, home ownership and the asset it represents have not been a central object of study in either the economic or social sciences. In the last decade or so this has begun to change. In part, this shift lies with the Global Financial Crisis and its association with the 'irrational exuberance' in mortgage lending and housing speculation that preceded it. It also resonates with shifting global economic conditions in the post-crisis era and, in particular, the role that residential real estate markets (especially urban ones) appear to have assumed as a means to store wealth, not only for owner-occupying households but also for investment companies and equity funds. Housing property has also become an important target of the internationally footloose capital of both high-net-worth individuals and the super-rich. This volume attempts to sketch a particular picture of the state of housing wealth that reflects the historic rise of private home ownership and the dynamics of housing markets and policies under contemporary neoliberalism. Our specific focus is the relationship between housing, housing wealth and welfare.

While housing and welfare have always been connected – either as a source of wellbeing or as a form of social or fiscal welfare policy – this relationship has been deeply altered by the increased centrality of housing wealth (typically via owner-occupied housing) for economies, governments and households. At the same time, processes of commodification and housing financialization in recent decades have been uneven across institutional contexts in terms of the depth of change and specific manifestations. All chapters in this edited volume seek to explore these new, more complex interactions between housing, housing wealth and welfare across a diverse range of historic, social and economic contexts. Processes of welfare state restructuring and rollback have now spread beyond the liberal English-speaking nations to also include a cluster of Northern European countries historically more wedded to the principles of universality and equality in social and economic policy. In most English-speaking societies, the accumulation of private debt (and equity) through mortgages has been an important means in the realignment of welfare relations, as households have turned to housing property in managing the redistribution of social risks from the state to the individual. In the latter group of countries, new patterns of inequality have also begun to creep in – in terms of increased stratification of debt, wealth and assets – with the privatization and commodification of housing also playing an important role.

Although Western and Northern European countries have undergone significant transformations regarding relationships between housing, housing wealth and welfare, it is important to not overgeneralize these processes. In Eastern Europe in particular, the lack of development in housing finance following privatization of state-provided housing, combined with the patchy evolution of welfare benefits and services during and since transition from state socialism, resulted in the redistribution of housing itself (and welfare in general), built around reciprocal relationships within the extended family. Such a trend, however, also has implications for the welfare and wellbeing of families, households and individuals, potentially giving rise to new inequities and inequalities regarding housing and welfare.

In the epilogue to this text, John Doling critically reflects on the main findings from the different chapters and how they advance our understanding of the temporally and spatially contingent relationships between housing, housing wealth and welfare. He also identifies a number of new challenges and limitations arising from the transformation of these relationships in recent times.

Many people have been helpful in making this book possible. Editorial assistance from Rinus Verkooijen was greatly appreciated, as was the support and patience of Edward Elgar staff. Most contributors have been involved in some way or another with the European Network for Housing Research (ENHR) Working Group on Homeownership and Globalization during the past years. In particular, the meetings in Paris (2014, hosted by Christian Tutin) and Bucharest (2015, hosted by Liviu Chelcea) were fertile grounds for the development of several chapters and for the formulation of our own ideas and research agendas. The editors also gratefully acknowledge funding from the European Research Council (ERC), which allowed them to establish their own research teams and to pursue their research on institutional and social change with regard to housing, housing wealth, welfare states, welfare and inequality. We are grateful to all who have engaged with our research projects at one time or another (Stéfanie André, Rowan Arundel, Oana Druta, Ilse Helbrecht, Christa Hubers, Justin Kadi, Christian Lennartz, Philipp Lersch, Aram Limpens, Lidia Manzo, Teresio Poggio, Karen Rowlingson, Adriana Soaita and Barend Wind). With both of our projects coming to a close, a final Conference on Housing Wealth and Welfare was organized in Amsterdam (May, 2016). This successful event helped further demonstrate that relationships between housing, housing wealth and welfare will continue to inspire (or should we say 'trouble'?) researchers and policymakers in the years to come.

Last but not least, we gratefully acknowledge John Doling's contribution to this edited volume and to our research careers in general. He has inspired us, and many others, to engage with research on housing wealth and welfare.

*Caroline Dewilde and Richard Ronald**

NOTE

* Caroline Dewilde's research was supported by the European Research Council (ERC Starting Grant HOWCOME, Grant Agreement No. 283615, www.tilburguniversity.edu/howcome). Richard Ronald's research was supported by the European Research Council (ERC Starting Grant HOUWEL, Grant Agreement No. 283881, www.houwel.uva.nl).

Abbreviations

ABW	asset-based welfare
AISSR	Amsterdam Institute for Social Science Research
ALMP	active labor market policies
ANOVA	analysis of variance
CEE	Central and Eastern European
CHESS	Comparative Housing Experience and Societal Stability (Survey)
EC	European Commission
EMF	European Mortgage Federation
ENHR	European Network for Housing Research
ERC	European Research Council
EU	European Union
FRG	Federal Republic of Germany
FRS	Family Resources Survey
GDP	Gross Domestic Product
GDR	German Democratic Republic
GFC	Global Financial Crisis
GSOEP	German Socio-Economic Panel
ISA	individual savings account
LTC	long-term care
MBS	Mortgage Backed Securities
MHCs	Municipal Housing Companies
MITR	Mortgage Interest Tax Relief
MPPI	Mortgage Payment Protection Insurance
OECD	Organisation for Economic Co-operation and Development
OFMDFM	Office of the First Minister and Deputy First Minister (Northern Ireland)
SDA	Small Dwellings Acquisition
SHARE	Survey of Health, Ageing and Retirement in Europe
SHER	Survey of Housing Experiences in Russia
SIS	Social Investment Strategy
UK	United Kingdom
UN	United Nations

1. Why housing wealth and welfare?

Richard Ronald and Caroline Dewilde

INTRODUCTION

The relationship between housing and wealth lies at the heart of contemporary forms of capitalism, especially its global, neoliberal incarnation (see, for example, Harvey, 2005). Residential property has increasingly become a target of global capital, but at the same time remains the primary container of household and family wealth. Indeed, global residential real estate is currently estimated to be worth approximately US$136 trillion, equivalent to around 60 per cent of global mainstream assets (Savills, 2016). At the same time, the distribution of housing wealth has undergone important transformations in recent decades. Until recently, the proportion of home owners has been expanding with, for example, more than 70 per cent home ownership across the European Union (EU) (Eurostat, 2015), up from average rates of less than 50 per cent in the 1960s (Doling and Ford, 2007). Initially, most home buyers accrued some form of housing equity along with sector growth, with housing largely functioning as a wealth equalizer. In recent decades, however, relative property value increases have become particularly uneven across income groups and social classes, age cohorts and geographic regions (for example, Hamnett, 1999; Wind et al., 2016), especially in the years leading up to and following the Global Financial Crisis (GFC). Economic shifts have furthermore altered meanings, preferences and practices surrounding housing, with the home increasingly understood as a commodity and subjugated to market over broader social interests.

The relationship between housing wealth and welfare has been less obvious (yet equally central) to social relations in capitalist economies. Traditional conceptions of housing and welfare focus on either the welfare state – in particular as a provider of shelter for vulnerable or low-income households through social rental housing (for example, Harloe, 1995) – or, more implicitly, on the promotion of (outright) home ownership as an effective 'pension in stone', reducing housing costs in old age (Kemeny, 1981; Castles, 1998). However, since the end of the last century it has become increasingly obvious that a broader conception of this relationship is necessary. Indeed, whereas housing was once considered the 'wobbly' pillar under the welfare state (Torgersen, 1987) and mostly ignored in comparative welfare regime and stratification research, there has been a growing realization that transformations in housing markets and assets have underpinned important shifts in wealth and welfare relations. These shifts necessitate a better understanding of the connections between housing and welfare as well as of variegation across institutional contexts. Such is the ambition of this text, which aims to reflect new light on past and present debates, identify new developments and develop conceptual tools for future research.

Specifically, in many contexts, the housing equity held by owner-occupiers has been eyed by governments and policy makers as not merely an enhancement of, but integral to, welfare self-provision across the life course and a means to compensate for diminishing public provision more generally (Malpass, 2008; Watson, 2010; Lowe et al., 2011). In a context of expansion in owner-occupation and house price inflation, households have also been increasingly orientated around their housing wealth as a means to boost their consumption and take care of their own welfare needs (Smith et al., 2009; Doling and Ronald, 2010; Wood et al., 2013). At the same time, however, growing dependency on property values and house price increases has created enormous vulnerability to economic fluctuations – as demonstrated by the GFC – and stimulated significant indebtedness and potential for inequality (Stephens, 2007; Schwartz and Seabrooke, 2008; Kennett et al., 2013; Rolnik, 2013). The central concerns of this book are, therefore, the emerging links between housing wealth and welfare practices and how they have been shaped in and by different social and economic settings. Each chapter questions in various ways how housing wealth has become so entangled with welfare conditions and in many cases has become a feature of socioeconomic inequality.

While traditional studies of welfare states and social stratification focus on income, employment and other kinds of assets, this volume shifts attention to housing wealth as a critical axis of social, economic and welfare practices in the twenty-first century. This introductory chapter establishes crucial historic junctions and processes, as well as the literature that has emerged to explain recent social, economic and political realignments around housing wealth. We ask why home ownership and property assets have become so prominent and explore the various links between housing and welfare. In doing so, this chapter provides an analytical lens for the nine substantive chapters and epilogue that follow.

We begin by considering how the owner-occupied home has been appropriated as a commodity in recent decades, with the function of shelter giving way to other meanings and uses, such as security, investment, asset accumulation, speculation and so on. We also address processes of finan- cialization that preceded and eventually culminated in the GFC, as well as how housing markets and property accumulation practices have since reasserted themselves. Our attention subsequently turns to the welfare role of housing property, moving away from traditional policy conceptions of housing as a service towards an understanding of household property equity as a source of wealth and income; that is, 'asset-based welfare'. Regardless of historic levels of marketization and deregulation, as this volume demonstrates, such conceptions and practices have been evident across economically liberal, corporatist and social-democratic societies alike in recent decades, serving to support welfare state retrenchment and the shift in responsibilities toward the market. Increasingly – and in an increasing diversity of countries – un-mortgaged home ownership has come to represent a particular kind of asset: a means of investment in an otherwise uncertain economic climate; a household asset enabling house- holds and families to redistribute resources as a means of mitigating new insecurities and inequalities; a resource that can be tapped in support of welfare or consumption needs that arise over the life course. Ultimately we address the implications of a growing welfare emphasis on housing wealth and assets – and in particular how this has restructured the potential for socioeconomic inequalities in different countries. The final section of this chapter turns to the structure of the book and the various contributions ahead.

HOUSING WEALTH

From Housing Services to Housing Commodities

In the postwar years, housing in the industrialized world, especially in cities, was primarily rented and not a particularly attractive commercial investment (see Harloe, 1995). Housing shortages had also become a spe- cific concern of nation states in the context of war damage to residential infrastructure, booming birth rates and ongoing decline in the private rental sector. In Western Europe, governments responded in a variety of ways, with the United Kingdom (UK), France, Germany, the Netherlands and Sweden, for example, deeply expanding public or social rental housing provision. The Keynesian model of public demand management provided workers with security through social policies, which in many countries often took the form of subsidized housing construction that also con- tributed to the growth of the economy. Owner-occupied housing also supported rebuilding and growth efforts, often with the assistance of government incentives and tax subsidies (Fahey and Norris, 2010). However, the oil crisis of 1973 and its economic consequences, combined with the transition to a more post-industrial service-led economy, exposed the limits to the growth of social policy and state-driven housing supply.

In the meantime, appetites for privately consumed housing had deepened, in part as an achievement of postwar affluence, while the role of markets in welfare service provision was enhanced (Spicker, 2014; Birch and Siemiatycki, 2015). In the UK and Ireland, for example, governments started to scale down social housing in the 1980s through 'right-to-buy' schemes (for example, Forrest and Murie, 1988), and reduced new social housing provision, instead catering for low-income households through a wider range of public, non profit and private intermediaries. 'Bricks and mortar' subsidies were replaced by demand (and increasingly means-tested) subsidies, with private landlords housing an increasing number of low-income households on housing allowances. Similar transfers of state–market responsibilities were later adopted in other Western European economies, such as Sweden (for example, Turner and Whitehead, 2002; Holmqvist and Magnusson Turner, 2014) and the Netherlands (for example, Priemus and Dieleman, 2002; Elsinga et al., 2008), as the logic of marketization began to take hold. Housing was a particularly vulnerable element of social policy and, unlike most other social services, markets remained influential to the provision and allocation of housing, with policies often correcting rather than replacing the market in ensuring broader access to decent and affordable housing (Bengtsson, 2001, 2012). At the same time, the growing, state-directed commodification of housing helped legitimize marketization in other areas of social provision and the broader undermining of the postwar welfare state (Forrest and Murie, 1988). In the 1990s, mass housing privatization also became critical to the overall restructuring of post-socialist Eastern European economies (see Mandič and Mrzel; Soaita; Zavisca and Gerber, this volume) and, after 1998, in the accelerated transition of China toward an urban, market-driven economy (Wu, 2015). In the EU, meanwhile, by the end of the century almost two-thirds of households were owner-occupying property owners (Doling and Ford, 2007).

The shift in policy from housing as a service to housing as a commodity typically marked a golden era in the expansion of housing markets and owner-occupancy rates. Market stimulation also contributed to the spread of household assets in the form of owner-occupied housing equity in an increasingly diverse range of societies. Housing and home ownership thus began to move from the periphery to the centre of economic policy, helping reposition the state, the market and individual households around the potential value – real and imagined – in the homes that most people, by that time, more or less owned.

Housing Financialization

Forrest and Hirayama (2015) describe a shift from a 'social' home owner-ship project, in which governments sought to expand private consumption of owner-occupied housing as a compensation for the deeper liberalization of the economy, to a more financialized 'neoliberal' project, in which prof-itmaking is central. In the case of the former, the aforementioned expan-sion of mortgaged owner-occupation and augmentation of housing assets were assumed to both integrate households into the market and provide an economic buffer. In terms of the latter, the increasing focus on and value of property aligned with the global expansion of credit and lending, as well as with the integration of housing and mortgage markets within a global neoliberal framework of rent seeking and wealth accumulation. Indeed, Schwartz and Seabrooke (2008, p. 210) identify a commensurable shift from an era in which housing assets were essentially 'inert, immobile and illiquid' to one in which homes became 'live, cashable and liquid'. Despite policy and rhetoric that sought to advance the tenure as a means to spread the distribution of assets security and social equity (Ronald, 2008) – and along with increasing flows of finance into the sector and escalating house prices – home ownership was transformed into a neoliberal project that subverted these social objectives in the 1990s and 2000s.

In the United States (US), the foundation of a Federal National Mortgage Association (Fannie Mae) in the 1930s introduced mortgage securitization as Mortgage Backed Securities (MBS), expanding the capac-ity of mortgage lending and, much later, facilitating the penetration of global capital via financialization into household borrowing for home buying (Bratt, 2012b). Financialization is a process in which market deregulation and reregulation allows global capital seeking ever-higher returns to colonize and dominate other economic domains. A specific practice is the realization of profitmaking 'through financial channels rather than through trade and commodity production' (Krippner, 2005, cited in Aalbers, 2008, p. 148). In the case of housing, deregulated mort-gage securitization in the 1980s expanded the interconnectedness of global capital and local housing markets. Local and tangible property assets were transformed into liquid, globally tradable financial MBS products, facili-tating extraordinary augmentations in lending and borrowing on property and subsequently house prices in the late 1990s and 2000s.

Both housing and mortgage markets beyond the US were increasingly influenced by, and subjugated to, an international architecture of financial growth built on credit and real estate. National mortgage and finance institutions similarly came to rely on market funds and interbank lending (as opposed to their deposit base) to finance domestic activities (European Central Bank, 2009). In this process, households were exposed to greater housing market risks such as indebtedness, interest rate fluctuations and house price volatility, as well as labor market risks (Stephens, 2007; OECD, 2011). It was inevitably the integration of subprime lending with mainstream securitization, along with a downturn in the US labor market, which triggered a chain of foreclosures that exposed macroeconomic vulnerability arising from the centrality of inflated housing assets in the global economy and culminating in the credit and ensuing economic crises. Even housing markets and economies that had remained relatively insulated from securitization and over-exuberance in borrowing and lending on homes were eventually pulled into the boom and bust in one way or another.

Post-GFC Housing Wealth

Depending on their economic blueprint and housing and welfare systems, the economic crisis took on a different form, with variegated consequences in each country (for example, Forrest and Yip, 2011; Fuentes et al., 2013; Waldron and Redmond, 2015). Although more households have faced employment risks and negative equity in countries with more strongly financialized housing finance systems, the relationship between risky household positions (for example, mortgage arrears and repossessions) and urgent welfare problems has been moderated by various factors. The size and generosity of the welfare system, as well as the existence of other protective arrangements, have been critical to this. In the Netherlands, for example, income support for the unemployed and protective measures against foreclosure (for example, Mortgage Guarantees) have softened the impact of house price deflation (see Ronald and Dol, 2011). In other contexts, the extent to which the speculative house price boom stimulated excessive house building and whether public deficits required the implementation of austerity packages (as in Spain and Ireland) have also been significant in amplifying the effects of the crisis (for example, Waldron and Redmond, 2015).

   In some countries, economic fallout was more contained and, in the years that followed, housing markets became even more speculative in a context of low interest rates and continued demand for owner-occupied housing (as in Sweden). Even in Germany, where house price growth had long been subdued, Kemp and Kofner (2014) have reported how the economic crisis has increased the attractiveness of residential property (in particular portfolios of private rental housing) as a safe haven for investment, especially among international investors. Global capital and finance again appears to be reshaping housing conditions. In the post-GFC context, however, this process has been more direct: in terms of the actual procurement of residential real estate rather than investment in securities. According to Savills (2016), cross-border residential property investment increased 334 per cent between 2009 and 2015. Within economies, cities have also reacted unevenly. Here, the UK is exemplary (also see Wallace, this volume); while house prices almost halved in Belfast (−47.2 per cent) between 2007 and 2015, in London they increased by around 44 per cent over the same period (Hometrack UK, 2015).

Although housing financialization was clearly identified as a root cause of the GFC, this seems to have done little to undermine state commitment to the promotion of home ownership or faith in it as a means to either stimulate the economy or enhance the security of households (see Ronald and Elsinga, 2012). At the macro level, economic growth in the pre-crisis era came to rely on the performance of housing markets and inflated asset values (see Schwartz, 2009). In the post-crisis context, governments have typically returned to this as a default assumption, and have now locked themselves into situations where they can do little to dissipate market over-heating or promote alternative tenures in such a way that access to decent and affordable housing remains safeguarded.

At the individual level, mortgaged owner-occupation, despite market volatility surrounding the GFC, has become strongly normalized, with the meaning of home – in the sense of haven – embedded with understandings of housing as a family asset or financial good (for example, Ronald, 2008; Naumanen and Ruonavaara, 2015; Poppe et al., 2015). As Smith (2015, p. 64) puts it, 'the functional and financial hybrid known as owner-occupation persists unquestioned as a cultural norm'. Decades of increasing home ownership along with ostensible long-term house price augmentation, in a context of intensified social and economic risk, has arguably contributed to the financialization of the self, reaffirming home owners as a key investor subject of neoliberalization (see Smith, 2008; Langley, 2010; Watson, 2010). New financial possibilities have changed households' management and consumption patterns in regard to their home, with many becoming more proactive in terms of accessing their housing assets (via equity release products and so on), or aggressive in terms of property accumulation and even landlordism[1] (Ronald et al., 2015). At the same time, as Wallace (this volume) shows in the case of Northern Ireland, not all home owners actively engage with their homes as financial assets; many low-income households prioritize the use-value, especially during economic downturns.

Another element of transformation in housing wealth has been the structure of outright, un-mortgaged home ownership. According to Eurostat (2015), among EU Member States, while seven in ten people live in an owner-occupied home, over one-quarter of the population dwell in a mortgaged home while more than two-fifths occupy a mortgage-free property (27.1 per cent compared to 43.0 per cent). Although the rate of mortgaged home ownership is higher in more financialized housing economies, with mortgage lending, as measured against gross domestic product (GDP), increasing up to the crisis, in many contexts house price advances have actually undermined this debt. Figure 1.1 provides an aggregated view

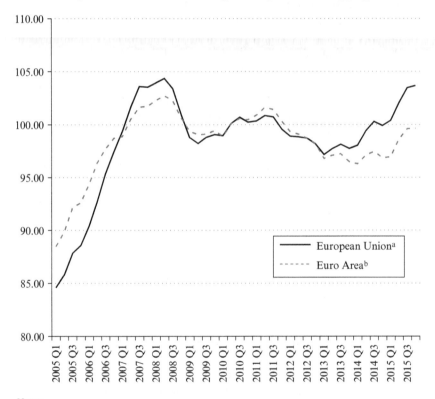

Notes:
a. European Union: EU6–1972, EU9–1980, EU10–1985, EU12–1994, EU15–2004, EU25–2006, EU27–2013, EU28.
b. Euro Area: EA11–2000, EA12–2006, EA13–2007, EA15–2008, EA16–2010, EA17–2013, EA18–2014, EA19.

Source: Eurostat (2015).

Figure 1.1   European house price index (2010=100)

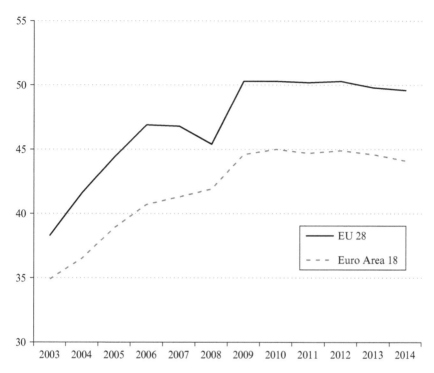

Sources: Hypostat sources listed (EMF, 2015): European Mortgage Federation National Experts, European Central Bank, National Central Banks, Eurostat, Bureau of Economic Analysis, Federal Reserve.

Figure 1.2   Total outstanding residential loans to Gross Domestic Product (GDP) ratio (%)

of house price developments. Although the crisis had a particular impact between 2008 and 2010, property values have typically been resilient, with a longer-term upward trend becoming more evident. Many countries – including Austria, Germany, Sweden, Norway and the UK, for example – have individually experienced value increases of more than 20 per cent since 2010 (see Table 1.1). Figure 1.2 meanwhile illustrates how house price recovery has not been led by a credit revival, with mortgage debt to GDP ratios remaining flat since 2009. The figures imply that recent house price increases represent a flow of capital from other domains to housing, feeding equity accumulation.

The balance of housing equity, however, is quite variegated across Europe (see Table 1.1). In Denmark and the Netherlands, the boom in home ownership was quite late and highly financialized, meaning

Table 1.1 Home ownership and related housing market characteristics across the EU around 2015 (%)

Country	Residential mortgage debt/GDP[a] (%)	House price change 2010-2015 (relative % change)[b]	Home-ownership rates[c] (%)	Home-ownership rates (%). Low-to-moderate income households (deciles 1-4)[c]	Outright home ownership (% of home owners)[c]	Outright home ownership (% of home owners). Elderly households (60+)[c]
Romania	6.70	-9.02	95.5	96.7	99.0	99.9
Bulgaria	8.30	-4.58	84.8	83.1	97.7	99.6
Slovenia	14.40	-15.90	75.3	68.0	89.6	97.9
Lithuania	16.40	20.78	91.3	88.7	93.4	99.8
Czech Republic	16.60	6.78	77.9	73.1	81.7	97.4
Hungary	16.60	6.29	88.5	85.5	82.2	95.0
Croatia	18.30	-10.80	88.9	88.5	97.6	99.7
Latvia	19.50	30.83	79.8	73.9	91.0	99.0
Poland	20.00	-4.52	81.4	75.3	89.0	98.8
Italy	22.20	-13.45	71.9	61.8	80.1	95.9
Slovakia	23.10	3.88	90.6	88.2	91.5	99.2
Austria	27.50	38.04	50.0	35.7	59.3	84.7
Estonia	31.10	59.85	76.5	72.3	81.6	98.8
Greece	38.80	–	72.8	69.6	82.9	91.9
Germany	42.40	21.72	44.5	29.0	55.6	82.3
France	43.30	3.90	61.0	44.7	62.4	93.6

Finland	43.70	7.90	67.3	52.0	51.9	83.8
Malta	45.40	8.75	76.6	68.7	77.8	99.7
Belgium	49.10	12.23	66.8	51.1	50.2	92.0
Ireland	49.40	−3.23	70.4	58.1	58.8	95.3
Luxembourg	50.70	26.02	69.0	50.4	46.3	92.6
Spain	55.40	−24.45	77.7	66.4	63.1	92.6
Portugal	59.20	−5.48	73.1	65.0	59.0	92.7
Cyprus	66.40	−11.79	66.4	52.5	76.1	98.5
Iceland	71.70	43.63	72.9	58.6	24.1	46.5
UK	75.00	27.70	63.5	49.5	51.8	89.8
Norway	75.80	34.96	77.1	60.1	29.5	57.5
Sweden	78.80	44.21	62.6	44.6	16.9	33.2
Netherlands	95.70	−8.78	56.4	34.1	14.9	35.4
Denmark	114.00	12.18	53.4	36.3	28.6	47.1

Sources: a. European Mortgage Federation, Hypostat (EMF, 2015); b. Eurostat (2015) (14 May 2016); c. EU–SILC (2013, own calculations, household level). EU–SILC data provided by Tilburg University.

residential mortgage debt to GDP ratios have continued to hover around the 100 per cent mark since the early 2000s. On the other hand, many Southern and Eastern European countries rely on family wealth to finance house purchases. In Italy, for example, mortgage debt still represents around one-fifth to one-quarter of GDP, while in Romania, just 1 per cent of home owners (who make up more than 90 per cent of households) are mortgaged (also see Soaita, as well as Zavisca and Gerber (for Russia), this volume). Table 1.1 also reveals how important home ownership and housing wealth are to the older population and across income categories in many countries; indeed, they are actually more prominent in less financialized contexts, particularly among lower-income households. Even though it is often pointed out that housing wealth in these less financialized contexts is also less accessible, house prices in these countries rose significantly, particularly during the period before the GFC and in urban settings. Furthermore, in these countries the housing–welfare link is of a qualitatively different nature (discussed later).

HOUSING AND WELFARE

In view of the growing prominence of housing wealth and its centrality to twenty-first-century socioeconomic transformations – specifically globalization and financialization – a broader 'political economy' perspective on housing has emerged (for example, Schwartz and Seabrooke, 2008; Aalbers, 2008; Aalbers and Christophers, 2014; Ansell, 2014), moving the spotlight from 'owner-occupation' as a source of shelter and stability to 'residential real estate' as an investment product, a store of housing wealth and a driver of economic and political change. Nonetheless, there has long been an awareness of the broader role of housing and housing wealth in the social structure. A specific point of reference has been the role of private housing assets in the restructuring of welfare relations as the traditional Keynesian social policy model has faded.

At an anecdotal level, Saunders (1990) alluded to this when he pointed out how the generation of his parents – lower-middle-class non-manual employees who started a family in the postwar years – managed to gain access to home ownership in the mid-1950s, and how they accumulated wealth in their home over time, which, based on labor market participation, they never could have otherwise achieved. Their unexpected housing wealth meant they were less dependent on either their income or the welfare state in satisfying their welfare needs, especially in later life. Kemeny (1981) and later others (Castles, 1998; Fahey, 2003; Dewilde and Raeymaeckers, 2008; Delfani et al., 2014) provided a more critical review of this process, focusing on the prevalence of home ownership and the accumulation of housing equity impacting on welfare structures, political relations and welfare outcomes.

Kemeny (1981) initially hypothesized that the expansion of the welfare state in countries with high levels of owner-occupation had been hampered by the frontloading in the family lifecycle of the costs of acquiring home ownership: the considerable financial means needed to purchase a house would compromise the willingness to accept the high tax burdens necessary to finance generous social transfers – in particular those benefiting the older population, most of whom are outright owners at retirement. Accounting for the comparatively low social spending in 'New World' English-speaking welfare states, Castles (1998) subsequently argued that widespread home ownership functions as a 'quasi' old-age insurance: home owners can get by on lower pensions because home ownership limits their housing costs in old age, hence, they do not press for more generous pensions. Essentially, this literature established an important country-level association (or so-called 'trade-off') between housing wealth and the structure and development of postwar welfare systems (in particular welfare state generosity in later life), but also failed to unravel the underlying dynamics and explanatory mechanisms.

Recent theoretical and empirical work has questioned a number of implicit assumptions with regard to the distributional outcomes of different housing–pension welfare mixes (Dewilde and Raeymaeckers, 2008) and its causality in terms of housing wealth driving retrenchment of pension provision (De Deken et al., 2012; Delfani et al., 2014). Contributions to the first part of this volume (that is, Norris; Bengtsson, Ruonavaara and Sørvoll; Lennartz; Köppe and Searle) equally challenge the idea that this relationship, or trade-off, can be formulated in causal or linear terms. They nonetheless continue to emphasize the relationship between housing wealth and welfare, but in terms of more embedded social and institutional arrangements surrounding housing regimes, welfare states and redistributive processes, mortgage and financial markets, politics, labor markets and family structures. They furthermore contribute to our understanding of the relationship between housing (wealth) and welfare (provision) by combining new interpretations of old debates with a reconceptualization of the main issues; for example, by recasting home ownership policies in some contexts as having predominantly redistributive goals, or by broadening the focus from pensions (which are notoriously hard to retrench) to other domains of welfare provision.

Critically, then, this volume seeks to move beyond the simple association between housing wealth and pensions and explores the more complex interactions between housing and welfare arrangements in different social and historic contexts. As we have argued from the beginning of this chapter, housing wealth appears to have not only expanded but also adopted a particular centrality in recent years, helping to forge important social, economic and political realignments that lie at the heart of contemporary social relations. Arguably, the most important of these are the restructuring of welfare regimes and decline of welfare states, the influence of housing markets on political dynamics and the subsequent emergence of new patterns of socioeconomic inequality, as we now consider in more detail.

Welfare Regimes

'Welfare' is an ambiguous term with various meanings and connotations. Within the context of advanced welfare states there is a consensus that 'welfare' equates to someone's wellbeing, which is determined not only by the fulfillment of basic needs (that is, physical survival), but also by the realization of life chances or capabilities (for example, Sen, 1983). The term 'welfare' is also often used to denote public systems of welfare provision,[2] in other words the 'welfare state' and its associated social services. More critically, the idea of 'welfare regime' has come to the fore since the early 1990s to explain how different 'types' of societies modify the distributional outcomes of (labor) markets. While notions of welfare regimes predate Esping-Andersen's 1990 work,[3] the original 'three worlds of welfare capitalism' he identified have since dominated comparative understandings of structures of inequality and wellbeing. Numerous authors have contributed to a diversification of this typology in response to critical differences in welfare arrangements (for example, Castles and Mitchell, 1993; Orloff, 1993, 1996; Arts and Gelissen, 2002; Gough et al., 2004; Scruggs and Allan, 2006; Hudson and Kühner, 2009). Housing was notably absent in early welfare regime constructions, but has – along with the changing nature of state provision and market consumption – become more prominent in explaining variations in welfare conditions and regime structures (see Hoekstra, 2003, 2010; Allen et al., 2004; Kurz and Blossfeld, 2004).

The alignment between welfare regimes and housing is by no means clear-cut. Housing systems in each society diverge in complex and meaningful ways, reflecting differences in organizing principles of housing provision, among other factors (for example, Barlow and Duncan, 1994). Well-known, concrete instances of such organizing principles pertain to the constitution of rental sectors in terms of dual or unitary (integrated) markets (Kemeny, 1995), the role of the (extended) family in housing provision (for example, Allen et al., 2004), and ways of promoting and financing home ownership (for example, Ronald, 2008). Kemeny (1992) initially posed housing and welfare regimes in countries such as the UK and Australia against those of Sweden and the Netherlands. In the former, the prevalence of home ownership and the structure of housing costs over the life course favored individualization, suburbanization and market-orientated welfare structures, while in the latter, widespread low-cost renting supported urbanization and more collectivized welfare practices.

While housing policies and practices remain highly differentiated, since the 1990s there has been growing international alignment in terms of housing financialization and property ownership (as discussed earlier). A specific way this transformation has been understood has been the advance of 'asset-based' welfare state restructuring. This describes a process in which individuals are encouraged to accept more responsibility for satisfying their own welfare needs by investing in financial products and assets that are expected to increase in value and be drawn upon in times of need. The term largely derives from Sherraden's (1991) approach to individual asset accumulation, in a broader sense, as a means to enhance personal capacity and as an alternative to welfare benefits. As housing assets became the main mode of asset accumulation in the late twentieth century, alongside the advance in property markets and values, asset-based welfare became increasingly manifest as a form of 'property-based' or even 'home-ownership-based' welfare (Doling and Ronald, 2010) and was more or less explicitly pursued in policy agendas (Watson, 2010).

Augmentations in housing wealth in different economies were thus increasingly associated with 'welfare switching' practices – from housing equity into private consumption, welfare services or even income – with advances in owner-occupancy and property values helping to 'legitimize' and 'incentivize' a shift away from collective social insurance to welfare self-provision (Smith et al., 2009). A similar process was conceptualized by Crouch (2009) as a form of 'privatized Keynesianism'. In this account, the postwar Keynesian growth model, in which the welfare system was sustained by a tax transfer mechanism, gave way to a new growth model based on credit. Specifically, in extending credit (debt) for home buyers and sustaining house price increases – facilitated through greater integration of commercial and investment banking – housing equity came to represent a means to improve asset wealth and sustain consumption, supporting economic growth more broadly. In this regard, economically liberal governments have specifically sought to nurture lower taxation, to roll away state welfare support and to reduce public debt in favor of extended market provision and private debt management, with households expected to either build up or release their housing equity according to changes in their own welfare needs.

While 'privatized Keynesianism' and 'asset-based welfare' have provided conceptual lenses for understanding welfare regime transformations in economically liberal, English-speaking societies in particular, they also provide insights into shifting welfare relations elsewhere. For example, the decline of large social housing sectors and the rapid advance of mortgaged home ownership in corporatist and social-democratic regimes – such as the Netherlands, Denmark and Sweden, where recent increases in home ownership have been even more pronounced – have provided a means to sustain and legitimize extensions of market practices and shift responsibilities from the state to private entities and households. Indeed, housing wealth, financialization and welfare relations appear to have aligned in different ways in different contexts, but with convergence among certain groups of countries. Schwartz and Seabrooke (2008) therefore distinguish between varieties of 'residential capitalism' – with, for example, 'liberal market' societies featuring a strong trade-off between owner-occupied housing equity and pension systems (such as Australia and the UK) – and 'corporatist market', low-housing-equity countries that have both large social rental housing sectors and substantial mortgage debt (such as Denmark and the Netherlands). It has been further argued that housing financialization has been particularly effective in stimulating rapid change and realignment in welfare state and institutional relations (Fernandez and Aalbers, 2016), connecting states and households to housing markets and global finance in different ways with important political implications at various levels.

The Politics of Housing Wealth

Malpass (2008) has argued that the advance of home ownership has not just been a way of promoting individual welfare autonomy, but has also represented a force for deeper state restructuring, with governments increasingly looking to housing markets 'to pursue non-housing goals in regard to key areas of personal well-being such as health, education and pension provision' (p. 3). The financialization of mortgage markets has been similarly associated with a deregulatory agenda that has sought a deeper embedding of market relations in social and institutional relations (for example, Aalbers, 2008; Langley, 2006). The assumption, then, is that policies surrounding the privatization of housing lie at the heart of recent political realignment. In this volume, the relationships between housing and politics are more explicitly examined by Bengtsson, Ruonavaara and Sørvoll (Chapter 3) and Lennartz (Chapter 5), who frame housing privatization against a backcloth of policy transformations and state–market restructuring in a number of European contexts.

There is, nonetheless, an historic line of argument that has focused on the political outcomes of housing property ownership at the individual level going back to Engels (1872), who identified how home ownership locked buyers into petit bourgeoisie property relations and limited potential for radical political action. More contemporary thinkers have argued, for better or for worse, that home buyers become stronger stakeholders and are therefore likely to be more politically conservative (Saunders, 1990) and resistant to taxation and welfare state spending (Kemeny, 1981). On the other hand, a considerable amount of literature has celebrated the influence of home ownership and how it sharpens autonomy and shapes individual traits (see Rohe et al., 2002). Empirical research concerning the social or political 'effects' of tenure on owner-occupiers, however, has been plagued by normative biases and weak empirical designs, rendering it difficult to disentangle causation from selection (Dietz and Haurin, 2003; Zavisca and Gerber, 2016). However, being in or entering home ownership does not change one's character or nature, but rather one's interests. Furthermore, for heavily indebted low-income home owners, feelings of 'ontological security' can often give way to financial insecurity and stress, with adverse impacts on subjective wellbeing (for example, Nettleton and Burrows, 1998).

More contemporary research on the politically divisive nature of housing-based wealth accumulation has typically been embedded within a more general theoretical narrative on neoliberalism and financialization (for example, Harvey, 2005). In this discourse, social change is often discussed in terms of largely impersonal forces arising from the changing nature of capital accumulation or as the result of a 'neoliberal project'. According to Mau (2015), however, neoliberal policies are driven (at least in part) by the changing interests and concomitant political alliances of the middle classes, as it is unlikely that such a political project can be carried out without the support of the majority of voters. Mau argues that the incorporation of the middle classes into the welfare state – allowing for collective upward mobility – ultimately resulted in their disengagement from socialized welfare arrangements. The middle classes have thus developed a self-economized orientation in which they 'repeatedly update, renew and update these resources [their social, economic and cultural capital] in order to be able to realize their life goals of increased prosperity, security and participation' (Mau, 2015, p. xi). To this end, they have increasingly invested their household assets in the market, by means of stocks and shares, participation in private pensions saving plans and also investment in home ownership – or, more broadly, residential real estate. The middle classes have therefore developed rentier interests that are at odds with their investments in collective welfare state arrangements, with consequences for voting behavior, electoral outcomes and ultimately government policies.

Although empirical research into the micro-level foundations of the transformation of the housing–welfare relationship is scarce, recent work has started to address these macro–micro links in more detail. Housing market financialization and concomitant gains and losses in housing wealth have been associated with (changes in) social policy preferences – in particular support for government redistribution (Ansell, 2014; André and Dewilde, 2016). During housing booms, right-wing parties have been shown to respond to changes in voter preferences aligned around house wealth by cutting down redistributive spending (Ansell, 2014). Comparative welfare state research has, however, also shown that more socialized welfare arrangements, entailing a higher level of risk pooling and redistribution among a larger number of social groups, are key to reducing poverty and inequality.

Housing Wealth as Driver of Greater Socioeconomic Equality or Inequality?

From a critical perspective, the advance of home ownership has embodied a historical alignment in political relations and wealth accumulation processes in which the focus on residential property as a means of accruing household assets has supported the advance of neoliberal forces: sustaining the commodification of the home, advancing financialization and the penetration of global capital, and legitimizing the withdrawal of collective provision in the form of the welfare state. Nonetheless, from a less critical angle it has also represented a socially progressive policy agenda: a means for governments to advance economic inclusion and the distribution of assets. Indeed, in its original formulation, the 'asset-' or 'property-based' welfare agenda assumed enhanced welfare and autonomy for those at whom it was targeted – the poor, low-income households and ethnic minorities – ultimately resulting in greater equality and prosperity (Sherraden, 1991; Retsinas and Belsky, 2005; Bratt, 2012a). Over time, however, many authors have identified weaknesses in this line of reasoning, especially when the 'assets' concerned typically refer to 'housing assets'.

For one, the distribution of housing wealth does not reflect need, and 'usable' housing wealth tends to be concentrated in the hands of those who already dispose of other resources (for example, occupational pensions). Moreover, strong house price inflation tends to advantage housing market insiders and wealthier households, while regional variations in house price booms and busts structure other inequities (see Hamnett, 1999; Dorling et al., 2005; Malpass, 2008). Housing markets have become remarkably uneven; gains are most intense in prime sectors in which higher-income home owners are more concentrated, and losses (or softer growth) characteristic of the homes and neighborhoods associated with lower-income owner-occupiers. Furthermore, housing market developments are not counter-cyclical to developments in the wider economy, with home ownership being limited as an economic buffer or welfare shock absorber. Indeed, it is just when housing wealth is needed most – such as during the last economic crisis – that it is likely to diminish or even be inaccessible (see Ronald and Doling, 2012).

Furthermore, in recent decades, returns on housing and other capital assets have been much greater than increases in incomes – with a disproportionate advantage for the holders of capital (Piketty, 2014), who have increasingly adapted urban real estate as a store of wealth – enhancing inequalities and diminishing possibilities to access housing asset wealth among lower-income households. It has therefore been argued that housing financialization and growth in housing equity has inevitably resulted in stronger possibilities for enhanced rent extraction and economic stratification (for example, Aalbers and Christophers, 2014). Critically, differential housing wealth gains and losses have contributed to other social and economic inequalities and transformed into additional forms of (dis) advantage and opportunities. This dynamic furthermore appeared to be reinforced in the aftermath of the GFC (Kennett et al., 2013; Rolnik, 2013; Forrest and Hirayama, 2015).

Two core dimensions of socioeconomic inequality can thus be associated with recent developments in housing wealth, both pertaining to a growing precarity in developed economies. The first of these concerns is the emergence of strong intergenerational divisions in access to housing and housing wealth. The second relates to the exacerbated condition of the poor and vulnerable.

The boom in home ownership rates among advanced economies in the late twentieth century was often characterized by growth among younger adult owner-occupiers, who previously had more limited access to credit and less motivation to leave renting. Despite easier access to mortgage credit during the period 1990–2007, the affordability of home ownership faded again following steep house price inflation. This contributed to increasing average age of entry to home ownership and the reassertion of social class differentials. This was further exacerbated by the labor market, with declining job security especially affecting new entrants (see Kurz and Blossfeld, 2004; Forrest and Yip, 2013). After the GFC it became even more difficult to enter home ownership, as conditions for mortgage lending became stricter, welfare transfers were curtailed (for example, for education) and labor market conditions of young people deteriorated further. Subsequent declines in home ownership rates among younger cohorts across Europe have been accompanied by commensurable revival of younger adults co-residing with parents or renting privately. According to Lennartz, Arundel and Ronald (2015), between 2007 and 2012, home ownership rates among independent 18- to 34-year-olds fell by an average of 3.3 per cent across the original 15 EU member countries, and by as much as 5 to 10 per cent in countries with high rates of financialization (mortgage debt) such as Denmark, the Netherlands, Sweden and the UK.

Much debate has subsequently focused on the housing situations of young people (for example, McKee, 2012; Lersch and Dewilde, 2015; Arundel and Ronald, 2016; Filandri and Bertolini, 2016; Kolb and Buchholz, this volume). A specific research focus has been children's dependency on parental help and resources to become and remain home owners. Several countries have witnessed an increase in the association between the home ownership of parents and that of their offspring (for example, Searle and McCollum, 2014; Mulder et al., 2015; Druta and Ronald, 2016), with housing emerging as an important medium in the restructuring of socioeconomic inequality. Indeed, to the extent that home ownership is more common among older higher-income groups, who can provide increasingly large amounts of housing wealth (achieved by market entry under an earlier regime of easy finance and lower relative prices) for their own children, intergenerational transfers threaten to deepen existing structures of inequality.

Some commentators have also focused on intergenerational conflicts derived from housing wealth disparities between older and younger generations. More melodramatic approaches conjure up a contemporary battleground featuring self-interested housing and pension wealthy baby boomers on one side and impoverished, employment-insecure 'generation renters' on the other (for example, Willetts, 2010). While the conflict has been somewhat overplayed in light of kinship-based transfers in housing wealth and assistance, research does indicate an increasing mobilization of housing assets by older people who have been advantaged by diminishing prospects of home ownership among the young (Ronald et al., 2015). In its most obvious form, this involves older cohorts buying up housing – helping to sustain higher house prices – to rent out to younger people locked out of owner-occupation.

While the young have featured in public discourses as those affected most by housing access and wealth inequalities, conditions for low-income households more generally have been eroded substantially by housing market transformations in the policy climate of deregulation, austerity and asset-based welfare. Although the vulnerable are often housed in other tenures, they have not remained immune from the financialization of housing and its impact on welfare regimes and housing market dynamics (for example, Dewilde and De Decker, 2016). The increased policy focus on, and use of, housing as an investment asset has compromised access to decent and affordable housing through processes such as privatization of the public housing stock; new urban strategies aimed at enabling the mobilization and circulation of global capital, such as institutional investment in private rental housing (for example, Fields and Uffer, 2016); welfare cuts and austerity measures (for example, Kennett et al., 2013) and greater spatial segregation and concentration of wealth (for example, Walks, 2016). In the post-crisis context, despite the prominence of mortgage finance as the root of the GFC, governments have been resistant in developing other tenures, especially social renting. The promotion of home ownership and housing commodification has thus progressed largely unabated. Moreover, in light of emerging market exclusion, subsidies have flowed towards initiatives to sustain home-ownership rates rather than ameliorating poor housing conditions or access to affordable homes, especially among those on low incomes.

WHY HOUSING WEALTH AND WELFARE?

In this introductory chapter, we have so far sketched out the contours of a new and more comprehensive framework that illustrates the multiple dimensions of the housing and welfare nexus. While housing and welfare have always been connected – either as a source of wellbeing or as a form of social welfare policy (that is, through social housing or state-supported outright home ownership in later life) – this connection has been deeply altered by the increased centrality of *housing wealth* (rather than 'home ownership' or 'housing') for economies, governments and households. Broadly speaking, processes of economic globalization and financialization – enabled by government reregulation – have driven an upward trend in aggregate and individual housing wealth holdings, supporting the shift from state welfare provision to more commodified forms of self-provision featuring house-buying and welfare-switching strategies across the life course.

Inflation – both real and imagined – in housing wealth has altered interests and practices involving its uses and meanings, with actual consequences for welfare regimes – in terms of political relations and advances in socioeconomic inequalities – before, but also after, the economic crisis. At the same time, the commodification and financialization of housing has been particularly uneven across institutional contexts in terms of the depth of change and specific manifestations. In Eastern Europe in particular, the lack of development in housing finance following privatization of state-provided housing, combined with the patchy evolution of welfare benefits and services during and since transition, have resulted in the redistribution of housing itself (and welfare in general) based on reciprocity within the extended family. All chapters in this edited volume seek to explore these new, more complex interactions between housing, housing wealth and welfare across a variegated range of historic, social and economic contexts.

OUTLINE OF THE BOOK

This edited volume addresses housing wealth and welfare relationships across various developed societies and interprets the concept of 'welfare' in its diverse manifestations and meanings. It thereby provides diverse empirical contexts for examining and understanding the complex relations between housing wealth and welfare. Of particular concern are the interactions between social, economic and housing policies and welfare state transformations, wellbeing and housing outcomes. The chapters are divided into two complimentary parts, although there is considerable overlap. Part I (chapters 2 to 5) addresses old and new conceptions in housing and welfare and is constituted of diverse contributions that provide a broad overview of debates placed in more historical, theoretical and cross-national relief. These opening chapters thus establish the critical theoretical tools and a more comparative empirical sensibility from which to address the more context-focused chapters that follow. Indeed, Part II of the book (chapters 6 to 10) goes on to explore different dimensions of housing wealth and welfare relations at various social and spatial scales and in a diversity of social, economic and political contexts.

The opening chapter of Part I revisits 'old conceptions' of housing and welfare by taking a longer historical look at the broadening distribution of housing assets and the role of public policy therein. Michelle Norris, in this case, examines the changing character of home ownership and its relationship with the welfare state in the Republic of Ireland over a century-long era, starting from the end of the nineteenth century. This longer-term vista provides a contrast to prevailing interpretations in Anglophone countries that links the growth of home ownership with neoliberalization and the weakening of the state's role in welfare provision. Norris argues, in terms clearly reminiscent of Forrest and Hirayama (2015), that the early promotion of mortgages, grants and tax subsidies that facilitated the expansion of owner-occupation was primarily 'socialized' rather than 'marketized'. Ireland's distinctive home-ownership regime emerged from a wider suite of policies that supported capital redistribution, particularly in the form of farmland, and was associated with welfare expansion in terms of a rudimentary asset-based welfare system. From the 1970s onward, however, this approach began to dissipate in conjunction with acute fiscal crises and ideological shifts in approaches to housing and the wider economy. Since the mid-1980s, various parts of the social system of home ownership have been rolled back in favor of a more speculative and market-orientated approach. By the end of the century, home ownership had been transformed and, while not entirely liberalized, has proven to be particularly speculation-orientated. It has also become characteristically fragile, as has been demonstrated by the collapse in the Irish housing market and the sharp fall in home ownership rates (from around 80 per cent in the 1990s to just over 68 per cent in 2015). While being a quite remarkable case, Norris's chapter provides fertile ground for evaluating the social and political roots of home-ownership-focused policies, as well as how they have interacted with a more globalized market context and the influence of neoliberal ideas and practices.

The second chapter in this section, and Chapter 3 in this volume, also takes a longer-term view of developments in housing policy and welfare – albeit over a shorter time frame – but with a focus on Nordic countries that have stronger social-democratic welfare traditions and deeper welfare states, especially in regard to housing. Sweden in particular has a long social rental housing tradition and, until recently, municipal housing companies have dominated provision in cities. This chapter specifically examines whether political processes related to the provision of owner-occupied housing in Finland, Norway and Sweden follow similar or different logics of path dependence compared with those of housing provision in general. Bo Bengtsson, Hannu Ruonavaara and Jardar Sørvoll argue that in all three of these countries, regardless of cultural and ideological differences, the discursive strength of political ideas surrounding home ownership and the potential power of home owners has increasingly taken hold despite considerable differences in policy regimes and trajectories. While the development of housing policies and institutions typically demonstrates strong elements of path dependence, this comparison of selected Nordic countries illustrates how powerful the 'myth of home ownership' (Kemeny, 1981) has become. Neoliberal conceptions of housing wealth and asset-owning home owners have also begun to permeate these societies, undermining the logic of equality and justice in the provision of housing, as well as tenure neutrality in policy, to forge alignment around home ownership as the state-favored tenure.

Chapter 4 takes us in a much more conceptual direction and sets out a new framework from which to understand and analyse processes involved in, and the impact of, housing wealth accumulation in some detail. Stephan Köppe and Beverley A. Searle specifically draw from the empirical literature on housing wealth transitions in English-speaking home-owning

societies in developing a framework that captures housing wealth and
welfare processes at different stages of the life course. The gAMUT
approach they set out focuses on four key stages: accumulation, managing,
using and transferring housing wealth. Based on these four stages, welfare
opportunities and risks across the life course are identified. A particular
finding in this research has been that while housing wealth has the potential to improve welfare security in later life, home owners are typically
more exposed to other social risks throughout their lives than they would
be otherwise. At the same time, risks are often highly individualized and
housing wealth is a particularly vulnerable form of personal insurance. For
example, while those who incur few care costs in late life can usually transfer the full value of their home to their children, those who have intensive
care needs are unlikely to fully pass on the wealth they may have amassed
in housing property. Koppe and Searle conclude that housing wealth
accumulation has potentially large individual benefits if managed well, but
is dependent on economic environments and, in the end, often functions
poorly as a means to cover social risks. The implications are then, that the
alternatives to the welfare state represented by housing-derived forms of
asset-based welfare are often of limited use.

The increased centrality of housing assets in the political economies
of Western welfare states and in securing the welfare position of households has gone hand in hand with new government approaches to welfare
provision. In Chapter 5, Christian Lennartz analyses the complemen-
tarity between the advent of property-based welfare strategies and the
Social Investment Strategy (SIS) propagated at the European level. Social
investment refers to a process of welfare state restructuring aimed at
curbing traditional, protectivist spending on so-called 'old' social risks
(for example, unemployment), while investing in more productive- and
employment-orientated social policies aimed at tackling so-called 'new'
social risks (for example, in-work poverty). Based on a 'directions of
change' matrix, devised in terms of protective and productive spending,
it is possible to distinguish between four different welfare state strategies:
welfare retrenchment (cutting down on both types of spending), welfare
expansion (increasing both types of spending), welfare protectionism
(increased spending on protectionist policies, decreased investive spending)
and welfare readjustment (increased spending on productivist policies,
decreased protective spending). In Lennartz's empirical analysis, there is
a striking association between welfare state retrenchment (especially in
Nordic countries) and readjustment (especially in liberal English-speaking
nations and the Netherlands) on the one hand, and the accumulation
of private debt through mortgages (coupled with increased housing
wealth following house price inflation) on the other hand. The housing

property-based welfare approach may therefore potentially be understood as part of a welfare restructuring process that advances a more productive welfare state, in which governments encourage citizens to assume large mortgage debts, with the accumulation of housing assets assuming a privatized security role, facilitating the redirected flow of public resources from 'old' to 'new' welfare state functions.

Part I of this volume thus moves us, conceptually speaking, from examples of older traditional modes of housing wealth as a feature of welfare policy to more recent and complex ones in which housing property cuts more deeply across the political economy and is more intertwined with social and economic practices. Part II provides a broader comparative and empirical basis for exploring and understanding institutional influences, socioeconomic and sociostructural variegation and the broader significance of context. It also deals with housing wealth and welfare as a more imminent concern that has critical salience to the development of capitalist societies and emerging drivers and relations of inequality.

Previously, we noted how property-based welfare policies clash with the concentration of housing market rewards and risks. In Chapter 6, Alison Wallace analyses how low-income home owners in Northern Ireland have managed the severe housing market downturn in the region. Specifically, she explores whether housing assets played a role in supporting vulnerable home owners through the economic downturn and what the removal of this resource in the falling market meant for home owners. Northern Ireland has been hit hard by the housing, financial and economic crisis, and has experienced a strong decline in house prices, coupled with high levels of negative equity, mortgage debt and arrears as well as a strong decline in property transactions. Quantitative and qualitative data sources, however, both point to a fair degree of resilience of low-income households. Although the region experienced the greatest incidence and magnitude of negative equity, home owners in Northern Ireland exercised greater caution towards the use of riskier forms of home finance than across the UK as a whole. When they did engage, however, they did so later in the housing market cycle and were therefore more vulnerable in the falling market. The ramifications of the market downturn on residential mobility, negative equity, mortgage arrears or repossession were deeply felt by a minority. However, resilience in the face of adversity was bolstered by adopting a conservative approach to the financialization of the home, as the private asset model of welfare was rejected and the use-value of the home was prioritized above its exchange value. Resistance to contemporary home economics increased their resilience in an uncertain market. The author, however, notes that such a strategy may offer security and control to home owners for the time being, but the extent to which the

global trend toward the financialization of housing can be reversed is more
questionable.

Due to institutional constraints, Germany has remained less exposed
to the vagaries of economic and financial deregulation, particularly in the
housing domain. Real house prices have remained constant for the last
three decades and residential mortgage debt still stands at a fairly low level
(see Table 1.1). This does not mean, however, that nothing has changed
in terms of housing wealth and welfare. In Chapter 7, Kathrin Kolb and
Sandra Buchholz focus on the development of social inequality in home
ownership and housing values by means of an intra-German comparison.
Using longitudinal (life course) data, they investigate the influence of
central socioeconomic characteristics on the likelihood of being a home
owner, the value of residential real estate and access to home ownership (in
terms of transition rates) in East and West Germany. Even 25 years after
reunification, home ownership rates and housing values remain markedly
higher in West Germany compared to the eastern part of the country.
With regard to being a home owner, the impact of labor market status,
in particular unemployment, has increased during the time period under
study, as has the importance of intergenerational transfers (only for West
Germany). The main result with regard to the transition to home ownership is that for the youngest cohort studied, transition is not significantly
lower in East compared with West Germany. This may indicate some
convergence in home ownership processes. Notwithstanding the latter
finding, the general picture suggests a growing influence of socioeconomic
characteristics on (access to) home ownership and housing wealth in
more recent times. For people with little education in lower-paid occupations, it has become more difficult to build up assets via home ownership,
disadvantaging them in regard to welfare provision in later life. This is
becoming increasingly salient, as pension benefits in Germany are contribution (or earnings-based), and therefore already quite stratified. Housing
market inequalities are thus exacerbating labor market inequalities and
stratification through housing has become more intense.

As demonstrated earlier (see Figure 1.1), transformations in the housing
domain look very different in Eastern compared with Western Europe.
Stephens et al. (2015) identify how the family increasingly protects people
from the risks that either the state no longer tends to or are left uncovered
by the market. Sustaining the family in taking on these challenges has
been an extraordinarily high distribution of home ownership and housing
equity among these societies. The diversity underlying 'super high' outright home ownership rates across former socialist countries since the transition to a free-market economy after 1989 is also quite striking. The final
three chapters of the book focus on post-socialist countries in particular,

illustrating the central and explicit role housing property has taken in the development of welfare systems in these contexts.

In Chapter 8, Srna Mandič and Maja Mrzel address the role of (family) housing (wealth) in the welfare of older people in post-socialist countries, starting from the argument that these societies are characterized by a structural 'old-age welfare gap'. The authors identify that welfare state arrangements in post-socialist countries have not been modernized in order to cope with demographic ageing, a societal issue located within the paradigm of 'new social risks' (see also Chapter 5). They explain the structural 'old-age welfare gap' in terms of the wider social costs arising from the transition to a free-market economy and political democracy after 1989 and the shock this presented. While economic restructuring and decline in welfare spending and programs had adverse social consequences, these were partly cushioned by the privatization of state-owned housing and the public pension system. Welfare system change was furthermore characterized by the growing significance of the informal sector, family and kinship networks. This chapter empirically explores the gap in old-age welfare provision across different European countries and welfare regime clusters (characterized by different levels of defamilialization of care in later life), as well as the potential of owned homes to help bridge this gap. The data presented documents substantial differences in the availability of old-age care services in post-socialist countries in comparison to the continental (especially social-democratic) countries, but also the potential role of housing in supporting older people. Nonetheless, while home ownership rates are often substantial, the incidence of unfit housing is high, as is housing suitable (or adaptable) to the needs of the aged (for example, for those physically impaired). What stands out is the high level of co-residence with adult children who can provide support but at the same time limits the options for consuming the housing wealth stored in the home. All in all, with the exception of the Czech Republic, the post-socialist countries examined in this chapter strongly resemble the Southern European situation and hence present similar challenges with regard to elderly care provision. Home ownership and housing wealth can only partly address some of these challenges.

The 'post-socialist' family is also the focus of Chapter 9. Jane R. Zavisca and Theodore P. Gerber trace the housing experiences of Russians since the collapse of the Soviet Union. In order to adequately explain the contemporary Russian housing situation, the authors make a distinction between residing in an owned home (de facto) and owning the title to a residence (de jure), as these two states do not always overlap. Put differently, not all adult household members necessarily share title, which may alternatively be shared with non-resident family. The chapter therefore draws on both qualitative and quantitative (life course) data in charting the structure of familial property rights and uses alternative measures of home ownership that are more consistent with local meanings. In their study, the authors found that although most people were living in privately owned homes, less than half of middle-aged urban adults had achieved 'full' ownership, with dispersed property rights often spread across a wide kinship network. High levels of co-ownership with extended family has produced intra-family inequalities that particularly affect younger generations, who have a hard time acquiring a home of their 'own'. Charting paths into residence and property rights reveals extensive 'behind the scene' transitions in tenure and independence, which are often less reflective of one's own life course transitions than those of other family members. The attainment of ownership in Russia is thus far less dependent on human capital or occupational achievements. Although market moves are on the rise among younger cohorts, this type of move is still far from the modal experience as most housing is still acquired – directly or indirectly – from the state or the family. Furthermore, the majority of changes in property rights over the past decades have been achieved without moving house. While state privatization is the main driver of transitions to ownership, family reciprocity is still the main means of transition to residential independence.

In Chapter 10, 'post-socialist' family-based housing provision is linked more explicitly to different types of housing inequalities and the potential (or lack of potential) for housing-based welfare strategies. Adriana Mihaela Soaita takes on the case of Romania, providing a long overview of the interrelated development of the housing system and the emergence of a family-based welfare regime. In doing so, Soaita traces the enduring legacies of historic forms of housing provision – pre- and post-communist – in the features of the current housing system. A critical outcome in this context has been the contrast between widespread debt-free home ownership (more than 90 per cent of Romanian households are un-mortgaged property owners) and the limitations of housing assets as a resource for family welfare. Specifically, housing access, quality and affordability, along with mobility practices, tend to undermine use of the owner-occupied home as a form of wealth that can be mobilized or monetized to provide for family welfare other than shelter. Soaita's analysis also delineates between the two faces of inequality engendered by the contemporary Romanian housing system: exclusion and unequal inclusion. Regarding the financial possibilities facilitated by home ownership, *exclusion* distinguishes home owners from non-home-owners. While non-home-owners are generally taken to be renters and the homeless, the label can also refer to the many individuals living rent-free in complex family households without ownership rights. The category of *unequal inclusion*, meanwhile, highlights inequalities among owner-occupiers – not only in terms of housing quality and suitability to household characteristics, but also in terms of single- or multiple-dwelling ownership. The chapter concludes by arguing that the nature of home ownership in Romania affords passive and reactive approaches rather than proactive strategies for mobilizing housing wealth as a source of family welfare.

While there is no concluding chapter by the editors, John Doling provides a short Epilogue to the book. He critically reflects on the main findings from the different chapters and how they advance our understanding of the temporally and spatially contingent relationships between housing, housing wealth and welfare. The logic of property-based welfare seems to have spread – albeit in an adapted, more 'obscured' way (though more identifiable in terms of policies and other indicators than in terms of an explicit public debate) – from the English-speaking liberal countries to a number of Northern European countries of a more social-democratic nature. Apart from the inherent contradictions within the asset-based welfare approach identified in this introductory chapter, Doling points out that, in these countries, asset-based welfare strategies may be further compromised by stalling or falling home ownership rates combined with the increased concentration of housing wealth. In other settings, particularly post-socialist countries, housing-based welfare continues to revolve around the house itself rather than around housing wealth. Given that the family as welfare provider even seems to gain in importance over time and extends to new domains of welfare provision (for example, long-term care), this situation is likely to persist in the foreseeable future.

NOTES

1. In the UK, for example, the number of private landlords has more than doubled since 2002 (to 2.1 million in 2014), with the majority of rental properties now let by owner-occupiers who own just one or two extra properties (Lord et al., 2013).
2. However, welfare is also provided by other institutions such as the family, the market and civil society.
3. For example, see Wilensky (1975).

REFERENCES

Aalbers M B (2008) The Financialization of Home and the Mortgage Market Crisis. *Competition & Change* 12(2): 148–166.
Aalbers M B and Christophers B (2014) Centring Housing in Political Economy. *Housing, Theory and Society* 31(4): 373–394.

Allen J, Barlow J, Leal J, Maloutas T and Padovani L (2004) *Housing and Welfare in Southern Europe*, Oxford: Blackwell Publishing/RICS Foundation.

André S and Dewilde C (2016) Home-Ownership and Support for Government Redistribution. *Comparative European Politics* 14(April): 319–348.

Ansell B (2014) The Political Economy of Ownership: Housing Markets and the Welfare State. *American Political Science Review* 108(2): 383–402.

Arts W and Gelissen J (2002) Three Worlds of Welfare Capitalism or More? A State-of-the-Art Report. *Journal of European Social Policy* 12(2): 137–158.

Arundel R and Ronald R (2016) Parental Co-Residence, Shared Living and Emerging Adulthood in Europe: Semi-Dependent Housing across Welfare Regime and Housing System Contexts. *Journal of Youth Studies* 19(7): 885–905.

Barlow J and Duncan S (1994) Comparing European Housing Systems. In: Barlow J and Duncan S (eds) *Success and Failure in Housing Provision: European Systems Compared*, Oxford: Pergamon, pp. 26–52.

Bengtsson B (2001) Housing as a Social Right: Implications for Welfare State Theory. *Scandinavian Political Studies* 24(4): 255–275.

Bengtsson B (2012) Housing Politics and Political Science. In: Clapham D F, Clark W A V and Gibb K (eds) *The Sage Handbook of Housing Studies*, Los Angeles: Sage, pp. 206–229.

Birch K and Siemiatycki M (2015) Neoliberalism and the Geographies of Marketization: The Entangling of State and Markets. *Progress in Human Geography* 40(2): 177–198.

Bratt R G (2012a) Home Ownership as Public Policy in the United States. In: Ronald R and Elsinga M (eds) *Beyond Home Ownership: Housing, Welfare and Society.* London: Routledge, pp. 130–145.

Bratt R G (2012b) Home Ownership Risk and Responsibility Before and After the U.S. Mortgage Crisis. In: Ronald R and Elsinga M (eds) *Beyond Home Ownership. Housing, Welfare and Society*, London: Routledge, pp. 146–169.

Castles F G (1998) The Really Big Trade-Off: Home Ownership and the Welfare State in the New World and the Old. *Acta Politica* 33(1): 5–19.

Castles F G and Mitchell D (1993) Worlds of Welfare and Families of Nations. In: Castles F G (ed) *Families of Nations: Patterns of Public Policy in Western Democracies*, Aldershot: Dartmouth, pp. 93–128.

Crouch C (2009) Privatised Keynesianism: An Unacknowledged Policy Regime. *The British Journal of Politics and International Relations* 11(3): 382–399.

De Deken J, Delfani N and Dewilde C (2012) The Relationship between Pensions and Homeownership Since 1990: What is the Longitudinal Evidence? *Retraite et Société* 62(February): 33–57.

Delfani N, De Deken J and Dewilde C (2014) Home-Ownership and Pensions: Negative Correlation But No Trade-Off. Why Asset-Based Welfare Only Fits Specific Institutional Settings. *Housing Studies* 25(5): 657–676.

Dewilde C and De Decker P (2016) Changing Inequalities in Housing Outcomes across Western Europe. *Housing, Theory and Society* 33(2): 121–161.

Dewilde C and Raeymaeckers P (2008) The Trade-Off between Home-Ownership and Pensions: Individual and Institutional Determinants of Old-Age Poverty. *Ageing & Society* 28(6): 805–830.

Dietz R D and Haurin D R (2003) The Social and Private Micro-Level Consequences of Homeownership. *Journal of Urban Economics* 54: 401–450.

Doling J and Ford J (2007) A Union of Home Owners (Editorial). *European Journal of Housing and Planning* 7(2): 113–127.

Doling J and Ronald R (2010) Home Ownership and Asset-Based Welfare. *Journal of Housing and the Built Environment* 25(2): 165–173.

Dorling D, Ford J, Holmans A, Sharp C, Thomas B and Wilcox S (eds) (2005) *The Great Divide: An Analysis of Housing Inequality*, London: Shelter.

Druta O and Ronald R (2016) Young Adults' Pathways into Homeownership and the Negotiation of Intra-Family Support: A Home, the Ideal Gift. *Sociology*, DOI: 10.1177/0038038516629900.

Elsinga M, Haffner M E A and van de Heijden H M H (2008) Threats for the Dutch Unitary Rental Model. *European Journal of Housing Policy* 8(1): 21–37.

EMF (European Mortgage Federation) (2015) *Hypostat 2015: A Review of Europe's Mortgage and Housing Markets*, Brussels: EMF.

Engels F (1872) *The Housing Question*, Leipzig: Volksstaat.

Esping-Andersen G (1990) *The Three Worlds of Welfare Capitalism*, Cambridge: Polity Press.

European Central Bank (2009) *Housing Finance in the EURO Area*, Frankfurt: Task Force of the Monetary Policy Committee of the European System of Central Banks.

Eurostat (Statistical Office of the European Union) (2015) Housing Statistics, accessed 11 June 2016 at http://ec.europa.eu/eurostat/statistics-explained/index.php/Housing_statistics.

Fahey T (2003) Is There a Trade-Off between Pensions and Home Ownership? An Exploration of the Irish Case. *Journal of European Social Policy* 13(2): 159–173.

Fahey T and Norris M (2010) Housing. In: Castles F G, Leibfried S, Lewis J, Obinger H and Pierson C (eds) *Oxford Handbook of the Welfare State*, Oxford: Oxford University Press, pp. 479–493.

Fernandez R and Aalbers M B (2016) Financialization and Housing: Between Globalisation and Varieties of Capitalism. *Competition and Change* 20(2): 71–88.

Fields D and Uffer S (2016) The Financialization of Rental Housing: A Comparative Analysis of New York City and Berlin. *Urban Studies* 20(2): 71–88.

Filandri M and Bertolini S (2016) Young People and Home Ownership in Europe. *International Journal of Housing Policy* 16(2): 144–164.

Forrest R and Hirayama Y (2015) The Financialisation of the Social Project: Embedded Liberalism, Neoliberalism and Home Ownership. *Urban Studies* 52(2): 233–244.

Forrest R and Murie A (1988) *Selling the Welfare State: The Privatisation of Public Housing*, London: Routledge.

Forrest R and Yip N-M (2011) Households, Homeownership and Neo-Liberalism. In: Forrest R and Yip N-M (eds) *Housing Markets and the Global Financial Crisis: The Uneven Impact on Households*, Cheltenham, UK and Northampton, MA, USA: Edward Elgar Publishing, pp. 1–19.

Forrest R and Yip N-M (2013) *Young People and Housing: Transitions, Trajectories and Generational Fractures*, London: Routledge.

Fuentes G C, Aitziber E E, Dol K and Hoekstra J (2013) From Housing Bubble to Repossessions: Spain Compared to Other West European Countries. *Housing Studies* 28(8): 1197–1217.

Gough I, Wood G, Barrientos A, Bevan P, Davis P and Room G (2004) *Insecurity and Welfare Regimes in Asia, Africa and Latin America: Social Policy in Development Contexts*, Cambridge: Cambridge University Press.

Hamnett C (1999) *Winners and Losers: The Housing Market in Modern Britain*, London: UCL Press.

Harloe M (1995) *The People's Home? Social Rented Housing in Europe and America*, Oxford: Blackwell.

Harvey D (2005) *A Brief History of Neoliberalism*, Oxford: Oxford University Press.

Hoekstra J (2003) Housing and the Welfare State in the Netherlands: An Application of Esping-Andersen's Typology. *Housing, Theory and Society* 20(20): 58–71.

Hoekstra J (2010) *Divergence in European Welfare and Housing Systems*, Delft: Delft University Press.

Holmqvist E and Magnusson Turner L (2014) Swedish Welfare State and Housing Markets: Under Economic and Political Pressure. *Journal of Housing and the Built Environment* 29(2): 237–254.

Hometrack UK (2015) Property Price Index, accessed 11 June 2016 at https://www.hometrack.com/uk.

Hudson J and Kühner S (2009) Towards Productive Welfare? A Comparative Analysis of 23 OECD Countries. *Journal of European Social Policy* 19(1): 34–46.

Kemeny J (1981) *The Myth of Home Ownership: Private versus Public Choices in Housing Tenure*, London: Routledge & Kegan Paul.

Kemeny J (1992) *Housing and Social Theory*, London: Routledge.

Kemeny J (1995) *From Public Housing to the Social Market: Rental Policy Strategies in Comparative Perspective*, London: Routledge.

Kemp P A and Kofner S (2014) Germany. In: Crook T and Kemp P A (eds) *Private Rental Housing: Comparative Perspectives*, Cheltenham, UK and Northampton, MA, USA: Edward Elgar Publishing, pp. 27–47.

Kennett P, Forrest R and Marsh A (2013) The Global Economic Crisis and the Reshaping of Housing Opportunities. *Housing, Theory and Society* 30(1): 10–28.

Krippner G (2005) The Financialization of the American Economy. *Socio-Economic Review* (3): 173–208.

Kurz K and Blossfeld H-P (2004) *Home Ownership and Social Inequality in Comparative Perspective*, Stanford: Stanford University Press.

Langley P (2006) The Making of Investor Subjects in Anglo-American Pensions. *Society and Space* 24: 919–934.

Langley P (2010) The Performance of Liquidity in the Subprime Mortgage Crisis. *New Political Economy* 15(1): 71–89.

Lennartz C, Arundel R and Ronald R (2015) Younger Adults and Homeownership in Europe Through the Global Financial Crisis. *Population, Space and Place* 22(8): 823–835.

Lersch P M and Dewilde C (2015) Employment Insecurity and First-Time Homeownership: Evidence from Twenty-Two European Countries. *Environment and Planning A* 47(3): 607–624.

Lord C, Lloyd J and Barnes M (2013) *Understanding Landlords: A Study of Private Landlords in the UK Using the Wealth and Assets Survey*, London: Strategic Society Centre.

Lowe S, Searle B A and Smith S J (2011) From Housing Wealth to Mortgage Debt: The Emergence of Britain's Asset-Shaped Welfare State. *Social Policy and Society* 11(1): 105–116.

Malpass P (2008) Housing and the New Welfare State: Wobbly Pillar or Cornerstone? *Housing Studies* 23(1): 1–19.

Mau S (2015) *Inequality, Marketization and the Majority Class*, Basingstoke: Palgrave Macmillan.

McKee K (2012) Young People, Homeownership and Future Welfare. *Housing Studies* 27(6): 853–862.

Mulder C H, Dewilde C, Van Duijn M and Smits A (2015) The Association Between Parents' and Adult Children's Homeownership: A Comparative Analysis. *European Journal of Population* 31(5): 495–527.

Naumanen P and Ruonavaara H (2015) Why Not Cash Out Home Equity? Reflections on the Finnish Case. *Housing, Theory and Society* 33(2): 162–177.

Nettleton S and Burrows R (1998) Mortgage Debt, Insecure Home Ownership and Health: An Exploratory Analysis. *Sociology of Health and Illness* 20(5): 731–753.

OECD (Organisation for Economic Co-operation and Development) (2011) Housing and the Economy: Policies for Renovation. *Economic Policy Reforms 2011: Going for Growth*, Paris: OECD.

Orloff A S (1993) Gender and the Social Rights of Citizenship: The Comparative Analysis of Gender Relations and the Welfare State. *American Sociological Review* 58(June): 303–328.

Orloff A S (1996) Gender in the Welfare State. *Annual Review of Sociology* 2251–78.

Piketty T (2014) *Capital in the Twenty-First Century*, Cambridge, MA: Harvard University Press.

Poppe C, Collard S and Jakobson T B (2015) What Has Debt Got to Do with It? The Valuation of Homeownership in the Era of Financialization. *Housing, Theory and Society* 33(1): 59–76.

Priemus H and Dieleman F (2002) Social Housing Policy in the European Union: Past, Present and Perspectives. *Urban Studies* 39(2): 191–200.

Retsinas N P and Belsky E S (eds) (2005) *Building Assets: Building Credit*, Washington, DC: Brookings Institution Press.

Rohe W, van Zandt S and McCarthy G (2002) Home Ownership and Access to Opportunity. *Housing Studies* 17(1): 51–61.

Rolnik R (2013) Late Neoliberalism: The Financialization of Homeownership and Housing Rights. *International Journal of Urban and Regional Research* 37(3): 1058–1066.

Ronald R (2008) *The Ideology of Home Ownership: Homeowner Societies and the Role of Housing*, Houndmills: Palgrave Macmillan.

Ronald R and Dol K (2011) Housing in the Netherlands Before and After the Global Financial Crisis. In: Forrest R and Ngai-Ming Y (eds) *Housing Markets and the Global Financial Crisis: The Uneven Impact on Households*, Cheltenham, UK and Northampton, MA, USA: Edward Elgar Publishing, pp. 93–112.

Ronald R and Doling J (2012) Testing Home Ownership as the Cornerstone of Welfare: Lessons from East Asia for the West. *Housing Studies* 27(7): 940–961.

Ronald R and Elsinga M (2012) *Beyond Home Ownership: Housing, Welfare and Society*, London: Routledge.

Ronald R, Kadi J and Lennartz C (2015) Homeownership-Based Welfare in Transition. *Critical Housing Analysis* 2(1): 52–64.

Saunders P (1990) *A Nation of Homeowners*, London: Unwin Hyman.

Savills (2016) *Around the World in Dollars and Cents: Trends in International Real Estate Trading*, accessed 11 June 2016 at http://www.savills.co.uk/research_articles/188297/198667-0.

Schwartz H (2009) Global Capitalism: Its Fall and Rise in the Twentieth Century. *Globalizations* 6(3): 408–409.

Schwartz H and Seabrooke L (2008) Varieties of Residential Capitalism in the International Political Economy: Old Welfare States and the New Politics of Housing. *Comparative European Politics* 6: 237–261.

Scruggs L and Allan J (2006) Welfare-State Decommodification in 18 OECD-Countries: A Replication and Revision. *Journal of European Social Policy* 16(1): 55–72.

Searle B A and McCollum D (2014) Property-Based Welfare and the Search for Generational Equality. *International Journal of Housing Policy* 14(4): 325–345.

Sen A (1983) Poor, Relatively Speaking. *Oxford Economic Papers* 35: 153–169.

Sherraden M (1991) *Assets and the Poor*, New York: M.E. Sharpe.

Smith S J (2008) Owner-Occupation: At Home with a Hybrid of Money and Materials. *Environment and Planning A* 40(3): 520–535.

Smith S J (2015) Owner Occupation: At Home in a Spatial, Financial Paradox. *International Journal of Housing Policy* 15(1): 61–64.

Smith S J, Searle B A and Cook N (2009) Rethinking the Risks of Home Ownership. *Journal of Social Policy* 38(1): 83–102.

Spicker P (2014) *Social Policy: Theory and Practice*, Bristol: Policy Press.

Stephens M (2007) Mortgage Market Deregulation and Its Consequences. *Housing Studies* 22(2): 201–220.

Stephens M, Lux M and Sunega P (2015) Post-Socialist Housing Systems in Europe: Housing Welfare Regimes by Default? *Housing Studies* 30(8): 1210–1234.

Torgersen U (1987) Housing: The Wobbly Pillar under the Welfare State. In: Turner B, Kemeny J and Lundqvist L J (eds) *Between State and Market: Housing in the Post-Industrial Era*. Göteborg: Almqvist & Wiksell, pp. 116–126.

Turner B and Whitehead C (2002) Reducing Housing Subsidy: Swedish Housing Policy in an International Context. *Urban Studies* 39(2): 201–217.

Waldron R and Redmond D (2015) Stress in Suburbia: Counting the Costs of Ireland's Property Crash and Mortgage Arrears Crisis. *Tijdschrift voor Economische en Sociale Geografie* 107(4): 484–501.

Walks A (2016) Homeownership, Asset-Based Welfare and the Neighbourhood Segregation of Wealth. *Housing Studies*. Published Online.

Watson M (2010) House Price Keynesianism and the Contradictions of the Modern Investor Subject. *Housing Studies* 25(3): 413–426.

Wilensky H (1975) *The Welfare State and Equality: Structural and Ideological Roots of Public Expenditure*, Berkeley, CA: University of California Press.

Willetts D (2010) *The Pinch: How the Baby Boomers Took Their Children's Future – And Why They Should Give It Back*, London: Atlantic Books.

Wind B, Lersch P and Dewilde C (2016) The Distribution of Housing Wealth in 16 European Countries: Accounting for Institutional Differences. *Journal of Housing and the Built Environment*. Published Online.

Wood G, Parkinson S, Searle B A and Smith S J (2013) Motivations for equity borrowing: A welfare switching effect. *Urban Studies* 50: 2588–2607.

Wu F (2015) Commodification and Housing Market Cycles in Chinese Cities. *International Journal of Housing Policy* 15(1): 6–26.

Zavisca J R and Gerber T P (2016) The Socioeconomic, Demographic and Political Effects of Housing in Comparative Perspective. *Annual Review of Sociology* 42(1): 347–367.

PART I

Old and new conceptualizations of housing
and welfare

2. The rise and fall of Ireland's property-based welfare state: home-ownership rates, policies and meanings in a historical perspective

Michelle Norris

INTRODUCTION

In most comparative analysis of governance and policy systems, English-speaking countries are categorized together on the grounds that they share similar arrangements for the delivery of public services and tax and benefit systems as well as a common language and legal system. For instance, Esping-Andersen's (1990) influential typology of welfare states categorizes these countries as 'liberal welfare regimes', in which households rely mainly on the market to maintain their standard of living (or in his parlance, 'de-commodification' of labour is low) because social security benefits are ungenerous and target low-income households. This contrasts with the corporatist–statist welfare regimes of Central Europe and the social democratic systems employed in Scandinavian countries, where more generous and universally available benefits enable higher decommodification.

In comparative analyses of housing systems too, English-speaking countries are regarded as similar primarily on the grounds of the dominance of home ownership compared to other housing tenures. In this vein, Ronald (2008) characterizes Anglophone countries as 'home owner societies' (Barlow and Duncan (1994) and Kurz and Blossfeld (2004) adopt a similar approach), while Kemeny (1995) suggests that these countries operate a 'dual' housing tenure regime in which home ownership dominates and renting is a small residual tenure (although in later work, Kemeny (2006) includes some non-English-speaking countries in this category).

A number of influential authors also argue that the correlation between high levels of home ownership, ungenerous social security benefits and social services in English-speaking countries – flagged in these typologies and confirmed by numerous other statistical analyses (for example,

Conley and Gifford, 2003) – is not merely coincidental; rather, there is a causal relationship between these two phenomena. This thesis was first proposed by Kemeny (1978; 1980; 1981), who argues that home-ownership-dominated societies not only reflect an individualist culture but also encourage individualist rather than collective solutions to social problems. This is because, for instance, the potential to live mortgage-free in an owner-occupied dwelling during old age means that pension savings are not prioritized. Castles (1998) famously summarized this thesis as 'The Really Big Trade-Off' between home ownership and the welfare state, and he and many other researchers have attempted to test its valid-ity, usually by means of comparative statistical testing of public spend-ing data (for example, Fahey, 2003; Doling and Horsewood, 2011). This debate has recently been resurrected in Ronald's (2007) work on housing and welfare systems in English-speaking and Southeast Asian countries. He concludes that the growth of home ownership in the former group of countries 'constitutes a form of convergence around a system of tenure that propagates the ideological and economic structures central to the logic of neo-liberalism. This logic constitutes a basis for liberal [welfare] regimes and lies at the heart of processes of globalisation' (Ronald, 2007, p. 480).

This chapter aims to contribute to this debate on the relationship between home ownership and the welfare state in English-speaking countries, but unlike most other instalments in this literature it does not offer a comparative analysis or statistical testing of survey or public spend-ing data. Rather, it examines the size and character of tenure in a single country – the Republic of Ireland – and the policy and finance regimes that shaped it in a very long-run historical perspective, beginning in the 1880s and ending in the 1980s. This country is commonly characterized as the archetypical Anglophone home ownership society and liberal welfare system (Esping-Andersen, 1990; Kemeny, 1995; Ronald, 2007) and these interpretations are supported by the fact that Irish home-ownership rates expanded steadily throughout the 20th century to among the highest levels in the developed world. In 1971, 70.8 per cent of Irish households were home owners, compared to 50 per cent and 35 per cent of their counter-parts in the United Kingdom (UK) and Sweden respectively; by 1991, Irish home-ownership rates had risen to 80 per cent, compared to 65 per cent in the UK and 39 per cent in Sweden (Kemeny, 1981; Boverket, 2006; Central Statistics Office, various years). However, the analysis presented here challenges the prevailing view that Ireland's ownership and welfare systems are similar to other English-speaking countries. Furthermore, on the basis of this case a more broad-ranging critique of housing and social policy researchers' dominant interpretation of this tenure's meaning and role (as a (neo)liberal project with the potential to undermine the welfare state) is also put forward (Ronald, 2007; 2008).

The argument presented in this chapter is that, until the mid 1980s, home ownership in Ireland was not a commodified tenure underpinned by low government intervention, market-based funding and housing development mechanisms. Rather, it was a decommodified or 'socialized' tenure characterized by mainly publicly funded inputs, redistributive ideological drivers and redistributive outcomes. Socialized home ownership was part of a wider project to progressively redistribute other types of property – primarily farmland – which emerged from agrarian agitation in the 19th century and played a central role in the Irish nationalist movement. Due to this combination of socialized home ownership and government subsidization of land redistribution, this chapter argues that Ireland operated a property-based welfare state for most of the 20th century, rather than merely a weak version of the social services- and benefits-focused model typical of other Western European countries. In the 1960s and 1970s, the property-based welfare state weakened; in conjunction with an acute fiscal crisis, this ultimately led to the rolling back of many elements of this regime from the mid 1980s. Nonetheless, some socioeconomic and policy legacies of the socialized home ownership system remain, which mean this tenure is not entirely 'neoliberal' in the Irish case.

The analysis of these issues draws on 'path dependence' (the view that once a particular policy direction is chosen, policies tend to remain stable because past policy decisions limit the options available to current policy-makers by increasing the effort and costs of changing direction) and associated concepts from the historical institutionalist literature (Mahoney, 2000). The main body of the chapter is organized chronologically and periodized around the phases of housing policy development devised by Bo Bengtsson (2008) and colleagues as part of their comparative, historical institutionalist analysis of Nordic countries. These are: establishment (when housing was transformed from a field of periodic crisis management to a permanent item on the policy agenda), construction (when the housing policy apparatus and many dwellings were constructed), saturation (when housing needs were largely met and the focus of policy moved away from new building) and retrenchment (when government housing subsidies and institutions were cut back). Also drawing on historical institutionalist theory, the next part of the chapter links the distinctive purpose and focus of the Irish welfare regime to its atypical origins and to factors relating to power, legitimacy and efficiency, which reinforced adherence to this unusual 'path' once it had been selected. The collapse of this regime in the 1980s is linked to the weakening of these bulwarks coupled with an external shock (a 'contingent break point', in historical institutionalist parlance) in the form of prolonged economic stagnation and an acute fiscal crisis (Mahoney, 2000; Bengtsson, 2008). The conclusions to the chapter set out the key findings and reflect on the implications of the Irish case for the international literature on home ownership and welfare systems.

THE RISE AND FALL OF IRELAND'S PROPERTY-BASED WELFARE SYSTEM

Pre-1922: Establishment of the Property-Based Welfare System

Stories about the emergence and evolution of welfare systems in developed countries typically start in cities and factories and end in benefits systems and social services. Historians commonly link the establishment and expansion of public welfare systems to the emergence and growth of the urban labour movement that followed industrialization, urbanization and the extension of the franchise to non-property-owners during the late 19th century (see Korpi, 1978, Castles, 1998 and Esping-Andersen, 1999, among many others). The focus of embryonic public welfare systems in many countries testifies to the influence of these factors; early housing policies usually targeted urban slums and access to social insurance schemes was often limited to industrial workers (Pooley, 1992; Balier, 2010). In mature welfare systems, most public spending is devoted to financing the systems for redistribution of income (via taxation and social security benefits) and provision of social services such as healthcare and education, which emerged from this urban working-class agitation (OECD, various years). This focus is reflected in the key concerns of most contemporary social policy analysis, such as Esping-Andersen's (1990) aforementioned typology of welfare states, which is derived mainly from analysis of social security policies and spending.

The story of Ireland's welfare system differs from the North-Western European norm. It ends in a property-based welfare regime rather than a benefits- and services-focused system; this distinctive end point reflects its unusual starting point in rural areas and agrarian social movements. When government first started to provide welfare services in the late 19th century, Ireland was part of the UK. Ireland was also a strongly rural society, with few urban centres of any scale; a small class of landlords (largely Protestant, aristocratic and loyal to the UK) owned most farmland, but the tenant farmers who rented their land were mainly Catholic and increasingly nationalist in outlook. By the late 1870s, tenant farmers' discontent with this landholding system inspired the establishment of an unprecedented mass political mobilization known as the Land League, the influence of which was enhanced when Irish nationalist members of the UK Parliament realized that taking up the cause of land reform would help to unite the bulk of the population behind their banner. Depending on their political hue, a series of UK governments proved willing to support land reform in Ireland (but not Britain) in order to procure nationalist support in Parliament, smother nationalist sentiment, 'bail out' bankrupt landlords or simply as the only viable means to foster a sustainable agricultural economy (Fahey, 2002).

These forces inspired a series of radical legislative interventions (the Land Acts), which facilitated a revolution in Irish property ownership. Starting in 1870, these Acts first regulated the letting of land by controlling rents and protecting tenants' security (thereby bankrupting many landlords); they then enabled – and finally heavily subsidized (using low-interest government loads) – the transfer of land ownership from landlords to tenant farmers (Clark, 1987). In 1870, only 3 per cent of Irish farmers owned their land and fewer than 800 landlords owned half the country. By 1929, the vast majority of the landed estates had been broken up and 97 per cent of farmers were owner-occupiers (Dooley, 2004).

These measures are significant for the discussion at hand, most obviously because they enabled mass rural home ownership and were important redistributive and decommodifying social policies in their own right, but more significantly because they had a defining influence on the welfare and broader social system that developed in Ireland during the 20th century. This is because, by conceding the principle of significant government involvement in the redistribution of land ownership from landlords to tenant farmers, the Land Acts opened a floodgate of knock-on demands – first for the provision of higher and higher public subsidies for peasant proprietorship and subsequently for support for the redistribution of other types of property, principally dwellings. It was from concessions to these demands that Ireland's property-based welfare system emerged during the first half of the 20th century.

This demonstration effect process was first manifest in social housing policy. The Land Act precedent was quickly cited by landless farm labourers, who were excluded from the benefits of land reform but were too numerous to be ignored by politicians. Their lobbying resulted in the introduction of generous rural social housing subsidies in the early 1880s and their extension by legislation introduced in 1906 and 1911 (Fraser, 1996; Fahey, 2002). As a result, by 1914, 45,000 social rented dwellings had been provided by Irish local government, 82 per cent of which were located in rural areas – compared to 24,000 units provided by their British counterparts, 98 per cent of which were in cities (Fraser, 1996; Malpass and Murie, 1999).

Despite the widespread slumification of Irish cities, the UK Government did not afford them the same special treatment as rural areas. Urban social housing subsidies in late-19th- and early-20th-century Ireland were almost identical to those applied to Britain; this was the primary reason why significantly less social housing was built in cities than in the countryside during this period (Fraser, 1996). In Ireland and Britain, local government was also empowered to provide mortgages by the 1899 Small Dwellings Acquisition (SDA) Act (but advanced few SDA loans until after World War I) and grants for private home owners were introduced in 1919 (O'Connell, 2004).

1922 to the late 1940s: Construction of the Property-Based Welfare System

Ireland seceded from the UK and became an independent state in 1922. However, the finances of the embryonic state were precarious and the first independent government (led by the Cumann na nGaedheal party) was socially and fiscally conservative (Ferriter, 2004). Thus, to balance the national accounts, swingeing public spending cuts were introduced during the 1920s, as some subsidies for urban social house building were abolished and old-age pensions reduced (Powell, 1992). However, the new government maintained – and in some cases increased – spending on the redistribution of capital assets.

For instance, the 1923 Land Act funded the remaining tenant farmers in buying their holdings but also radicalized the land reform project by funding the compulsory purchase, breakup and redistribution of large farms to smallholders. The redistributive nature of this policy was amplified by the fact that it was partly funded by the land owners whose land was being appropriated, while the recipients of the land (called 'allotees') were heavily subsidized by government. The former were paid 'fair value' for their land (which was significantly below market value) and compensated not in cash but in government-issued 'land bonds' (which yielded a fixed rate of return and could be sold back to government at face value, but government decided when and how many) (Seth Jones, 2001). The state generally sold on the land to allotees for significantly less than its purchase price and the allotees repaid this sum in instalments, known as 'annuities', rather than upfront in a cash lump sum or by using a mortgage (Dooley, 2004).

In addition, the framework of home ownership supports established before 1922 was expanded significantly in terms of spending, coverage and the array of policy instruments employed. In the decade after Irish independence, these instruments were expanded in four key directions. First, the state began to build dwellings for home owners. This began in 1922 when the 'Million Pound Scheme' enabled local government to

construct 2,000 new dwellings, mostly for sale. This type of output continued at varying rates for the following 50 years (National Economic and
Social Council, 1977; Aalen, 1992). Second, grants for home owners were
significantly expanded. The 1924 Housing Act increased existing grants
to approximately one-sixth of average house-building costs at the time
(Norris, 2003). Third, the Government enabled owner housing development by cooperatives called 'public utility societies'. The 1925 Housing Act
made these societies eligible for home owner grants and free government
land and they built 27 per cent of all private housing in Dublin between
1933 and 1938 (McManus, 1996). Government also provided the credit
necessary to enable households to purchase a dwelling, but with limited
success initially (O'Connell, 2004).

There was a change of government in 1932, when the populist and more
pro-public-spending Fianna Fáil party took office. It increased spending
on 'mainstream' welfare services and benefits but also continued to expand
the socialized home ownership regime. Fianna Fáil increased home owner
grants in 1932, established the Local Loans Fund in 1935 – to borrow
money from commercial sources and lend it on to local government to
fund SDA mortgages (and social house building) – and made SDA mortgages available for the purchase of new dwellings in the 1940s. Take-up
of SDA mortgages subsequently increased radically – from an average of
100 loans per annum in the 1920s to 5,309 loans in 1936/37, for example.
Consequently, local government was the main source of loan finance in the
1940s and 1950s (Daly, 1997).

The Fianna Fáil Government also fulfilled a key election promise to
its core support base of small farmers in 1933 when it cut by half the
outstanding annuity repayments they were obliged to pay arising from
the Land Act settlements. This further amplified the redistributive and
decommodifying effects of land reform policy (because the former tenant
farmers, who generally had low to moderate incomes, paid even less to buy
their land) – but it also inspired complaints of unfairness by rural social
housing tenants, who campaigned for the right to buy their dwellings on
similar subsidized terms. Once again, citing the precedent of the Land Acts
reaped benefits for this cohort and the 1936 Labourers Act afforded rural
social tenants the right to buy their dwellings, with annuity repayments set
at 75 per cent of pre-purchase rents. Thus another policy instrument was
added to the arsenal of home ownership supports; by the mid 1960s, 80
per cent of rural social housing was owner-occupied, accounting for 11.6
per cent of all home owners identified in the 1966 census (Central Statistics
Office, various years).

By the mid 1950s, the United Nations (1958) calculated that state
housing subsidies in Ireland were the highest among 15 European countries

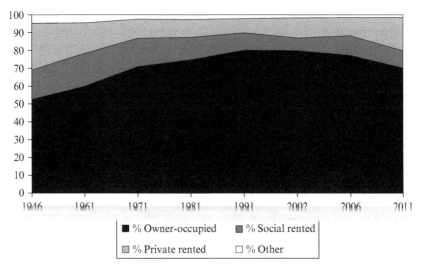

Source: Central Statistics Office (various years) and Threshold (1981).

Figure 2.1 Tenure patterns in Ireland, 1946–2011

examined, in terms of the proportion of both housing capital derived from the exchequer (75 per cent) and new dwellings that received public subsidies (97 per cent). The level of these subsidies, their universal availability and the variety of policy instruments employed to promote home ownership indicates that, in terms of inputs, the home ownership policy regime was comprehensively socialized by this time. By removing the key barriers to accessing home ownership, namely credit availability (addressed by SDA mortgages) and the need to accumulate a deposit (the United Nations (1958) study revealed that deposits averaged 5 per cent for SDA mortgages, compared to 10 per cent to 30 per cent elsewhere in Europe), Irish Government home ownership subsidies helped to grow this tenure to 52.6 per cent of households by 1946, with rates even higher in rural areas (Andrews and Sánchez, 2011) (see Figure 2.1).

Late 1940s to Mid-1970s: Saturation of the Property-Based Welfare System

Between the 1950s and 1970s, the socialized home ownership element of the property-based welfare system continued to expand, particularly in urban areas, so urban and rural home-ownership rates began to converge (see Figure 2.1). This development was initially flagged in the 1948 housing policy statement, which complained that urban middle-income households were continuing to rent privately (sometimes in poor conditions due to the impact of rent controls) while their working-class counterparts were being moved from the private rented slums to new social housing (Minister for Local Government, 1948). In response, the 1948 Housing (Amendment) Act further increased grants for individual home buyers and public utility societies and introduced supplementary grants for low-income households. 1956 legislation index-linked these grants and doubled the SDA loan limit. Subsequently, according to O'Connell (2004, p. 26), 'By the early 1960's . . . almost 30% of the cost of a standard suburban house could be recouped [from government] by the purchaser.'

Urban home-ownership rates received a further boost in the mid 1950s, when Dublin and Cork City Councils gained access to Local Loans Funds to finance SDA loans, as well as when the right to buy was extended to urban social housing tenants in 1966. The latter was supported by parliamentarians principally on the grounds of fairness; one claimed it 'would give them [urban tenants] the same right of ownership, at a reasonable cost, as is given to their brethren in rural Ireland' (Tully, cited in Dáil Éireann, 1966, vol. 200, no. 7, col. 1054). Like in rural areas, the right to buy significantly increased urban home ownership; nationwide, the tenure expanded to 60 per cent by 1961 (Central Statistics Office, various years) (see Figure 2.1).

Government involvement in land redistribution also continued to expand at this time, although it was becoming increasingly evident that this policy had reached its viable limits. The expansion of land reform policy was strongly promoted by a small farmers' party called Clann na Talmhan (literally 'family of the land'), which was active between the mid 1930s and late 1960s and participated in two coalition governments during this period. The party used its participation in government to reanimate land redistribution activities, which had been restricted during World War II in order to safeguard food production. On this basis in 1940, the wartime restrictions on the land redistribution were lifted, the state's legal powers to compulsorily acquire and redistribute land extended and the funding required to enable this increased. As a result the number of acres of land redistributed doubled between 1947/48 and 1949/50 (Dooley, 2004). However, despite vociferous lobbying by Clann na Talmhan, the budget for land redistribution remained static during the 1950s. Consequently, land redistribution rates did not increase any further. As explained shortly, these budgetary constraints partly reflected concerns about the continued value and enormous costs of this project, which were voiced publicly by a minister for land for the first time in the late 1950s (Dooley, 2004).

Late 1970s to 1980s: Retrenchment of the Property-Based Welfare State

Land reform was the first element of the asset-based welfare state to emerge in the 1880s and also the first to recede a century later. This policy was wound down significantly in the 1960s but its abolition was first officially sanctioned by a government committee report on land struc-ture reform in 1978 (Dooley, 2004). The report dismissed the aims of the preceding 50 years of land reform policy by linking Ireland's agricultural problems and rural population decline not to the lack of small farms but to their overabundance. It also raised questions about the cost and value of state investment in land redistribution. On these grounds, it recommended that the Government's land acquisition and redistribution activities be discontinued and 'in the future the land market should be conducted, as far as possible, without the state becoming involved in land acquisition and allocation' (Inter-Department Committee on Land Structure Reform, 1978, pp. 56–7). Most of their recommendations were implemented imme-diately and land redistribution largely ceased at this time. However, a succession of governments proved unwilling to publicly acknowledge this fact by shutting down the agency responsible for land reform – the Land Commission – which did not finally close until 1992, 111 years after its establishment (Dooley, 2004).

Ireland's socialized home ownership system proved more resilient; as a result, the proportion of the population accommodated in this tenure continued to expand during the 1970s and 1980s, albeit at half the rate seen in the 1950s and 1960s (see Figure 2.1). However, the first signs of weak-nesses in this element of the property-based welfare regime also appeared in the 1970s, as evidenced by uneven efforts to retrench some public sub-sidies for home owners while expanding others. This process was initially manifested in funding crises caused by persistent breaches of Local Loans Fund borrowing limits by local government due to high take-up of SDA loans (Daly, 1997). To address this problem, central government tried to encourage building societies to provide more mortgages (with limited success) until the 1950s, when access to SDA loans was limited for the first time to households with lower incomes. Consequently, SDA lending declined from 31.6 per cent of mortgages (by value) in 1966/67 to 17.9 per cent in 1972/73. Throughout the 1970s, the Government also intervened repeatedly in building society mortgage lending practices and subsidized their mortgage interest rates directly in an effort to further reduce reliance on SDA mortgages (Carey, 2007).

The 1970s also saw the first efforts to control subsidization of home ownership; home purchase grants were limited to first-time buyers in 1977 and, in 1974, a limit was placed on the amount of mortgage interest that was tax deductible (O'Connell, 2004). Mortgage Interest Tax Relief (MITR) has existed since the income tax system was first established, but for decades its cost was limited by the small number of home owners and low interest rates and offset by the taxation of imputed rent (Baker and O'Brien, 1979). This changed as home ownership expanded, tax on imputed rent was abolished in 1969 and interest rates rose during the 1970s, with the result that MITR spending increased by 61 per cent between 1975 and 1977; in response, government introduced a ceiling on the amount of interest that was tax deductible (National Economic and Social Council, 1977). However, the ceiling was high initially and MITR still covered up to 22.6 per cent of the total costs of servicing the average building society mortgage in 1975 (National Economic and Social Council, 1977).

Ireland enjoyed strong economic growth in the 1960s and early 1970s, but the oil crises had a particularly severe economic impact and the economy alternated between recession and stagnation for most of the late 1970s and 1980s (Bielenberg and Ryan, 2013). This precipitated a severe fiscal crisis; by 1987, 17 per cent of the workforce was unemployed, public debt was 150 per cent of gross domestic product (GDP) and debt servicing took up 27 per cent of public spending, which created obvious challenges for funding the state (Powell, 1992). The fiscal crisis was a contingent break point, which effected a critical juncture in home ownership policy because efforts to cut revenue spending were stymied by a marked rise in benefit claimants. Furthermore, following nationwide tax justice protests in the late 1970s and early 1980s, a widespread consensus emerged among policymakers that taxes could be raised no further and public spending would have to be reduced (Bielenberg and Ryan, 2013). Capital spending on major infrastructure was cut severely in the early 1980s; by 1987, having exhausted all of the other options available to balance the books, the Government decided that home owner subsidies (and subsidies for social house building) must be radically reduced (Honohan, 1992). As a result, the socialized system of home ownership that had been slowly constructed during the previous half century was largely dismantled in just a couple of years. The key milestones in this process were:

- The abolition of three of the four home owner grants in 1987/88.
- To restrain the spiralling national debt, the income limit for access to SDA mortgages (which was included in this debt) was significantly reduced in 1988. SDA lending therefore fell from a quarter of mortgages in the early 1980s to 2 per cent by the end of this decade and has remained below this level ever since (Norris and Winston, 2004).
- The hitherto highly regulated Irish commercial banking and building society sector was also deregulated during the 1980s; to encourage

greater lending competition, fiscal subsidies for building societies were also withdrawn, after which banks slowly took over as the primary source of mortgages (Murphy, 2004).

DRIVERS OF THE RISE OF THE PROPERTY-BASED WELFARE STATE

Power

The most significant driver of the continued growth of the property-based welfare state between the mid 19th and mid 20th centuries was the growing numerical and political power of small to medium scale farmers. The population decline wrought by the potato famine of the 1840s was felt most severely by landless labourers and the 'cottier' class (who, like sharecroppers in the United States, worked for a share of the crop or access to land on which to grow one), which reinforced small farmers' position as the numerically dominant class. Their influence was further increased by the intensification of the already strongly rural nature of Irish society after Irish independence in 1922. Belfast, which was the only significant industrial centre on the island, remained in the UK, while the cities of the newly independent state were small and – as trading, rather than industrial, centres – unable to support large numbers of well-paid, steady, working-class jobs (Ó Gráda, 1992). Gaining access to land was the only one of the few available routes to a living (and also to social status) for most people; this imperative drove the 'land hunger' that inspired agrarian campaigning for ever-higher spending on land distribution (Dooley, 2004).

Garvin (1981) argues that the numerical weight of small farmers was reinforced by their political skills. Drawing on a strong tradition of political mobilization accrued during their long campaign for land reform, they were far more skilled and effective advocates of their concerns than their urban class counterparts. Unlike many other European countries, in Ireland this mobilization was not expressed primarily by establishing dedicated agrarian parties (although three small parties of this type emerged and dissolved between the 1920s and 1960s). Rather, it was expressed by mobilizing behind the two parties that dominated Irish politics during this period (Fianna Fáil and Cumann na nGaedheal – later called Fine Gael) and campaigning to influence these parties' policies, as well as by establishing non-party-political campaign groups (Varley, 2010). Dooley (2004) links the changing electoral landscape between the 1920 and 1950s to the willingness of small farmers to block vote in favour of the parties that best reflected their interests; this in turn explains the willingness of politicians of all political hues to support land redistribution.

The introduction of the right to buy rural social housing in the mid 1930s was also shaped by electoral competition – not between the major parties, but rather between Fianna Fáil and the much smaller Labour Party. Despite its strong trade union links, during the opening half of the 20th century Labour failed to establish itself as a significant urban electoral force; its parliamentary representatives remained heavily concentrated in the rural counties of the east and the south, where they attracted a substantial vote from current and former farm labourers (O'Connor, 2011). Thus, between the 1920s and the 1940s, Labour Members of Parliament worked tirelessly to protect the interests of this class (and thereby their votes) from Fianna Fáil's charms, while Fianna Fáil worked tirelessly to attract the votes of this shrinking – but, until the mid 20th century, still relatively numerous – cohort (Hayden, 2013).

As well as the agrarian lobby, the building industry lobby had a significant influence on the introduction, persistence and expansion of home ownership subsidies. This was due in part to energetic and sustained lobbying by their representatives (described in Daly, 1997) and in part to the weakness of the Irish economy and the chronic oversupply of labour for much of the 20th century. As a result of the latter, the potential of home building and renovation to generate construction jobs was regularly used to justify exchequer subsidies for home building (O'Connell, 2004).

Legitimacy

In addition to small farmers' numerical power and lobbying skills, widespread political consensus regarding the legitimacy of their demands helped to drive the expansion and radicalization of the land reform programme between the 1920s and the 1940s. Both of the dominant political parties during this period were strongly committed to finishing the process of redistributing land title from landlords to tenants – a process that had commenced prior to Irish independence. They viewed this as necessary to reverse the historic wrongs perpetuated against the Irish by colonial oppressors, as well as due reward for the key role the support of small farmers had played in the success of the nationalist movement (Dooley, 2004).

However, Éamonn de Valera – Fianna Fáil's founder and leader until 1959 and the most senior figure in his party – held a more radical interpretation of the purpose of land redistribution. He viewed land redistribution as key social policy – a means of ensuring the economic viability of the agrarian–familist social model to which he was strongly committed and which enjoyed wide political, societal and religious support during this period (Seth Jones, 2001; Dooley, 2004). De Valera's commitment to this familist–agrarian social model was exemplified by the Irish Constitution he introduced (and was largely responsible for drafting) in 1937, which committed the state to recognizing 'the family as the natural primary and fundamental unit group of Society' and ensuring 'That there may be established on the land in economic security as many families as in the circumstances shall be practicable' (Government of Ireland, 1937, art. 41, 45). Government subsidization of property redistribution reinforced familial (in practice, usually patriarchal) authority since their further redistribution to inheritors was at parental discretion. Subsidies for the purchase of family farms and low debt also supported the stem (or three-generational) family system, which became widespread in Ireland after the potato famine (Gibbon and Curtin, 1978). Commonly, sons who hoped to inherit the family farm would work (unpaid) on the farm for many years, delaying marriage until they were deemed fit to inherit and the farm income could support an additional family. The unpaid labour of heirs and other assisting relatives made subsistence farming viable and provided a valuable form of welfare in the context of limited alternative employment options.

Politicians also supported land redistribution and the other aspects of the property-based welfare system because they complemented other important ideological and policy objectives. For instance, the redistribution of land from large farmers (who serviced export markets) and to smallholders (who serviced local markets or lived a subsistence lifestyle) complemented Fianna Fáil's economic policy during the 1930s and 1940s, which was protectionist and focused on promoting national self-sufficiency (Ferriter, 2004). Land reform and home ownership supports complemented the Catholic social teaching – and particularly the related economic philosophy of distributism, which encouraged governments to promote the widest possible distribution of property ownership across society (Garvin, 1981). In the 1930s and 1940s, distributism was promoted by Catholic intellectuals (for example, De Blacam, 1944) in Ireland as a 'third way' between unfettered free markets and communism – one that promoted social cohesion rather than class conflict – and by a clergy strongly rooted in the farming and small business classes and therefore intuitively sympathetic to this approach (O'Dowd, 1987). Although the specific term 'distributism' rarely permeated Irish policy debates, the influence of its principles was clear. For instance, the Government commission set up to examine the proposed sale of rural social housing to tenants argued: 'The history of our country had been one of continuous struggle both on the land and in the town to gain the freedom and security that go with ownership. This we regard as a basic and essential principle in any Christian State that bases social order on justice' (Saorstát Éireann, 1933, p. 1).

Efficiency

The property-based welfare system expanded faster than social security benefits and social services in Ireland because the former had some 'efficiency' benefits over the latter. Ireland's economy underperformed during the first half of the 20th century; the resultant strains on exchequer finances, coupled with a strong commitment to fiscal rectitude and deflationist economic policies on the part of senior civil services, are commonly cited as key reasons for the underdevelopment of the social services and benefits system in this country (see Fanning, 1978; Garvin, 1981 and Cousins, 2003 among many others). These efficiency concerns failed to stymie the growth of the property-based welfare system, in part because of land reform and house building's wider socioeconomic function as an employment generator and also because the distinctive arrangements for funding the implementation of this policy were less likely to attract the opposition of the disciples of fiscal rectitude. Prior to the introduction of insurance-based benefits in the 1950s, social security was funded from direct public spending, which had to be paid for through taxation and was visible in the national accounts. In contrast, spending on land reform was in part funded by those whose land was appropriated and the exchequer subsidy less visible because it was funded by borrowing in the form of land bonds. SDA mortgages were also funded by local government borrowing. Neither of these categories of debt were formally considered part of the national debt until national accounting standards started to be standardized in the 1950s (Eason, 1931 points that this was not the case in Britain or Northern Ireland). Thus, while exchequer subsidization of property-based welfare was costly, it was less costly and – crucially – less visible than the costs of effecting a revolution of similar scale in social security. As a result, land reform attracted less concerted opposition from the civil service than 'mainstream' welfare spending and – unlike social security, for instance – the power and legitimacy supports for land reform were sufficiently strong to overcome this opposition.

DRIVERS OF THE FALL OF IRELAND'S PROPERTY-BASED WELFARE STATE

Power

While the power of farmers (and to a lesser extent the construction industry) and the relative lack of power of the urban working class drove the growth of Ireland's property-based welfare state, by the 1980s the declining influence of agriculture enabled government to think the previously unthinkable and end the land redistribution project. The number of males working in agriculture, forestry and fishing fell by 29.3 per cent between 1971 and 1981 and this sector accounted for just 15.6 per cent of the workforce by the latter year (Central Statistics Office, various years).

Concurrently, Ireland finally began to urbanize and industrialize. For the first time in the history of the state, a majority of the population (53.1 per cent) lived in towns and cities of 1,500 people or more by 1956; this trend of urbanization continued during the decades which followed (Central Statistics Office, various years).

Legitimacy

Urbanization inspired the aforementioned expansion of subsidies for home owners; however, it also produced a marked increase in spending on social security benefits, education and major public infrastructure – particularly in the 1970s – which obviously reduced the potential for spending on the property-based welfare system. Increased social security spending was promoted by the Labour Party, which wanted to deliver for its now predominantly urban-based voters and was ideologically committed to developing a conventional European welfare model in Ireland (O'Connor, 2011). However, increased infrastructure and education expenditure also reflected the election of a new generation of political leaders in the two dominant parties who questioned the benefits of promoting smallholdings and wanted to encourage more efficient, large farms and industrial development (Garvin, 1981). The displacement of agrarian familism and distributism by this developmentalist/modernizing political ideology was a key reason why land reform was wound down in the 1960s and abandoned in the 1970s (Dooley, 2004). The influence of this paradigm shift on socialized home ownership was less direct, but nonetheless significant, over the long term. As the developmentalists increased spending on education and infrastructure to encourage industrial development, the level of public spending on home owner supports became increasingly unsustainable. Thus, from their perspective, the disadvantages of adhering to this policy path now outweighed the benefits (Malpass, 2011).

Efficiency

Concurrently, the efficiency bulwarks that had supported the asset-based welfare system also weakened. Standardization of national account-ing practices, which accelerated following Ireland's accession into the European Union (EU) in the early 1970s, reduced the potential for hiding public spending on the property-based welfare system 'off balance sheet' (in modern terminology). In addition, the rationale for this welfare model declined in tandem with the various 'market failures' it was designed to fix. Following Ireland's accession to EU membership, farm incomes were supported by the Common Agricultural Policy price supports – which reduced the need for land redistribution – and bank and building society mortgage lending increased significantly during the 1970s. Thus, the Housing Minister justified the virtual abolition of SDA mortgages in the mid 1980s on the grounds that it would reduce the national debt, with banks and building societies providing 'an adequate supply of mortgages for all income groups in all areas' (Flynn, cited in Dáil Éireann, 1987, p. 983). This call proved correct, and new mortgages increased from 27,632 in 1986 to 38,580 by 1989 (Department of the Environment, Community and Local Government, various years).

CONCLUSIONS

This chapter has examined the changing size and character of home owner-ship in the Republic of Ireland, the policy and finance regimes that shaped this tenure and its relationship with the welfare state between the late 19th and late 20th centuries. The interpretation of the Irish case proposed here contrasts to the prevailing interpretation of Anglophone countries in the comparative literature on housing and welfare systems (Barlow and Duncan, 1994; Kemeny, 1995; Kurz and Blossfeld, 2004; Ronald, 2008). Rather than a liberal housing system characterized by low government intervention, the preceding analysis has linked expanding home owner-ship in Ireland during the first two-thirds of the 20th century to a policy regime that was socialized in terms of inputs (most finance was derived from government), redistributive ideological drivers (agrarian–familism and the Catholic social philosophy of distributism) and reasonably pro-gressive redistributive outcomes (in 1994, 88.5 per cent of households in the highest income quintile were home owners, as were 63.6 per cent of

households with incomes in the bottom income quintile, so home ownership did not vary substantially according to income) (Fahey et al., 2004).
Rather than undermining the welfare system or supporting the emergence
of a (neo)liberal version, this chapter argues that Ireland's home ownership regime was associated with welfare system expansion – albeit in an
unusual, property-focused format, rather than the social-services- and
benefits-focused model typical of Western Europe.

Although these property and land redistribution policies are not conventionally categorized as social policies, in terms of scale of government
intervention in the economy required and the outcomes achieved, the Irish
property-based welfare system has significant similarities with more conventional benefits- and social-services-focused European welfare systems.
Land reform in particular was a progressive form of redistribution and an
effective way of protecting low-income households from the vagaries of
the market, and its decommodifying effects were amplified by the large
public subsidy received by allotees of farmland, which radically reduced
allotees' debt. Land reform required government intervention in the
property rights of land owners, which was just as radical as the taxation
applied to the incomes and assets of middle and higher earners to establish
the mainstream welfare states. Thus, although Éamonn de Valera and the
other architects of the land reform movement are now remembered as conservatives who sought to preserve traditional lifestyles, values and settlement patterns, in other respects this ideology was very radical. Indeed, the
view expressed by one of the few critics of land reform elected to the Irish
Parliament in the 1930s that the policy 'could not be framed or conceived
by any body of men except men imbued with a communistic outlook'
contains more than a grain of truth (Belton, in Dáil Éireann, 1933, vol.
49, no. 9, col. 937). Home ownership subsidization was admittedly less
decommodifying and less redistributive than land reform because, unlike
farmers, most home owners do not generate a cash income from their
dwelling and lower-income households are less likely to be able to purchase
their home. However, the very high levels of public subsidization of this
tenure did have significant decommodifying effects by reducing the debt
Irish households needed to shoulder in order to purchase their home, enabling relatively high home-ownership rates among low-income households.

Following the collapse of Ireland's socialized home ownership regime
in the 1980s, this tenure was significantly marketized and grew incremen-
tally more so over the decades that followed. As explained previously,
this process began with the withdrawal of most universal grants for home
owners, cuts to MITR and the almost complete withdrawal of local-
government-provided SDA mortgages in the 1980s. It continued in the
1990s and 2000s, when mortgage lending was further deregulated, most

building societies were converted into banks and MITR was reduced further, which coupled with the house price boom that commenced in the mid 1990s. This shift forced recent home buyers to take on much higher levels of debt than their counterparts in previous generations (Norris and Winston, 2012). Ireland's home ownership regime has thus become more neoliberal in terms of inputs and outputs in recent decades and therefore more similar to the norm in other Anglophone countries. This convergence is incomplete, however, because strong vestiges of the previous socialized system persist in Irish housing policy. The most obvious manifestation of these is the numerous targeted government supports for low-income home buyers, which have replaced the universalist subsidies (Norris et al., 2007). Norris and Byrne (2015) argue that credit deregulation, liberal land use planning and tax subsidies for housing development in urban and rural renewal areas are vestiges of socialized home ownership, because both sets of measures were partially inspired by the desire to use housing development as an economic and employment stimulant.

Although the introduction to this chapter explained that Ireland's socialized home ownership regime and property-based welfare systems are atypical, particularly in Western Europe, they are not unique. According to Gulbrandsen (2004, p.166), in Norway, historically 'housing policy was designed to combat the property rights of the few (the landlords) by spreading ownership among the many (the tenants)'. There are also clear parallels between the socialized home ownership in Ireland and the asset- or property-based welfare states common in Southeast Asia, as well as between Irish land reform and the very similar policies instituted in Japan, Taiwan and South Korea after World War II (Dore, 1959; Fei et al., 1979; Shin, 1998; Ronald, 2007; Ronald and Jin, 2010).

The Irish case has important implications for debates about the relationships between home ownership and welfare, as well as those surrounding housing and neoliberalization, in the international literature. The Irish case suggests that a more nuanced reading of these issues is required; one that takes account of home ownership's different meanings and roles in different cultures. The history of home ownership in Ireland demonstrates that this is not necessarily a neoliberal tenure that facilitates the rolling back of the welfare state. Home ownership can be socialized rather than marketized and has the potential to support the growth of the welfare state (albeit an unconventional property-focused one in Ireland's case) rather than undermining it. A more nuanced reading of home ownership should also take account of the numerous mechanisms governments can employ in its support. A key reason why the neoliberal aspects of home ownership policy are overemphasized by housing researchers relates to the number, variety and complexity of instruments governments can use to intervene in this tenure and the difficulties in identifying these – not to mention quantifying their scale and impact (Fahey and Norris, 2010). As detailed in this chapter, to increase home ownership the Irish Government has employed indirect subsidies (grants and tax reliefs), direct and indirect mortgage lending (SDA loans and tax subsidization of building societies), direct and indirect construction (by local government and public utility societies) and regulation/deregulation of mortgage lending by the private sector. The very in-depth, longitudinal examination of this wide variety of home ownership subsidies presented in this chapter has reached conclusions regarding the nature and function of home ownership in Ireland, which are very different from those reached by less comprehensive analyses of this case.

REFERENCES

Aalen, F (1992), Ireland, in C Pooley (ed), *Housing Strategies in Europe, 1880–1930*, Leicester: Leicester University Press, pp. 132–164.
Andrews, D and Caldera Sánchez, A (2011), *The Evolution of Homeownership Rates in Selected OECD Countries*, Paris: OECD.
Baker, T and O'Brien, L (1979), *The Irish Housing System: A Critical Overview*, Dublin: ESRI.
Balier, B (2010), Ordering Change: Understanding the 'Bismarckian' Welfare Reform Trajectory, in B Balier (ed), *A Long Goodbye to Bismarck?: The Politics of Welfare Reforms in Continental Welfare States*, Amsterdam: Amsterdam University Press, pp. 19–43.
Barlow, J and Duncan, S (1994), *Success and Failure in Housing Provision*, Trowbridge: Redwood.
Bengtsson, B (2008), 'Why so different? Housing regimes and path dependence in five Nordic countries'. Paper presented at the European Network for Housing Research Conference, 6–9 July, Dublin.
Bielenberg, A and Ryan, R (2013), *An Economic History of Ireland Since Independence*, London: Routledge.
Boverket (2006), *Housing Statistics in the European Union*, Stockholm: Boverket.
Carey, S (2007), *Social Security in Ireland, 1939–1952: The Limits to Solidarity*, Dublin: Irish Academic Press.
Castles, F G (1998), 'The Really Big Trade-Off: Home Ownership and the Welfare State in the New World and the Old', *Acta Politica*, 33(1): 5–19.
Central Statistics Office (various years), *Census of Population of Ireland*, Dublin: Stationery Office.
Clark, S (1987), The Political Mobilisation of Irish Farmers, in A O'Day (ed), *Reactions to Irish Nationalism, 1865–1914*, London: Hambleton Press, pp. 61–78.
Conley, D and Gifford, B (2003), *Home Ownership, Social Security and the Welfare State*, New York: New York University.
Cousins, M (2003), *The Birth of Social Welfare in Ireland: 1922–1952*, Dublin: Gill and Macmillan.
Dáil Éireann (1933, 1966, 1987), *Díospóireachtaí Dála* [Parliamentary Debates], Dublin: Houses of the Oireachtas.

Daly, M (1997), *The Buffer State: The Historical Origins of the Department of the Environment*, Dublin: IPA.

De Blacam, A (1944), 'An Outline of Distributivism', *The Irish Monthly*, 72(856): 430–441.

Department of the Environment, Community and Local Government (various years), *Annual Bulletin of Housing Statistics*, Dublin: Stationery Office.

Doling, J and Horsewood, N (2011), 'Home Ownership and Pensions: Causality and the Really Big Trade-Off', *Housing, Theory and Society*, 28(2): 166–182.

Dooley, T (2004), *'The Land for the People': The Land Question in Independent Ireland*, Dublin: UCD Press.

Dore, R (1959), *Land Reform in Japan*, London: Oxford University Press.

Eason, C (1931), 'Should the List of Authorised Trustee Investments in the Irish Free State be Extended?', *Journal of the Statistical and Social Inquiry Society of Ireland*, XV(2): 1–9.

Esping-Andersen, G (1990), *Three Worlds of Welfare Capitalism*, Princeton: Princeton University Press.

Esping-Andersen, G (1999), *The Social Foundations of Post-Industrial Economies*, Oxford: Oxford University Press.

Fahey, T (2002), 'The Family Economy in the Development of Welfare Regimes: A Case Study', *European Sociological Review*, 18(1): 51–64.

Fahey, T (2003), 'Is There a Trade-Off between Pensions and Home Ownership?: An Exploration of the Irish Case', *Journal of European Social Policy*, 13(2): 159–173.

Fahey, T and Norris, M (2010), Housing, in F Castles, S Leibfried, J Lewis, H Obinger and C Pierson (eds), *The Oxford Handbook of the Welfare State*, Oxford: Oxford University Press, pp. 479–494.

Fahey, T, Nolan, B and Maître, B (2004), *Housing, Poverty and Wealth in Ireland*, Dublin: IPA.

Fanning, R (1978), *The Irish Department of Finance (1922–58)*, Dublin: Institute of Public Administration.

Fei, J, Ranis, G and Kuo, S (1979), *Growth with Equity: The Taiwan Case*, New York: Oxford University Press.

Ferriter, D (2004), *The Transformation of Ireland, 1900–2000*, London: Profile Books.

Fraser, M (1996), *John Bull's Other Homes: State Housing and British Policy in Ireland, 1883–1922*, Liverpool: Liverpool University Press.

Garvin, T (1981), *The Evolution of Irish Nationalist Politics*, Dublin: Gill and Macmillan.

Gibbon, P and Curtin, C (1978), 'The Family in Social Context: The Stem Family in Ireland', *Comparative Studies in Society and History*, 20(3): 429–453.

Government of Ireland (1937), *Bunreacht na hÉireann: Constitution of Ireland*, Dublin: Stationery Office.

Gulbrandsen, L (2004), Home Ownership and Social Inequality Norway, in K Kurz and H-P Blossfeld (eds), *Home Ownership and Social Inequality in Comparative Perspective*, Stanford: Stanford University Press, pp. 166–186.

Hayden, A (2013), *Tenant Purchase in Ireland: A Study of Path Dependency*, unpublished PhD thesis, Dublin: University College Dublin.

Honohan, P (1992), 'Fiscal Adjustment in Ireland in the 1980s', *Economic and Social Review*, 23(3): 258–314.

Inter-Department Committee on Land Structure Reform (1978), *Final Report*, Dublin: Stationery Office.

Kemeny, J (1978), 'Forms of Tenure and Social Structure', *British Journal of Sociology*, 29(1): 41–56.

Kemeny, J (1980), 'Home Ownership and Privatisation', *International Journal of Urban and Regional* Research, 4(3): 372–388.

Kemeny, J (1981), *The Myth of Home Ownership: Private versus Public Choices in Housing Tenure*, London: Routledge.

Kemeny, J (1995), *From Public Housing to the Social Market: Rental Policy Strategies in Comparative Perspective*, London: Routledge.

Kemeny, J (2006), 'Corporatism and Housing Regimes', *Housing, Theory and Society*, 23(1): 1–18.

Korpi, W (1978), *The Working Class in Welfare Capitalism*, London: Routledge and Kegan Paul.

Kurz, K and Blossfeld, H-P (eds) (2004), *Home Ownership and Social Inequality in Comparative Perspective*, Stanford: Stanford University Press.

Mahoney, J (2000), 'Path Dependence in Historical Sociology', *Theory and Society*, 29(4): 507–548.

Malpass, P (2011), 'Path Dependence and the Measurement of Change in Housing Policy', *Housing, Theory and Society*, 28(4): 305–319.

Malpass, P and Murie, A (1999), *Housing Policy and Practice*, Basingstoke: Macmillan.

McManus, R (1996), 'Public Utility Societies, Dublin Corporation and the development of Dublin, 1920–1940', *Irish Geography*, 29(1): 27–37.

Minister for Local Government (1948), *A Review of Past Operations and Immediate Requirements*, Dublin: Stationery Office.

Murphy, L (2004), 'Mortgage Finance and Housing Provision in Ireland, 1970–90', *Urban Studies*, 32(1): 135–154.

National Economic and Social Council (1977), *Report on Housing Subsidies*, Dublin: NESC.

Norris, M (2003), The Housing Service, in M Callanan and J Keogan (eds), *Local Government in Ireland*, Dublin: IPA, pp. 165–189.

Norris, M and Byrne, M (2015), 'Asset Price Keynesianism, Regional Imbalances and the Irish and Spanish Housing Booms and Busts', *Built Environment*, 41(2): 156–189.

Norris, M and Winston, N (2004), *Housing Policy Review, 1990–2002*, Dublin: Stationery Office.

Norris, M. and Winston, N. (2012), 'Home-Ownership, Housing Regimes and Income Inequalities in Western Europe', *International Journal of Social Welfare*, 21: 127–138.

Norris, M, Coates, D and Kane, F (2007), 'Breaching the Limits of Owner Occupation? Supporting Low-Income Buyers in the Inflated Irish Housing Market', *European Journal of Housing Policy*, 7(3): 337–356.

O'Connell, C (2004), The Housing Market and Owner Occupation in Ireland, in M Norris and D Redmond (eds), *Housing Contemporary Ireland: Policy, Society and Shelter*, Dordrecht: Springer, pp. 46–92.

O'Connor, E (2011), *A Labour History of Ireland, 1824–2000*, Dublin: University College Dublin Press.

O'Dowd, L (1987), 'Town and County in Irish Ideology', *Canadian Journal of Irish Studies*, 13(2): 43–53.

OECD (various years), *Socio-Economic Statistics*, Paris: OECD.

Ó Gráda, C (1992), *Money and Banking in the Irish Free State 1921–1939*, School of Economics WP92/3, Dublin: University College Dublin.

Pooley, C (1992), Housing Strategies in Europe, 1880–1930: Towards a Comparative Perspective, in C Pooley (ed), *Housing Strategies in Europe, 1880–1930*, Leicester: Leicester University Press, pp. 325–348.

Powell, F (1992), *The Politics of Irish Social Policy 1600–1990*, New York: Edwin Mellen Press.

Ronald, R (2007), 'Comparing Homeowner Societies: Can We Construct an East–West Model?', *Housing Studies*, 22(4): 473–493.

Ronald, R (2008), *The Ideology of Home Ownership: Homeowner Societies and the Role of Housing*, London: Macmillan.

Ronald, R and Jin, M-Y (2010), 'Home Ownership in South Korea: Examining Sector Underdevelopment', *Urban Studies*, 47(11): 2367–2388.

Seth Jones, D (2001), 'Divisions within the Irish Government over Land Distribution Policy, 1940–70', *Eire–Ireland*, XXXVI: 83–109.

Shin, G-W (1998), 'Agrarian Conflict and the Origins of Korean Capitalism', *American Journal of Sociology*, 103(5): 1309–1351.

Threshold (1981), *Private Rented: The Forgotten Sector*, Dublin: Threshold.

United Nations (1958), *Financing of Housing in Europe*, Geneva: UN.

Varley, T (2010), 'On the Road to Extinction: Agrarian Parties in Twentieth-Century Ireland', *Irish Political Studies*, 25(4): 581–601.

3. Home ownership, housing policy and path dependence in Finland, Norway and Sweden

Bo Bengtsson, Hannu Ruonavaara and Jardar Sørvoll

INTRODUCTION

While housing policy debates have been historically dominated by discussions of rental tenures, more recent attention has turned to the role of home ownership, especially in regard to so-called asset-based welfare (see Ronald and Dewilde, this volume). So far, most contributions to discourses on home ownership and welfare have understandably focused on social and economic aspects. In contrast, this chapter takes a perspective of *housing politics* (cf. Bengtsson 2015) and discusses power and political processes related to housing policies that include home ownership. In doing this, we explore what specific expressions of path dependence housing provision would take in relation to such a policy. The argument draws on observations from three Nordic housing regimes: Sweden, Norway and Finland.[1] In all these countries, home ownership has indeed been seen as an important ingredient in general housing policies, although from different cultural and ideological standpoints and within different institutional frameworks. Policies of asset-based welfare related to home ownership have so far not been coherently formulated in any of these countries, although in more general terms, the issue has recently entered public debates.

To our knowledge, this chapter represents the first attempt within housing studies to examine whether political processes related to the provision of owner-occupied housing follow similar or different logics of path dependence compared to those of housing provision in general. Our discussion is related to Jim Kemeny's (1981) well-known thesis on 'the myth of home ownership', and we explicate the political implications of this myth by linking it to empirical observations of political processes of housing provision in Finland, Norway and Sweden. In the following, three separate sections corresponding to each national context are presented followed by a concluding comparative discussion. This outline is in accordance with a methodological logic of 'comparative process tracing' that combines theory, chronology and comparison and where the primary focus is on the historical trajectories of policies and institutions (cf. Bengtsson and Ruonavaara 2011). Comparison is not based on static variables but on the social mechanisms of path dependence and theory-informed periodization. In contrast to other chapters of this book, the evidence is qualitative: political texts, statements and debates; unfortunately, space does not allow detailed references to our sources here.[2]

THE MYTH OF HOME OWNERSHIP REVISITED

More than 30 years ago, Jim Kemeny argued that the conventional view of the virtues of home ownership was a socially constructed myth (Kemeny 1981; cf. Ronald 2008). This myth was deeply embedded in the cultures and policies of a group of Western capitalist societies he called 'home owning societies' (the UK, the USA, Australia and New Zealand) whereas in what he called 'cost-renting societies' (Sweden, the Netherlands, the Federal Republic of Germany and Switzerland) the myth had much less power. Kemeny did not single out in detail what the myth consists of. However, as we see it, the core concerns are essentially long-run affordability and value increase, freedom of consumer choice, autonomy from outside control and resident responsibility.[3]

Kemeny argued that the alleged virtues of home ownership are socially and politically produced through institutional and legal arrangements that make owner-occupied housing an attractive and advantageous choice. These arrangements are ideologically justified by a discourse that constructs home ownership as the 'natural' type of tenure that everyone in her/ his right mind should strive for. Together with how ownership and other general institutions are defined legally and socially in a society, housing policy is obviously central in the social production of comparative advantages of home ownership. Subsidies to different forms of tenure are an obvious way to make one form more attractive than another, as well as the tax breaks that home owners in many societies enjoy.

However, political decisions are not the only means through which governments contribute to the myth of home ownership. Kemeny paid considerable attention to non-decisions and claims that the superiority of home ownership is largely produced by choosing not to create a cost-rental (limited profit) housing sector that would be able to compete on equal terms with home ownership. Thus, without a conscious political intervention to create a competitive sector of non-profit rental housing, home ownership would be the dominant tenure everywhere. This is also what Michael Harloe argues from a framework based on a theory of capitalist development (for example, Harloe 1995).

The most important policy measures targeted at existing home owners are various kinds of tax concessions; for example, lower taxes on housing property and rights to deduct mortgage interest payments from taxes or taxable income. Such subsidies are not always the result of conscious political decision-making and their size is often not even calculated in national budgets. Thus, much of the housing policy targeted at home owners consists of indirect measures under limited political control.

All over Europe home owners have, for several decades now, tended to be better off than tenants. However, with a growing share of home owners in the population, there will be more variation in their situations (see, for example, Forrest et al. 1990). In societies with mass home ownership, there will likely be a substantial group of home owners on the margins for whom maintaining their tenure status is a challenge. If the ongoing economic recession in Europe continues, more and more home owners will have problems (of the kind, for example, that home owners in Spain have already experienced), which calls for rethinking housing policies targeted at home owners. This development also has important implications for the prospects of a policy of asset-based welfare (Elsinga and Hoekstra 2015).

In this chapter, we look at housing policies targeted at home ownership in Finland, Norway and Sweden. Previous research has established the strong elements of path dependence in housing policies and institutions in all of these countries (Bengtsson et al. [2006] 2013), but the focus has largely been on the rental sector and the relation between rentals and other tenures. Would we expect path dependence to be stronger or weaker in the owner-occupied sector, for example due to a dominant 'myth of home ownership'? As mentioned, perspectives of path dependence have not been applied to home ownership policies.[4]

PATH DEPENDENCE AND HOME OWNERSHIP

In recent years, various studies have pointed to the strong degree of path dependence in housing provision (for example, Kleinman 1996; Kemp 2000; Lowe 2004, chapter 6; Kay 2005; Bengtsson et al. [2006] 2013; Holt-Jensen and Pollock 2009; Malpass 2011). A typical case of path dependence is where actors more or less deliberately design institutions at point A (a 'critical juncture'); institutions that at later point B (a 'political focus point') serve as restraints to political decision-making and thus make some policy alternatives impossible or implausible. The mechanisms of path dependence can be summarized as efficiency, legitimacy and power, implicating that events at point A would make some alternatives (appear to be) more efficient, more legitimate or more powerful at point B (Bengtsson and Ruonavaara 2010; cf. North 1990; Hall and Taylor 1996; Thelen 1999; Pierson 2000).

How, then, can the relatively strong path dependence in housing provision be explained? First of all, housing has some well-known special characteristics as consumption and investment good. Dwellings last long, they are tied to a specific place, slow to produce, expensive, not easily substituted with other goods and so on (Stahl 1985; Arnott 1987). A housing stock produced over decades and centuries represents a powerful physical, social and cultural heritage that no government can ignore when making policy decisions. Furthermore, the psychological and social 'attachment costs' related to a household's transfer from one dwelling in one housing area to another (Dynarski 1986) should also have a stabilizing effect on policy.

Second, market contracts serve as the main mechanism for distributing housing, while state intervention has the form of correctives, defining the economic and institutional setting of those contracts (Bengtsson 2001; Oxley and Smith 1996, 2–3, make a similar observation; cf. Torgersen 1987). This means the main institutions are those that define the rules of the game in that market: in housing, crucially, tenure forms and other types of regulations. Housing tenures help define the basic rights of possession and exchange that are fundamental to a capitalist economy, which should induce some political self-restraint.

Third, since housing is ultimately distributed via markets, change in tenant legislation must also be accepted in the market by consumers and producers. This need for 'double legitimacy' – both in the political and the market arena – may also contribute to the path dependence of housing provision.

So, would a housing policy directed (also) at home ownership be strongly path dependent? First, the special characteristics of housing markets are highly relevant to home ownership. Even though owner-occupied single-family houses may on average not last so long, be a little easier to move, take a little less time to produce and be a little less expensive to produce than large multifamily blocks, it is definitely not an easy thing to adjust the supply of owner-occupation to short-term changes in demand. And the emotional 'attachment costs' of abandoning one's home may even be higher, due partly to the prevalence of the myth of home ownership. So we should expect the special characteristics of the housing market to restrict change in the home-ownership sector as well.

Second, the legal and financial conditions of home ownership decide the economic welfare of a large share of the population, so political self-restraint may be expected in the general interest of predictability and transparency for home owners. Indeed, considerable state intervention to the disadvantage of home owners may easily be framed by critics as an intrusion on citizens' basic rights and economic conditions.

Third, the need for 'double legitimacy' for change (politics and market) should be of relevance to the home ownership market as well. The obstacles to change may indeed be particularly strong, considering that in most countries the majority of voters live in owner-occupied housing.

The myth of home ownership may in itself have path-dependent properties. If the mutual relation suggested by Kemeny between housing policy and the discursive power of the myth is indeed valid, this would be an example of a self-reinforcing circle, typical of path dependence. In sum, we would expect just as strong – if not stronger – path dependence in policies directed at home ownership, as has previously been observed in housing provision generally.

HOME OWNERSHIP AND HOUSING POLICY IN THREE NORDIC COUNTRIES: AN OVERVIEW

'Home ownership', or owner-occupation, is a general label for a type of tenure that exists in many particular forms (cf. Ruonavaara 1993). Karlberg and Victorin (2004) make an illuminating distinction between direct and indirect ownership of housing. The clearest case of *direct ownership* is a household individually owning a house and the land on which it stands and being individually responsible for the property and all its costs, as well as being the sole beneficiary of capital gains and other benefits. *Indirect ownership* refers to a situation where 'the building or property is owned by a legal entity of which the residents are members or joint owners' and 'shareholding in the legal entity is linked to the right to a certain dwelling' (ibid., 62). In indirect ownership, the owners' individual rights of use, control and disposition concern only their dwelling, whereas shared spaces and the property as a whole are owned jointly together with other residents and managed collectively. The distinction between direct and indirect forms is highly relevant to understanding owner-occupation in Finland, Norway and Sweden.

Sweden and Norway have substantial sectors of *cooperative housing*. Today, in both countries, the major cooperative tenure forms share many characteristics with home ownership, and Karlberg and Victorin (2004) classify them as 'indirect owner-occupation'. Besides the dominant tenure of direct owner-occupation in single-family houses, owner-occupation in multifamily housing is also allowed in both countries – in Norway since 1983 and in Sweden only since 2009.

In Finland, besides direct ownership of detached housing, there is also a specific form of tenure based on indirect ownership: *housing companies* (see Lujanen 2010 for a detailed description). Each resident owns a certain number of shares in the company and these shares entitle her/him to the possession of a specific apartment. The resident has rights of use and disposition of the apartment, whereas the ownership rights to the structure of the house and estate belong to the joint-stock company in which the residents are shareholders.

In all three countries, owner-occupation is the most common type of tenure – but there are important differences in the forms. In Norway, most people are owners of detached housing. Direct ownership in Finland and Sweden is on a rather similar level, but in contrast to Norway, Finland's reputation as a home-owning society rests on the large share of indirect, housing-company-based owner-occupation. Using the classification developed by Karlberg and Victorin (2004), Table 3.1 shows the tenure divisions of the three countries *c*.2010.

The role of home ownership has differed considerably between the three countries and, to some extent, also over time. In Finland, part of the home-ownership sector, together with part of the rental sector, has functioned as social housing with means testing for applicants. In Norway, housing policy was universal until the 1980s, without means testing and with price-controlled cooperative housing as the institutional mainstay. The rental sector then was a peripheral concern for politicians. In Sweden,

Table 3.1   Distribution of housing stock by category of owner, c.2010 (%)

	Owner-occupied		Rented		Other	All
	Direct ownership	Indirect ownership[a]	Public and social rented	Private for-profit		
Finland, 2010	36	30	15	16	3	100
Norway, 2011	63	14	5[b]	18[b]	–	100
Sweden, 2011	41	22	18	19	–	100

Notes:
a.   Finland: housing companies; Norway and Sweden: cooperatives.
b.   Distribution between public and private rented estimated.

Sources: Statistics Finland (2010, Table 216); Statistics Norway (2011); Bengtsson (2013, 122).

the universal housing policy pursued after the Second World War has, at least in principle, been directed at all tenures, without any means testing, under the principle of 'tenure neutrality'.

Although home ownership has had different functions within the different housing regimes, in all three countries it has continuously been on the political agenda and discussed explicitly in housing policy terms, often in relation to other tenures. This should make them fruitful as cases for the empirical study of housing policies directed (also) at home ownership. The main differences between the three housing regimes are summarized in Table 3.2.

Development in the three countries can be organized and periodized in terms of a phase model based on the structural and discursive development logic of housing provision in modern welfare states. In all Nordic countries (and probably other countries as well) four phases can be distinguished more or less clearly: (1) an introduction phase;

Table 3.2 Comparative overview of the housing regimes of Finland, Norway and Sweden

	Finland	Norway	Sweden
General logic	Selective	Universal → selective	Universal
Type of regime (Kemeny)	Home ownership	Home ownership	Cost-renting
Direct ownership share	Medium	High	Medium
Indirect ownership share	High	Medium	Medium
Indirect ownership form	Housing companies	Cooperatives	Cooperatives
Rental market (Kemeny)	Dualist	Dualist	Integrated
Means testing	(Ownership[a]); rentals	Public rentals	Not formally
Role of municipalities	Planning; owning estates; allocation	Planning; owning estates; allocation	Planning; owning MHCs; allocation
Housing organizations	Weak	Medium	Strong
Type of corporatism	Trade union	Housing	Housing

Note: a. Until 2007.

Sources: Bengtsson (2013); Ruonavaara (2013); Sørvoll (2014).

(2) a construction phase; (3) a management (or saturation) phase and (4) a retrenchment (or privatization) phase. In the first phase, housing becomes a political question and public interventions in the housing market are initiated. In the second phase, the main concern of housing policy is to produce as much housing as possible to combat shortages. By the third phase, intensive production in the previous phase has resulted in a largely saturated housing market and the concern shifts to the management and maintenance of the existing stock. In the fourth phase, housing provision is gradually marketized.

FINLAND: OWNER-OCCUPATION IN A DUALIZED HOUSING REGIME

The nature of the Finnish housing regime can be summarized by three features, which to a large degree characterize it from the beginning to the present day. First, owner-occupation has long been seen as the normal, desired form of housing tenure, whereas renting is something for those temporarily or permanently unable to access owner-occupation. Second, housing policy has been seen as a branch of social policy; that is, something that concerns primarily those with a weak position in the housing market. Third, public housing policies are targeted at those most in need of support, leading to increasing selectivity in housing policies – and this has been seen as fair and socially responsible.

Despite recent changes in housing policy, as discussed below, it can be argued that in Finland home ownership has been dominant not only numerically but also ideologically – even though it is difficult to find policy statements explicitly promoting home ownership. Throughout history, there has been a taken-for-granted consensus that the two major ways for households to satisfy their housing needs are either by renting or buying in the private market or by self-building. Of the two market forms of tenure, home ownership has been politically preferred (cf. Ruonavaara 2013). Housing provided and regulated by the state has been seen largely as a supplement to private forms of housing provision.

Finland industrialized later than many other countries in Europe and the development of housing policy also lagged behind. In the first half of the 20th century, the public involvement in housing provision remained marginal and restricted to acute crisis situations, like the housing shortage after the First World War. This was in line with the general welfare policy orientation: social policy was generally residual and control-spirited (ibid., 287–9.)

The end of the Second World War was a landmark for the development of the Finnish welfare state in general and housing policy in particular. During postwar reconstruction, the role of the state in housing provision became dominant: rents were controlled, new house building was subsidized in taxation and a new state housing loan system, ARAVA, was established (in 1949). This marked the first large-scale intervention in housing by urban and semi-urban municipalities. After rather modest beginnings, ARAVA became quite important. Whereas the other postwar policy measures were gradually abolished after the private housing market recovered, ARAVA was preserved. Over the following decades, the ARAVA share of housing production was larger when private production stagnated and smaller when it thrived (ibid., 296–309).

The establishment of the ARAVA system meant the introduction of a social rental sector in Finland, but ARAVA production was not targeted at any particular form of tenure. In practice, the loan policy supported above all the growing indirect ownership sector in the urban areas; during its first decade, as much as 80 per cent of housing produced with the help of state housing loans was for owner-occupation, mostly flats in housing companies. Although the share of rental housing increased in the state-financed production, it was not until the 1980s that it exceeded that of owner-occupied housing. At that time, however, the state financed little more than one-third of all production (ibid., 317–19). It can be safely concluded that, in the early postwar period, the new interventionist housing policy actually promoted the growth of home ownership – especially for low- and middle-income households.

With the revival of private housing production after postwar reconstruction, state intervention in housing tended to lose importance. This changed with the ideas of social planning and equality of the 1960s (ibid., 309–17). Now, for the first time, the state was seen to have responsibility for the workings of the housing provision system and its distributive outcomes. A social minimum for housing standards was defined and the state was understood as being responsible for guaranteeing that minimum to every citizen. The conceptual triad of social planning, social justice and economic efficiency characterized the new housing policy. The scope of public financing of housing production expanded radically. When benefiting from subsidized housing finance, developers also had to comply with state regulations concerning the standards of housing produced, house prices and rents, as well as choice of residents. Social justice was to be guaranteed by favouring the least well off.

The planning ideology of the 1960s, however, had already started to wane by the end of the 1970s. The 1980s was a time of very lively private housing production and growth of privately financed home ownership. Finnish housing policies shifted from supporting production to supporting

consumption. Selective and direct forms of subsidy increased their importance in state subsidy policies. However, at the same time tax subsidies
enjoyed by indebted home owners became the most important form of
subsidy to housing, outweighing public production support and housing
allowances (ibid., 309–16). In terms of our phase model, the period from
the early 1980s on had characteristics of both management and retrenchment phases. The orientation towards more market-based housing policy
typical of the retrenchment phase emerged already in the 1980s, whereas
some of the typical features of the management phase, like concern for
residential segregation and for the renovation of housing areas from the
construction period, emerged later.

In recent years, the role of the state in housing finance has diminished.
The ARAVA system, once the flagship of Finnish housing policy, was put
to rest by a government decision to not grant new ARAVA loans after
2007. The once substantial state financial support of owner-occupied
housing production has shrunk to include only interest subsidies for
first-time buyers and self-promoters of low-energy detached housing.
State financial support for housing supply is now targeted at social rental
housing and housing for special groups (ibid., 331–2). Moreover, since
2012, the Government has started to scale down the politically sensitive
tax subsidy to home owners: the right to deduct mortgage interests in taxation. In 2015, 65 per cent of interest payments were deductible, whereas
the percentage in 2011 was 100 per cent. The estimated size of this subsidy
in 2015 was still 350 million Euros (Ministry of Environment 2015). The
retrenchment phase has meant that the selective character of housing
policy has become stronger. For example, the ending of ARAVA loans was
justified in parliament by the argument that, instead of general production
subsidies, the housing budget should be targeted at needy 'special groups'
(Ruonavaara 2013, 332). Thus, housing policy has become more selective
and has even more of a social policy character than before.

The Global Financial Crisis (GFC) immediately affected the Finnish
economy, but its impact on home ownership was quite limited at first.
After an initial shock in 2009, dwelling prices continued to rise until 2013.
Since then, there has been a slight decrease in prices and demand. From the
early 2000s, the stock of outstanding housing loans – as well as the average
mortgage – increased, with the GFC making little difference. However,
in the year 2013 this trend stopped and for the first time the volume of
outstanding housing loans decreased. As in other European countries, the
prolonged economic crisis increased the number of home owners experiencing debt problems. For example, compensations paid through mortgage
payment protection insurance increased in Finland in 2013. Debt problems
have especially emerged in unemployment-ridden municipalities, where

large employers have cut down and/or relocated their activities. Overall, however, credit defaults have increased considerably slower in Finland than in most countries and mortgage repossessions have been relatively rare. This is partly due to the strong protection that Finnish law provides for residential property (Wennberg and Oosi 2014).

In the Finnish housing discourse, owner-occupiers are increasingly seen as people who are doing all right and are in no need of support through either direct or indirect housing policy interventions. Though the idea of asset-based welfare has not been raised explicitly, expert voices have suggested that people should provide at least part of their future care needs from their own sources – and what assets do ordinary people have, other than the wealth stored in their home? The most important housing policy response by the government to the problems caused by the GFC was the increase of financial support for production of social rental housing in the years 2009–2011. The main objective for this was to boost employment in the building sector. The previous government's (2012–15) housing policy programme did express concern for the debt problems of home owners – and these were indeed investigated (see Wennberg and Oosi 2014) – but this did not result in any specific policy measures.

NORWAY: THE SOCIAL DEMOCRATIC NATION OF HOME OWNERS[5]

The development of the Norwegian housing regime may be summarized with reference to three characteristics (cf. Sørvoll 2014). First, the universal policy of the postwar years was gradually replaced by a selective housing policy directed at underprivileged households from the 1980s. Second, despite a universal tradition of housing provision, individual and coopera-tive home ownership have been the dominant tenures since the postwar years. Both of these tenures were subject to price controls until the 1960s and 1980s respectively. Third, Norway is a classic example of a 'dualist' rental market, to use Kemeny's (1995) typology. Since the 1950s, a small sector of rented housing owned or controlled by the municipalities has catered primarily to the housing needs of the most marginalized members of society. In 2012, the municipal sector accounted for around 12 per cent of the rental market (Sørvoll and Sandlie 2015).

After the Second World War (and as in Sweden), Social Democratic governments led Norway. Both countries launched ambitious postwar pro-grammes aiming at comprehensive welfare state reforms in education, care, pensions, the labour market and so on. Considerable attention was paid to housing provision, which was seen as contributing to the conditions in other welfare state sectors. In both countries, housing policies before the war (the introduction phase) had been rather ad hoc and directed towards solving imminent problems of housing shortage, inadequate housing standards and sudden fluctuations in housing markets. Now was seen as the moment to lay the ground for more comprehensive and universal policies, where 'only the best is good enough for the people' – to quote an expression often attributed to a former Swedish Minister of Social Affairs.

When the construction phase started in Norway, the socially oriented housing sector that existed before the Second World War had successively developed from municipal renting towards cooperative tenant-ownership. The universal housing policy launched by the Labour Government in 1946 favoured cooperative and owner-occupied housing, the former mainly in the cities and the latter in the countryside. These tenures were supported through the new State Housing Bank subsidies to construction and munic-ipal land allocation. The establishment of the nationwide cooperative umbrella organization, NBBL, also contributed to the strong expansion of housing cooperatives in the construction phase; in 1980, cooperatives accounted for nearly 17 per cent of the housing stock (Kiøsterud 2005, 29). In Oslo, the cooperative sector grew from 16 to 45 per cent of the housing stock between 1950 and 1980 (Hansen and Guttu 1998, 354).

In contrast to the Social Democrats of neighbouring Sweden, the Norwegian Labour Party supported individual and cooperative owner-occupation on ideological grounds. This was not because they had fallen victims to the myth of home ownership; indeed, the policy was rather based on what can be seen as an anti-capitalist and anti-landlord ideology of housing provision. In a parliamentary debate in 1951, future Prime Minister Trygve Bratteli (1971–72, 1973–76) made it clear that owning other people's homes should not be accepted as a field for private business interests:

> To me it is a matter of principle, and I want to make this crystal clear. In the modern society there are certain fields where private business is conducted and other fields where private business is no longer conducted, or where it is being phased out, and I for one do not accept owning other people's homes as a field for private business. (Stortingsforhandlinger (1951); our translation)

The cooperative sector, as the 'non-speculative' mainstay of Norwegian universal housing policy, had strong links to municipalities. In the construc-tion phase, then, transfer prices of cooperative housing were controlled by the state via the municipalities. However, in the 1970s, with the passing from the construction to the management phase, this regulation came under pressure from many quarters. According to Gulbrandsen (1983), the effects of Social Democratic housing policy after 1945 – that is, the growth of the cooperative tenure and the decline of rented housing – led to a backlash against state regulation. Ironically, the Labour Party lost votes because of the success of its own policies. Most importantly, fast-growing numbers of cooperative dwellers in the capital increasingly began to regard themselves as home owners and therefore turned against many of the regulations governing the Norwegian cooperative tenure. In short, they wished to sell their apartments to the highest bidder, just like owners of single-family housing. Studies of electoral behaviour indicate that residents in the cooperative sector flocked to the Conservative Party between the late 1960s and early 1980s. This is argued to have been an outcome of the party promising to protect their interests as home owners (Gulbrandsen 1983; Bay 1985).

Despite growing pressure from residents, the system was not changed until a Conservative Government came into office in the early 1980s. During the Willoch Government (1981–86), the principle of market prices was established in large parts of the cooperative sector. Regulated prices survived for some time in the capital, where the cooperative tenure had its highest relative and absolute importance. However, after 1988, they were of negligible importance even in Oslo.

Since the 1980s, in the management and retrenchment phases, the former universal housing regime has successively developed into an almost completely dualist one; market-priced individual and cooperative ownership and private rentals dominate the supply of housing, while a small municipal sector provides housing to low-income households with special needs. Interestingly, no serious political efforts to turn the tide have been made – not even under the Labour-led Government of 2005–2013. When it entered the halls of power, this government promised to establish a large sector of non-commercial rented housing. However, it did not seriously pursue this ambition at any time (Annaniassen 2006; Sørvoll 2014).

In recent years, moreover, politicians have expressed concern for the almost continuous increase in property prices and household debt since 1993. This is not surprising, given that the Global Financial Crisis only affected the Norwegian housing market temporarily; after a modest downturn, the housing market recovered in 2009. Between 2009 and 2015, property prices surged to an all-time high (Statistics Norway 2016). However, the Government's response to spiralling debts and price increases has consistently been based on the general presumption that home ownership is the 'normal' tenure (that is, on Kemeny's myth of home ownership). The Labour-led Government in office from 2005 even considered policies that sought to increase the number of low-income home owners. Similarly, to the Finnish case, policy makers generally consider rental housing a tenure form suitable for households temporarily unwilling or unable to cover the costs of home ownership (Sørvoll 2011).

According to the present, Conservative-dominated Government's new strategy for the housing sector, home ownership is an entrenched part of the 'Norwegian national spirit' (KMD 2015, 1). In the view of the Government (ibid.), housing capital has become a source of economic security and freedom for many home-owning pensioners in light of the price increases in recent decades. Previously, the Conservatives argued that rented housing was a poverty trap because it does not promise capital gains (Sørvoll 2011). This suggests that, even though asset-based welfare is not high on the political agenda, housing wealth is implicitly regarded as a supplement to the welfare state, most notably on the Right.

While mainstream politicians seldom question the merits of home ownership, public debate reflects a slightly different reality. For instance, academics and journalists have recently sought to document the different forms of inequality characterizing the owner-occupied sector. Gulbrandsen and Sandlie (2015) highlight that the housing boom of recent years has increased both the need for and ability of parents to help their children establish themselves as home owners. The prevalence of intergenerational housing wealth transfers 'may reproduce or even increase social inequalities' (Gulbrandsen and Sandlie 2015, 74). The importance of inherited housing capital is a novel development at odds with the egalitarian ethos of the welfare state. This notwithstanding, the comprehensive and universal Norwegian welfare state is not in the process of being abandoned for a so-called property-owning welfare state, in which life chances are determined by 'the accidents of market-determined changes' (Groves et al. 2007, 2). Instead, housing wealth supplements relatively generous welfare state benefits and services.

Moreover, many economists claim that the tax system unduly favours relatively prosperous home owners and is a major cause of rising property prices and socioeconomic inequality. In Norway, there is no state property taxation and home owners have the right to deduct interest rate payments from their taxable income. In 2013, the estimated value of tax subsidies to the owner-occupied sector was approximately 7 billion Euros (Braanen Sterri 2014). Even though several government policy commissions – from the 1970s to the present time – have recommended increasing the tax burden of home owners, little has changed. This is another illustration of the strong position of home ownership in Norwegian politics: the National Federation of Homeowners and their allies in parliament have successfully defeated all proposals calling for housing taxation reform (Sørvoll 2011). In short, neither the financial crisis and increasing debt nor concerns about inequality have undermined political support for the promotion of home ownership. This suggests strong path dependence in the Norwegian owner-occupied sector. Indeed, the decisions taken at the critical juncture of 1945 empowered home owners and their organizations, weakened the political voice of tenants and contributed to the strong ideational legitimacy of home ownership in policy debates.

SWEDEN: OWNER-OCCUPATION AND TENURE NEUTRALITY

In Sweden (as in Norway), the construction phase in our phase model commenced in the late 1940s, when a comprehensive and universal housing policy was introduced by a Social Democratic Government. The Swedish housing regime from that date and up to the beginning of the 21st century can be summarized in terms of five distinctive characteristics or 'pillars' (cf. Bengtsson 2013).

1. A universally oriented housing policy directed at all tenure forms, without individual needs testing or means testing.
2. A public rental sector with municipal housing companies (MHCs) that are owned by the municipalities and professionally managed at arm's length from political influence. After new legislation from 2011, MHCs are to change from being cost-based to being 'business-like'.
3. A unitary rental market (Kemeny 1995) in which both public and private rental housing is available to all types of households and formal links exist between rent settings in the public and the private sector.
4. A 'corporatist' system of centralized rent negotiations between (public and private) landlords and representatives of a well-established national tenant movement with internationally unique membership rates.
5. A large cooperative sector based mainly on the specific tenure of 'tenant-ownership', which before the Second World War was the leading provider of socially oriented housing but today is a clear case of 'indirect ownership'.

Sweden has the largest share of cooperative housing in Europe, comprising more than 20 per cent of all dwellings. In the 1930s, the Swedish model of tenant-ownership was actually imported to Oslo where, as mentioned, it came to play a crucial role.

However, for its new universal housing policy after the Second World War, Sweden set out on a different institutional path to Norway. Sweden chose a system based primarily on rental tenure in municipally controlled MHCs, while also supporting cooperative tenant-ownership. Although the postwar decisions prioritized municipal rental housing, they also included an element of tenure neutrality. The new state loans were directed at all tenure forms, including individual home ownership. Together with the developer's own capital investment, the state offered top loans to cover the share of the building costs (about 30 per cent) that could not be borrowed in the general finance market. The MHCs, being publicly owned, received loans covering all of this 30 per cent. Cooperatives received up to 25 per cent and had to contribute 5 per cent of the total cost from equity. Private investors, including individual home owners, had to contribute 15 per cent as a down payment.

Importantly, state finance only included a small and provisional element of subsidies; the main function of the state loans was to guarantee the financial security of investments in housing. They were combined with state control of rents and transfer prices of cooperative and owner-occupied housing; there was also some municipal influence on the distribution and transfer of dwellings. The policy was universal and the commission behind the proposals eloquently emphasized the need for a comprehensive policy in order to avoid housing with 'institution or slum character'.

When wartime rent regulations were finally phased out, the regulation of transfer prices of tenant-ownership dwellings was also abolished (in 1969). Like in Norway 15 years later, over time this led to a complete marketization of the cooperative sector. The political debate over the deregulation was less infected than discussions over the corresponding decision in Norway in the 1980s; after the deregulation, returning to the previous cooperative price control was never a realistic political option (cf. Sørvoll 2014). This meant that tenant-ownership in Sweden was transformed into a form of indirect ownership; from this point on, it came to fill the market segment that in other countries consists of owner-occupation in multifamily housing. In consequence, MHCs in principle became the sole socially oriented organization and tenure form in the more universally orientated Swedish housing regime.

In the last and most intensive period of the construction phase, the intensive building production of the so-called Million Programme 1966–75 – first associated with large-scale multifamily housing – led to an expansion of all tenure forms, including home ownership. Soon, with inflation and rising interest levels, the right to deduct interest on housing loans from taxed incomes turned into a financial support to home owners. Individual home owners were actually 'paid for being housed' – the title of a book by two leading economists (Sandelin and Södersten 1978). The Social Democrat Government realized that something had to be done but saw it as politically too risky to undermine economic conditions for this large group of 'our people' – as the influential Minister of Finance labelled home owners. The solution was to reintroduce (in 1974) general subsidies to all housing under the parole of 'tenure neutrality'. The intention was that interest subsidies and tax deduction together should favour rental, cooperative and directly owned housing equally. Up to the early 1990s, tenure neutrality was actually highlighted in the state budget when the total size of the subsidies from tax deduction was presented alongside the costs of subsidies to housing production.

Before long, however, this generous 'neutrality' was to become a serious threat to Sweden's economy as state subsidies expanded beyond all limits. When a right-wing government took office in 1991, a 'system shift' in housing policy was immediately signalled, starting with the termination of the Ministry of Housing. This also represented the beginning of the retrenchment phase in Swedish housing policy; in the following years, state loans and housing subsidies were successively phased out. These reforms put an end to economic tenure neutrality. The galloping universal production subsidies were phased out, although tax deductions remained. In 2012, total tax subsidies for home ownership were estimated at 3 billion Euros (Svenska Dagbladet 2013). Private and public housing were, however, still to compete in the same unitary market, and selective means testing was not even discussed.

As Holmqvist and Magnusson Turner (2014) point out, encouraging ownership was an essential part of the housing policy of the Liberal/ Conservative Government in office from 2006 to 2014. Some examples of this were promoting conversions from rentals to cooperatives, abolishing the real estate taxes (in 2008) and making condominiums legal in new buildings (in 2009). Sweden went through the GFC comparatively unharmed. House prices only decreased by 5 per cent between 2008 and 2009 and then went up again. However, the recent promotion of home ownership may have made the Swedish economy more vulnerable to future housing-related crises (cf. Holmqvist and Magnusson Turner 2014).

The indebtedness of Swedish home owners is high by international standards (and growing), although some commentators find comfort in the fact that the debt ratio is highest for households with high incomes, while the Swedish economy is seen as generally sound. Nevertheless, a number of different measures have recently been suggested against potential bubbles, including loan caps, mandatory amortization on housing loans, cuts in tax deductions for home owners and limits to households' debt-to-income ratios. All such proposals are technically and legalistically complex, as well as politically sensitive, and the only step taken so far is a new amortization regulation that says mortgages taken from June 2016 have to be paid off 1 per cent per year if they exceed 50 per cent of the property value and 2 per cent if they exceed 70 per cent per year.

Tenure neutrality is no longer an explicit goal of Swedish housing policy – and tax deductions are no longer framed as subsidies in the annual state budget. However, the concept of tenure neutrality still seems to have some discursive power. Organizations representing the rental sector (private and municipal landlords as well as tenant unions) regularly point out that home owners are favoured by the taxation system, which is argued to be unfair.

On the other hand, the political will to restore tenure neutrality seems to be weak. Today, direct and indirect home owners represent an even stronger political pressure group than they did in the 1970s. And universal subsidies seem to be politically unacceptable after the subsidy crisis of the late 1980s. This would represent path dependence driven not only by the discursive myth of home ownership but also by the political strength of home-owning marginal voters. So far, however, the economic support of home ownership has not initiated any political debate on asset-based social welfare as an alternative to the traditional Swedish welfare policies, which are still universal although largely dressed in NPM clothing.

So far, Sweden is not a home-owning society in Kemeny's terms – home ownership is still not taken for granted as the 'natural' tenure form. Since 2011, after new legislation in adjustment to European Union (EU) competition law, MHC rents are no longer to be cost-based and MHCs are to be more 'business-like'. However, the outcome in the market of this reform is still uncertain (cf. Elsinga and Lind 2013). Thus, it is still too early to tell whether in the end Sweden will no longer have the competitive sector of non-profit rental housing that Kemeny sees as a necessary condition for keeping the dominance of home ownership at bay.[6]

CONCLUSION: OWNER OCCUPATION, PATH DEPENDENCY AND POLICY

The analyses in previous sections demonstrate the strong path dependence of housing provision in the three studied countries. In each of them, the institutions established in the postwar period were crucial to development over the following decades – through the phases of construction, management and retrenchment. Even when the previous institutions were radically changed, or even abolished, traces of them were still seen in the discourse and the new institutions. Table 3.3 summarizes the development in the three countries over the different phases of our periodization model.

The analysis also demonstrates how home ownership has played an important part in the housing policies of Finland, Norway and Sweden – in some periods as the centre of the political debate, in other periods

Table 3.3   The path-dependent development of the Finnish, Norwegian and Swedish housing regimes

Phase	Finland	Norway	Sweden
Introduction phase, *c.*1900–1945	Crisis management: self-build and rentals	Crisis management: municipal rentals	Crisis management; selective MHCs
Construction phase, *c.*1950–1980	ARAVA system: social ownership and rentals	Social ownership, direct and indirect	Support to all tenures; universal MHCs
Management phase, *c.*1980–2000	Phased out state finance; ownership expansion and tax subsidies	Deregulation of cooperative sector	Tenure neutrality; galloping subsidies
Retrenchment phase, *c.*1995–	deregulation of rental housing	Development of social rental sector	Ownership expansion; business-like MHCs

Sources: Bengtsson (2013); Ruonavaara (2013); Sørvoll (2014).

lurking in the background as a crucial constraint to what is politically possible. However, the role of owner-occupation in the historical development of the national housing regimes differs strongly between the three countries.

In sum, Finland has shifted from a two-tier selective housing policy with both means-tested rentals and means-tested owner occupation towards a system where owner-occupation is constructed as the privileged tenure form and the social sector is dominated by means-tested rentals. Norway, meanwhile, has gone from a universal housing regime with price-regulated cooperative housing, open to all households but under some municipal control, to a selective system with a small sector of means-tested municipal housing. Sweden, finally, has gone from a universal and tenure-neutral housing regime with cost-based MHCs (and previously also price-regulated cooperative housing) without means testing towards a modified universal system, still largely based on (now more 'business-like') MHCs but without tenure neutrality.

Despite the strong national differences in the social and institutional roles of home ownership, in none of our three countries have policies concerning asset-based welfare so far arisen on the political agenda in a prominent way. As the recent debate in Norway indicates, however, this may soon change. Although the role of home ownership has been continuously debated over the years, this has been under the auspices of housing policy rather than general social policy. The (still rather stable) 'home ownership policies' of the three countries may also be explained to some extent by the relatively limited impacts of the GFC, particularly in Norway and Sweden.

The perspective of path dependence has also ostensibly proved to be fruitful in analysing the development of home-ownership policies in three Nordic countries. Our periodization of housing provision appears to be relevant for the comparison between the national processes. In all three cases, path dependence and change can be related to the changing conditions of the construction, management and privatization phases.

As mentioned in note 4, Aalbers (2015) also suggests a periodization of developments in housing markets. He distinguishes between (1) a pre-modern period (before the Second World War); (2) a modern or Fordist period of 'building for the masses' (from the end of the Second World War); (3) a 'flexible neoliberal' post-Fordist period (from about 1980) and (4) an emerging 'late neoliberal' post-crisis period. Whereas our periodization is based on the structural conditions of modern housing provision, Aalbers (2015) takes the impact of transformations in global capitalism on housing markets as his point of departure. Interestingly, periods of transition largely occur at the same points of time.

The myth of home ownership is prominent in all three countries, although only Finland and Norway would qualify as home-owning societies in Kemeny's terms. The myth seems to have an important role in the path-dependent patterns we have observed, although it can probably be deconstructed in terms of the more established mechanisms of efficiency, legitimacy and power. Being an ideational phenomenon, the largest impact of the myth is probably via the mechanism of legitimacy.

Our analysis has identified another mechanism that has to do with the potential political power of home owners – should they be mobilized as an interest group. This was most obvious in the Norwegian case in the 1980s, when price controls in urban areas were abolished. Moreover, in all three countries politicians evidently fear the reactions of home owners to tax increases. In a sense, this is to be expected: home owners potentially constitute a large block of voters.[7] It is interesting to note here that in Finland, deductible interest payments have been cut from 100 to 65 per cent in the last few years. What mechanism has acted against the power of home owners here? Though we have not investigated this, it can be hypothesized that the prolonged economic crisis in Finland has opened a window of opportunity for politicians to drive through reforms that previously were politically impossible.

Price regulation and housing taxation could benefit prospective home owners and thus, indirectly, the wider society. For instance, previous price controls on cooperative shares in Norway and Sweden were expected to ensure low entry prices for first-time buyers. Proposals calling for heavier taxation of home owners' housing wealth or reducing the tax breaks they enjoy are frequently framed as methods to combat inequality and promote social justice, reduce price fluctuations in the housing market, minimize speculation in price increases and finance welfare services. In light of these alleged benefits, therefore, the question is why other groups have not acted as a counterweight to home owners' expressed and perceived anti-tax and anti-regulation attitudes. Drawing on the works of Pierson (1994; 1996), we suggest an answer to this question related to collective action theory. Whereas market prices and low levels of taxation constitute a tangible advantage that is channelled toward home owners and simple for them to understand, the perceived benefits of housing taxation and regulated prices are less tangible and harder to grasp for non-owners. They may not even have an established identity as 'prospective home owners' – and consequently may be unlikely to protest against the 'privileges of existing home owners' (cf. Tranøy 2000).

The Norwegian case illustrates another aspect of the political and cultural dominance of home ownership. The favouring of owner-occupied and cooperative housing after 1945 led to the marginalization of actors championing rented housing, such as the National Federation of Landlords, as well as the organization of tenants. This could be seen as an explanation of why recent proposals to revive private rental housing have found little support amongst politicians (Sørvoll 2015). In contrast, Sweden has a uniquely strong tenant movement that has consistently been playing the 'neutrality card' as an argument for more equal economic conditions between tenures. However, so far they have not been very successful either, illustrating the strength of power mechanisms that favour home ownership.

Both the myth of home ownership and the potential political power of home owners work in the same direction. Together, they represent a powerful force favouring path-dependent stability where a certain housing regime already supports ownership and path-dependent change where it does not (cf. Thelen 1999). If we add the myth of home ownership and home owners' political importance as voters to the general path dependence of housing provision, the path dependence of home ownership policies would seem to be exceptionally strong. Neither arguments about tenure neutrality, justice and equality nor arguments about increasing risks of housing bubbles have changed the current progress along the path of favouring home ownership in the otherwise quite different housing regimes of Finland, Norway and Sweden. Examining the future politics of home ownership, wealth and welfare in these countries, as well as in the context of other housing regimes, represents a critical task for future research.

NOTES

1. Following Jim Kemeny (1981), our definition of 'housing regime' is quite wide. We see a housing regime as 'the social, political and economic organization of the provision, allocation and consumption of housing' (Kemeny 1981, 13).
2. For empirical detail on the path dependence of the three housing regimes, see Bengtsson (2013) (Sweden), Ruonavaara (2013) (Finland) and Sørvoll (2014) (Norway).
3. A myth is here seen as a belief that is taken for granted by those concerned but may possibly be false in an empirical sense. Interestingly, Forrest and Hirayama (2015) discuss post-crisis home ownership in terms that can be understood as claiming that the elements of the myth of home ownership are to a growing extent empirically false within the current 'economic project of neoliberalism'.
4. Aalbers (2015) suggests a periodization of developments in housing markets on the basis of transformations in global capitalism, which may be interpreted in terms of path dependence.
5. The heading is inspired by the title of Annaniassen (2006).
6. Kemeny (2005) discusses how declines in welfare provision for the elderly may represent a threat to integrated rental markets like Sweden's. Presently, however, the EU represents a more imminent threat to that model.
7. Politicians' public choice-inspired perceptions of home owners punishing them on election day may be too simplified (cf. André and Dewilde 2014; Ansell 2014). But such perceptions matter. Key Nordic politicians have certainly been preoccupied with the potential electoral power of owner-occupiers (Sørvoll 2014, 483–4).

REFERENCES

Aalbers, Manuel B. 2015. 'The Great Moderation, the Great Excess and the Global Housing Crisis'. *International Journal of Housing Policy* 15(1): 43–60.

André, Stéfanie and Caroline Dewilde 2014. 'Home Ownership and Support for Government Redistribution'. *Comparative European Politics* 14(3): 319–348.

Annaniassen, E. 2006. *Én skandinavisk boligmodell? Historien om et sosialdemokratisk eierboligland og et sosialdemokratisk leieboligland*. NOVA temahefte 1/2006: Oslo.

Ansell, Ben 2014. 'The Political Economy of Ownership: Housing Markets and the Welfare State'. *American Political Science Review* 108(2): 383–402.

Arnott, Richard J. 1987. 'Economic Theory and Housing'. In Edwin S. Mills (ed.), *Handbook of Regional and Urban Economics, Vol. II: Urban Economics*. Amsterdam: North-Holland, pp. 959–988.

Bay, Ann-Helén 1985. *Boligstatus og stemmegivning: eller, boligpolitikkens betydning for høyrebølgen*. Oslo: University of Oslo.

Bengtsson, Bo 2001. 'Housing as a Social Right: Implications for Welfare State Theory'. *Scandinavian Political Studies* 24(4): 255–275.

Bengtsson, Bo 2013. 'Sverige – kommunal allmännytta och korporativa särintressen'. In Bo Bengtsson (ed.), Erling Annaniassen, Lotte Jensen, Hannu Ruonavaara and Jón Rúnar Sveinsson [2006] 2013. *Varför så olika? Nordisk bostadspolitik i jämförande historiskt ljus*. Malmö: Égalité.

Bengtsson, Bo 2015. 'Between Structure and Thatcher: Towards a Research

Agenda for Theory-Informed Actor-Related Analysis of Housing Politics'. *Housing Studies* 30(5): 677–693.

Bengtsson, Bo and Hannu Ruonavaara 2010. 'Introduction to the Special Issue: Path Dependence in Housing'. *Housing, Theory & Society* 27(3): 193–203.

Bengtsson, Bo and Hannu Ruonavaara 2011. 'Comparative Process Tracing in Housing Studies'. *International Journal of Housing Policy* 1(4): 395–414.

Bengtsson, Bo (ed.), Erling Annaniassen, Lotte Jensen, Hannu Ruonavaara and Jón Rúnar Sveinsson [2006] 2013. *Varför så olika? Nordisk bostadspolitik i jämförande historiskt ljus*. Malmö: Égalité.

Braanen Sterri, Aksel 2014. *Tilbake til Politikken. Hvordan Arbeiderpartiet igjen skal bli folkets parti*. Oslo: Kagge forlag.

Dynarski, Mark 1986. 'Residential Attachment and Housing Demand'. *Urban Studies* 23(1): 11–20.

Elsinga, Marja and Joris Hoekstra 2015. 'The Janus Face of Homeownership-Based Welfare'. *Critical Housing Analysis* 2(1): 32–41.

Elsinga, Marja and Hans Lind 2013. 'The Effect of EU Legislation on Rental Systems in Sweden and the Netherlands'. *Housing Studies* 28(7): 960–970.

Forrest, Ray and Yosuke Hirayama 2015. 'The Financialisation of the Social Project: Embedded Liberalism, Neoliberalism and Home Ownership'. *Urban Studies* 52(2): 233–244.

Forrest, Ray, Alan Murie and Peter Williams 1990. *Home Ownership in Transition: Differentiation and Fragmentation*. London: Unwin Hyman.

Groves, Richard, Alan Murie and Christopher Watson (eds.) 2007. *Housing and the New Welfare State: Perspectives from East Asia and Europe*. Aldershot: Ashgate.

Gulbrandsen, Lars 1983. 'Fra gårdeier til andelseier: om framveksten av nye konfliktlinjer på boligmarkedet i Oslo'. *Nordisk tidsskrift for politisk økonomi* 14: 77–88.

Gulbrandsen, Lars and Hans Christian Sandlie 2015. 'Housing Market and Family Relations in a Welfare State'. *Critical Housing Analysis* 2(1): 74–81.

Hall, Peter A. and Rosalind C. R. Taylor 1996. 'Political Science and the Three New Institutionalisms'. *Political Studies* 44(5): 936–957.

Hansen, Thorbjørn and Jon Guttu 1998. *Fra storskalabygging til frislepp. Beretningen om Oslo kommunes boligpolitikk 1960–1989*. Oslo: Norges Byggforskningsinstitutt.

Harloe, Michael 1995. *The People's Home? Private Rented Housing in the United States and Europe*. Oxford: Blackwell.

Holmqvist, Emma and Lena Magnusson Turner 2014. 'Swedish Welfare State and Housing Markets: Under Economic and Political Pressure'. *Journal of Housing and the Built Environment* 29(2): 237–254.

Holt-Jensen, Arild and Eric Pollock (eds.) 2009. *Urban Sustainability and Governance: New Challenges in Nordic–Baltic Housing Policies*. New York: Nova.

Karlberg, Björn and Anders Victorin 2004. 'Housing Tenures in the Nordic Countries'. In Martti Lujanen (ed.), *Housing and Housing Policy in the Nordic Countries*. Copenhagen: Nordic Council of Ministers, pp. 57–78.

Kay, Adrian 2005. 'A Critique of the Use of Path Dependency in Policy Studies'. *Public Administration* 83(3): 553–571.

Kemeny, Jim 1981. *The Myth of Home Ownership: Private versus Public Choices in Housing Tenure*. London: Routledge and Kegan Paul.

Kemeny, Jim 1995. *From Public Housing to the Social Market: Rental Policy Strategies in Comparative Perspective*. London and New York: Routledge.
Kemeny, Jim 2005. '"The Really Big Trade-Off" between Home Ownership and Welfare: Castles' Evaluation of the 1980 Thesis, and a Reformulation 25 Years on'. *Housing, Theory and Society* 22(2): 59–75.
Kemp, Peter A. 2000. 'Housing Benefit and Welfare Retrenchment in Britain'. *Journal of Social Policy* 29(2): 263–279.
Kiøsterud, Tore 2005. *Hvordan målene ble nådd. Hovedlinjer og erfaringer i norsk boligpolitikk*. Oslo: NOVA.
Kleinman, Mark 1996. *Housing, Welfare and the State in Europe*. Cheltenham, UK and Northampton, MA, USA: Edward Elgar Publishing.
KMD (The Ministry of Local Government and Modernisation) 2015. *Strategi for boligmarkedet*. Oslo: Departementene.
Lowe, Stuart 2004. *Housing Policy Analysis: British Housing in Cultural and Comparative Context*. Basingstoke and New York: Palgrave Macmillan.
Lujanen, Martti 2010. 'Legal Challenges in Ensuring Regular Maintenance and Repairs of Owner-Occupied Apartment Blocks'. *International Journal of Law in the Built Environment* 2(2): 178–197.
Malpass, Peter 2011. 'Path Dependence and the Measurement of Change in Housing Policy'. *Housing, Theory & Society* 28(4): 305–319.
Ministry of Environment 2015. Asumisen tuki-ja verojärjestelmien vaikuttavuus. Ympäristöministeriön raportteja 4/2015. Helsinki: Ministry of Environment. Accessed 11 October 2016 at https://helda.helsinki.fi/bitstream/handle/10138/153 468/YMra_4_2015.pdf?sequence=1.
North, Douglass C. 1990. *Institutions, Institutional Change and Economic Performance*. New York: Cambridge University Press.
Oxley, Michael and Jacqueline Smith 1996. *Housing Policy and Rented Housing in Europe*. London: E. & F. N. Spon.
Pierson, Paul 1994. *Dismantling the Welfare State? Reagan, Thatcher and the Politics of Retrenchment*. Cambridge: Cambridge University Press.
Pierson, Paul 1996. 'The New Politics of the Welfare State'. *World Politics* 48(2): 143–179.
Pierson, Paul 2000. 'Increasing Returns, Path Dependence and the Study of Politics'. *American Political Science Review* 94(2): 251–267.
Ronald, Richard 2008. *The Ideology of Home Ownership: Homeowner Societies and the Role of Housing*. Basingstoke: Palgrave Macmillan.
Ruonavaara, Hannu 1993. 'Types and Forms of Housing Tenure: Towards Solving the Comparison/Translation Problem'. *Scandinavian Housing and Planning Research* 10(1): 3–20.
Ruonavaara, Hannu 2013. 'Den dualistiska bostadspolitiken och jakten på det sociala'. In Bo Bengtsson (ed.), Erling Annaniassen, Lotte Jensen, Hannu Ruonavaara and Jón Rúnar Sveinsson [2006] 2013. *Varför så olika? Nordisk bostadspolitik i jämförande historiskt ljus*. Malmö: Égalité.
Sandelin, Bo and Bo Södersten 1978. *Betalt för att bo: värdestegring och kapitalvinster på bostadsmarknaden*. Stockholm: Rabén & Sjögren.
Sørvoll, Jardar 2011. *Norsk boligpolitikk i forandring 1970–2010. Dokumentasjon og debatt*. Oslo: NOVA.
Sørvoll, Jardar 2014. *The Politics of Cooperative Housing in Sweden and Norway: The Swedish Deregulation of 1968 and the Norwegian Liberalization of the 1980s*. Oslo: University of Oslo.

Sørvoll, Jardar 2015. *Staten, kommunene, private og leiemarkedet: Et større og mer profesjonelt leiemarked i norske byer?* Oslo: NOVA.

Sørvoll, Jardar and Hans Christian Sandlie 2015. 'The Return of Large-Scale Landlords in the Norwegian Private Rented Sector? Political Reform and Path Dependence in a Nation of Homeowners'. Paper presented at the European Network of Housing Research seminar, 'Private Renting After the Crisis', LSC, 19–20 March 2015.

Stahl, Konrad 1985. 'Microeconomic Analysis of Housing Markets: Towards a Conceptual Framework'. In Konrad Stahl (ed.), *Microeconomic Models of Housing Markets*. Berlin and Heidelberg: Springer-Verlag, pp. 1–26.

Statistics Finland 2010. *Statistical Yearbook of Finland 2010*. Helsinki: Statistics Finland.

Statistics Norway 2011. *Population and Housing Census*. Accessed 10 October 2016 at https://www.ssb.no/a/english/kortnavn/fobhushold_en/tab-2012-12-18-12-en.html.

Statistics Norway 2016. *House Price Index 1992–2015*. Accessed 11 October 2016 at http://ssb.no/en/priser-og-prisindekser/statistikker/bpi.

Stortingsforhandlinger 1951. Volume 7a (transcript from the debates of the Norwegian Parliament). Oslo: Norwegian Parliament.

Svenska Dagbladet 2013. 'Så mycket förlorar staten på svenskars ränteavdrag'. *Svenska Dagbladet*, 17 December 2013.

Thelen, Kathleen 1999. 'Historical Institutionalism in Comparative Politics'. *Annual Review of Political Science* 2: 369–404.

Torgersen, Ulf 1987. 'Housing: The Wobbly Pillar of the Welfare State'. *Scandinavian Housing and Planning Research* 3(1): 116–126.

Tranøy, Bent Sofus 2000. *Losing Credit: The Politics of Liberalisation and Macro-Economic Change in Norway 1980–92 (99)*. Oslo: University of Oslo.

Wennberg, Mikko and Olli Oosi 2014. *Selvitys taloudellisiin vaikeuksiin joutuneiden asuntovelallisten tilannetta helpottavista toimenpiteistä*. Helsinki: Ministry of the Environment. Accessed 11 October 2016 at http://www.ym.fi/fi-FI/Ajankohtaista/Julkaisut/YMra_162014_Selvitys_taloudellisiin_vaik(30065).

4. Housing wealth and welfare over the life course

Stephan Köppe and Beverley A. Searle*

INTRODUCTION

Advanced welfare states provide social protection to differing degrees, from cradle to grave and through various services and transfers. Historically, however, the emphasis has gradually shifted from the grave to the cradle. The first social protection schemes focused on pensions and the workplace. Since the Golden Age of the welfare state, subsequent generations have witnessed not only major policy changes but also changing life course patterns and risks (Rowlingson, 2009). Shifts in academic debates acknowledge a need for a strong state welfare focus on the young rather than the elderly (Van Kersbergen and Hemerijck, 2012) – although within policy discourse this is played out as a generational U-turn, with politicians trying to play off an ill-defined younger generation against the elderly 'welfare generation' (Walker, 2012).

This perspective on the life course is the backdrop to understanding how housing wealth is utilized from cradle to grave and how it is being given back, or more accurately passed forward, for welfare purposes. The move to asset-based welfare in some advanced welfare states (see specific country chapters in this volume) has to various degrees complemented or even replaced existing welfare schemes. Most social policy textbooks have neglected this trend by either focusing on housing policy as providing shelter and rental regulation or ignoring the topic altogether, without acknowledging the increased welfare function of property assets (for an exception, see Fahey and Norris, 2010). A few housing scholars have addressed housing transitions in different life stages (for example, Beer et al., 2011), but without a comprehensive framework to capture its complexities across time. Welfare state retrenchment, austerity and a neoliberal agenda in developed welfare states, and lack of welfare expansion in residual welfare states, have increased the pressure and incentives to draw on housing wealth to finance education, pensions or long-term care. Yet so far we have only limited understanding of how housing assets and wealth may impact the life-course approach and interact with existing social protection schemes, both theoretically and empirically. Furthermore, it is important to shed light on the old and new social risks (Bonoli, 2005) associated with housing wealth.

The aim of this chapter is to explicitly lay the theoretical foundations to conceptualize housing wealth as a means of welfare not only in old age, but also throughout the life course. Though the prime function of housing is shelter, home owners also acquire substantial wealth to use for welfare needs at different points in time. While acknowledging these extended welfare functions, we discuss critically the benefits and opportunities of having and using housing wealth and contrast it with risks, drawbacks and dysfunctions. We present an analytical framework based on four key stages of how housing wealth can be used by individuals. Our gAMUT framework aims to capture the gamut of housing wealth across the life course, stretching from Acquiring, Managing and Using to Transferring and how it relates to welfare. This analytical framework assists in understanding the interdependencies of housing wealth and welfare theoretically and provides links to wider welfare discourses around privatization and asset-based welfare. Related to the aim of this volume, we will embed this discussion in inequalities across the life course and how the financial crisis has reinforced them.

We discuss the opportunities and risks associated with a stronger reliance on housing wealth and reinforce this with reference to recent housing trends in Britain – though we think this accounts for other advanced home ownership societies as well. Moreover, we develop an interdisciplinary conceptual framework of housing wealth in order to find common ground within a diverse terminology. Ultimately, the analytical ideas presented here are the basis for further theoretical, empirical and methodological discussions on housing wealth in general and how we can explain changes in housing wealth over the life course.

To present our framework the chapter is structured as follows. In the second section we review the life-course approach and the notion of choice. In the third section we describe our analytical gAMUT framework. Here, we differentiate between four core life-course stages of housing wealth, namely (1) Acquiring; (2) Managing; (3) Using and (4) Transferring, and discuss how to operationalize these stages. Following this, we analyse and discuss the opportunities and risks associated with each stage. The final section draws some wider conclusions about cumulative research strategies, practical applications and potential amendments to this framework. We also discuss the broader interdependencies between basic protection schemes, social insurance and wealth accumulation to provide welfare.

HOUSING WEALTH OVER THE LIFE COURSE

In their lifetimes, people accumulate different assets and use them for various purposes. Typically, the life-course approach retrospectively describes pathways of individuals and tries to connect these to historical events and generational change (Elder, 1994). Individual life-course changes are crucial in understanding the interplay of choices, preferences, institutions, culture and life events (Hareven, 2000). Applied to personal wealth, traditional lifecycle models assume a linear accumulation of wealth during the working life and depletion of that wealth in retirement (Modigliani and Brumberg, 1954). With regard to housing, such an idealized trajectory implies that individuals will follow a well-defined pathway and housing career (Clark et al., 2003; Morrow-Jones and Wenning, 2005). Once on the housing ladder, the home becomes a flexible asset over the life course: 'the ownership of a house is a source of current services; it may be used to satisfy part of the consumption planned for after retirement; it may be bequeathed; and, finally, it is a source of funds in emergencies' (Modigliani and Brumberg, 1954, p. 393).

However, modern societies are increasingly individualized, which questions the implicit assumptions of a linear progression within the lifecycle hypothesis. Increasing individualization suggests that these stylized pathways disintegrate and become more plural (Vickerstaff, 2006). Standard biographies are allegedly shifting to 'choice biographies'; that is, social norms of expected transitions are deconstructed and more unique pathways can be observed (Brannen and Nilsen, 2005). However, increasing options may create the illusion of choice without offering real alternatives (Le Grand, 2007, p. 45) and individualization of risks (Hacker, 2006). These trends suggest that life stages increasingly overlap (for example, studying and working) or are experienced in reverse order (for example, renting after a period of home ownership) compared to the idealized linear pathways presumed in the lifecycle hypothesis.

Assuming that modern life trajectories form increasingly complex deltas of smaller creeks rather than a mainstream river where the majority drifts, then the key research focus shifts towards the bifurcations of individual pathways. This means critical junctures of status changes are key to understanding the whole life course. If people are faced with alternatives at certain life stages, they perform 'choices'; or, more realistically, they have to make a decision. Yet, we reject assumptions that rational actors always pick superior options for their own welfare. Extensive studies have shown that these individual choices or decisions are influenced by structural and situational factors such as norms, institutions, personal capabilities and resources, timing or location (for example, in social policy, Clarke et al.,

2006; in economics, Thaler and Sunstein, 2009; and in housing, McKee, 2012) – factors that contribute to different life-course trajectories in different countries. Still, our understanding of 'choice' implies that individuals have alternatives (albeit constrained) but may be unable to opt for their preferred option in practice; hence, we use the more realistic terminology of 'decision'. For instance, people who rent may lack the financial resources to buy a home; this means they have no alternative, unless their circumstances change. On the other hand, people may make the decision to rent temporarily in a cheaper area to save up for a deposit (a conscious 'choice' is made). We also acknowledge that earlier lifecycle decisions are critical junctures that may lock individuals into certain positions and influence subsequent decisions (Mahoney, 2000). The empirical question is what determines people's housing decisions and their norms and perceptions about housing options over the life course.

Based on these theoretical considerations, the following conceptual framework aims to understand housing *wealth* transitions and their welfare functions over the life course, which is embedded in – yet substantially different from – Clapham's (2002, 2005) concept of housing *pathways*. Although the focus is on housing wealth, other wealth forms (for example, savings and shares) are included in this framework when they are transferred into housing wealth and vice versa. We recognize that housing markets are linked to many other life decisions (such as education, work and family) and that our focus on housing wealth covers only one particular, albeit key, aspect of wealth accumulation. Yet, housing wealth offers many links to welfare services such as assisting family members in times of need, a pension nest egg, long-term care and others. Moreover, our conceptual framework remains open in order to incorporate complementary perspectives on housing wealth.

gAMUT FRAMEWORK

Following these considerations of the life course, we want to address the key stages of housing wealth in this section. Various measures of housing wealth are used in the housing literature, such as tenure type, gross/net housing assets or house prices (Clark et al., 2003; Morrow-Jones and Wenning, 2005); however, these are seldom situated in a comprehensive framework. This points to the 'dependent variable problem'; that is, how to measure complex social concepts (Clasen and Siegel, 2007). While this leads to the need for multiple indicators to operationalize a complex concept over time, care needs to be taken to be precise about what is measured. Our gAMUT framework aims to be comprehensive in capturing the complexities of housing wealth over the life course through multiple indicators and to illustrate the links between housing and welfare, while being parsimonious in design.

To illustrate our understanding of housing wealth and how it can be operationalized over the life course, consider a fictional – yet 'traditional' – couple, Mr and Mrs Jenkins, who (1) acquire a house with a mortgage; (2) repay their outstanding debt; (3) use their housing wealth in old age to finance long-term care; and (4) in their will, split the house equally between their three children. We propose to label these stages of housing wealth transitions (1) Acquiring; (2) Managing; (3) Using; and (4) Transferring (abbreviated to our gAMUT framework). These four categories encapsulate key transitions between housing wealth statuses, as illustrated by Mr and Mrs Jenkins' straightforward housing wealth pathway, while enabling it to include much more complex transitions (discussed shortly). The labels refer purposefully to everyday terms that speak to lay and expert audiences alike and bridge disciplines, language barriers and methodological approaches (Gerring, 2001). Figure 4.1 illustrates these four housing wealth stages and their interdependencies.

Generally, these four stages can overlap or occur in any order. While individuals are acquiring a new home, for instance, they may use proceeds of an inherited house to put down a deposit or borrow more than they need to enhance or add value to the property. In the same line of argument, people's perceptions may not differentiate between these analytical categories and they may intermingle the various steps that lead to sustained housing wealth. Finally, the numbering of the four stages might pre-empt an idealized order, as exhibited in the fictional example. Though this order could prove to be empirically dominant, multiple pathways in and out of housing wealth suggest more complex sequences, reverse transitions and recurring alterations between two categories.

The following paragraphs illustrate in detail what we understand by acquiring, managing, using and transferring and how each stage can be operationalized through various indicators.

Acquiring

The first step into housing wealth is the actual acquisition of a property. When an individual changes from renting to home owning, this marks the milestone into housing wealth. Hence, the main dependent variable is becoming an owner-occupier. Based on this indicator, the analysis can reveal who is entering into housing wealth when, how, where and why (or why not) and whether the decision reflected a real choice.

There is a growing literature on the pathways of young adults into

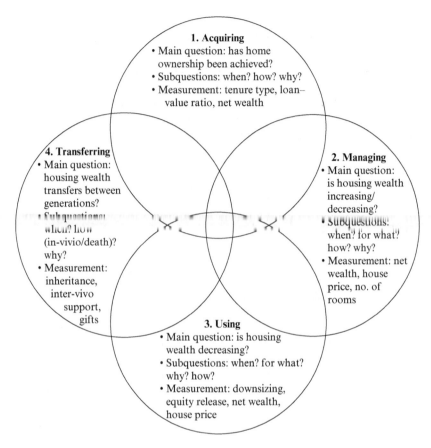

1. **Acquiring**
• Main question: has home
  ownership been achieved?
• Subquestions: when? how? why?
• Measurement: tenure type, loan–
  value ratio, net wealth

4. **Transferring**
• Main question:
  housing wealth
  transfers between
  generations?
• Subquestions:
  when? how
  (in-vivio/death)?
  why?
• Measurement:
  inheritance,
  inter-vivo
  support,
  gifts

2. **Managing**
• Main question:
  is housing wealth
  increasing/
  decreasing?
• Subquestions:
  when? for what?
  how? why?
• Measurement: net
  wealth, house
  price, no. of
  rooms

3. **Using**
• Main question: is housing
  wealth decreasing?
• Subquestions: when? for what?
  why? how?
• Measurement: downsizing,
  equity release, net wealth,
  house price

Note: The overlapping sections are only indicative and suggest no empirically observed
relationship.

Source: Author's own conceptualization.

*Figure 4.1   gAMUT framework: stages of housing wealth over the life
           course and the dependent variable problem*

housing wealth (see, for example, Kneale et al., 2010; Clapham et al., 2012).
However, a more fine-grained analysis of pathways into housing wealth
will help to understand strategies of housing wealth acquisition. For
instance, in the UK, a growing number of young adults are moving directly
from the parental home into owner-occupation (Köppe et al., 2013). It is
therefore as important to measure tenure type before the first acquisition
as it is after holding housing wealth. Furthermore, the amount of acquired
housing wealth would be a useful indicator for comparing long-term

pathways into home ownership – and, more generally, housing inequality. Estimates of housing wealth can be based on both official accounting measures and individual valuations.

A final note relates to the period prior to the first purchase of a home. In order to secure a mortgage, first-time buyers usually have to put down a deposit (although mortgages of 100% or higher have been available in the past). This period varies in length depending on how the deposit is acquired. Besides sufficient disposable income, saving for the deposit requires individual skills and characteristics, such as mental accounting and perseverance. Alternative indicators of intergenerational dependencies are also important where a deposit may be funded via a bequest or inter-vivo gift.

Managing

Once housing wealth is acquired, we consider that home owners are *managing* their wealth stock. This can be done successfully or unsuccessfully, explicitly or implicitly, actively or by doing nothing with the primary aim to sustain a home's value. Theoretically, there are various factors that may change one's holding in housing wealth. First, we should point out that the amount of housing wealth can both rise and fall at that stage, including falling into negative net wealth.

Second, housing wealth management involves both the physical and financial asset. Typically, changes regarding the *physical* dwelling (and its immediate surroundings) – such as moving home, refurbishing or extending property, unfortunate devastation or damage – may increase or decrease housing wealth, as can positive or negative neighbourhood changes through regeneration or social downturn. Upward or downward changes to the *financial* housing wealth may refer to individual decisions to alter the mortgage balance sheet; that is, by overpaying, taking mortgage holidays, re-mortgaging or 'shopping around' for better mortgage terms. A comprehensive understanding of housing wealth increases or decreases takes into account both physical and financial housing wealth.

Third, changes in the amount of housing wealth may be related to both the home owner's agency and external forces. Bizarrely, managing housing wealth involves also doing nothing, since nominal housing wealth increases on average in the long term by inflation despite successive booms and busts (see Doepke and Schneider, 2006). Therefore, managing housing wealth also involves the timing of selling and purchasing in highly volatile housing markets, which determines gains and losses to a large extent. For instance, selling at the height of a housing boom promises wealth gains without sophisticated management strategies, whereas buying at the pinnacle of a boom can lead home owners into negative equity (Ronald and Doling, 2012, p.953). In sum, managing housing wealth means sustaining the housing stock in the long run by active investments and changes in assets but also by doing nothing.

Quantitative indicators for change in housing wealth would be the frequency and amount of maintenance, undertaking improvements to the property, an increase or decrease in available living space or number of rooms, an increase or decrease in estimated property value or paying off a mortgage (see, for example, Smith and Searle, 2008; Parkinson et al., 2009). Despite these moves up and down, the primary aim would be to continue to possess housing wealth rather than selling in order to cash in.

In sum, managing one's housing wealth may involve increases and/or decreases in the amount accumulated, whether planned or unexpected. Managing also means dealing, whether proactively or passively, with the Janus-faced character of loss and gain in housing wealth accumulation.

Using

Using housing wealth overlaps strongly with the management stage and is not always clearly delineated from managing a decrease. Differences between these stages are perhaps more fuzzy and diffuse than between other stages and the motives for these decisions are often missing from social survey data. While the management stage aims to sustain and maintain housing wealth, we understand using housing wealth to be purposefully draining the wealth from property – to be transferred into other forms of financial assets (for example, pension, savings or shares), consumed for household purposes (goods or services) or channelled into household budget management (just getting by). Age is also a key criterion for distinguishing motives of managing and using, though it may only be a proxy for the underlying reasons for decreasing housing assets.

Individuals can plan to cash in some or all of their housing wealth, access it in response to an emergency or be forced to give it up when homes are repossessed (Searle, 2012). However, exempting compulsory repossessions, the use of housing wealth is here understood as a relatively voluntary act. For instance, British elderly people living alone are required by law to use their wealth – including selling their home – in order to finance long-term care services before they become eligible to receive means-tested support. Using also includes equity release products (for example, Overton, 2010). They free a predefined amount of the property value to be used for consumption or other purposes, while the remaining property value is protected and can be bequeathed to next of kin or as determined in a will.

Transferring

Finally, by housing wealth transfers we understand changes in wealth that involve more than one person. In such a zero-sum exchange, one person gains housing wealth while the other loses it. Research on transfers should therefore be attuned to both the individual who passes on a property (or part thereof) and the individual(s) who receives it (both inter-vivo and bequests transfers; for example, Kohli, 1999). Compared to the personal usage in the previous category, housing wealth transfers are characterized by passing on housing wealth to another individual(s). Indeed, the motives for housing wealth transfers are not altruistic per se; for example, parental bequest motives can demand care services in exchange for an inheritance (Angel and Mudrazija, 2011). Such ancillary benefits of the physical or financial transfer are left aside here, though they might be important drivers for the exchange.

We should also note that housing wealth transfers are bidirectional across generations, although downward intergenerational transfers (that is, from parents to children) are by far the dominant type (Kohli, 1999). In addition, these transfers often have a strong intragenerational component; that is, when a bequest is inherited by several siblings. It should also be noted that substantial housing wealth transfers occur between spouses after bereavement (estimates for the UK suggest about 30% of total transfer value is between spouses; calculations based on data from Karagiannaki, 2011).

Housing wealth transfers may link to any of the other three categories of housing wealth. The receivers may use the gift/bequest in order to (1) acquire a property; (2) increase their existing housing wealth – for instance, by home refurbishment or by paying off a mortgage; (3) use it to purchase any goods or services; or (4) transfer it further down another generation (see Figure 4.1).

WELFARE OPPORTUNITIES AND RISKS

Along the four gAMUT stages, housing wealth offers opportunities and risks for welfare. Like other assets, housing wealth offers direct in-cash welfare benefits and can be used for welfare services. However, with assets also come liabilities, especially when housing wealth accumulation is debt-financed and mortgagers are exposed to new risks.

First and foremost, housing provides shelter, which is one basic welfare need. However, shelter can also be provided in similar quality and for affordable prices in the rental sector. Therefore, we will focus our discussion on the additional welfare benefits that derive from owning a home. These welfare effects have been theorized in the asset-based welfare approach. The original theory of asset-based welfare is based on access to savings accounts as a means of alleviating poverty (Sherraden, 1991). This has been extended to other assets such as pension funds and housing wealth. Allegedly, assets provide a nest egg against social risks and contingencies to facilitate smooth consumption over the life course (for example, pensions) and prevent people falling into poverty (for example, precautionary saving). The key welfare effect of housing wealth relates to the accumulated net assets that can be used flexibly for welfare purposes, such as a net pension, financing long-term care and so forth. Further welfare benefits derive from welfare functions allegedly associated with holding assets, such as higher social conformity, wellbeing, democratic participation and autonomy (Sherraden, 1990, 1991, Prabhakar, 2009). In the following two sections we will discuss these alleged benefits and opportunities of property assets as well as potential new social risks (Bonoli, 2005). Where relevant, we will also address welfare adequacy, sustainability and access (Ronald and Doling, 2012). In this discussion we draw on our life-course perspective developed in the gAMUT framework and apply it to the asset-based welfare approach. Overall, we find little empirical evidence to support the theoretical claims made (Searle and Köppe, 2014).

Opportunities, Security and Wellbeing

The financial benefits of using housing assets as a nest egg from which to draw have been studied in various countries and for several welfare purposes (Ford et al., 2004; Hurst and Stafford, 2004; Clasen and Koslowski, 2013). From a life-course perspective, the acquisition stage lacks the benefits of accessing housing wealth for welfare purposes as insufficient net capital has been accumulated to draw on; instead, it rather amplifies risks (discussed shortly). Only later in the managing stage have households accumulated sufficient net wealth to capitalize on their property.

Empirical research suggests that mortgagors are increasingly drawing from their housing wealth during the managing stage (Lowe et al., 2012; Clasen and Koslowski, 2013; Wood et al., 2013). Research from the UK and Australia shows that equity withdrawal during the management stage is often used to finance family formation (Searle and Smith, 2010); this means younger households are more likely to increase their debt than older households, who potentially have other financial resources and lower consumption needs. Housing wealth serves as a financial buffer to cover social risks when public schemes are inadequate, which mainly accounts for residual and developing welfare states. However, the withdrawn housing assets are not only used in connection with social risks (such as unemployment); other non-welfare purposes (such as serving credit card debt, generational support or financing general household consumption) are also frequently mentioned. It is also evident that housing wealth is often only used as a last resort (Toussaint and Elsinga, 2009; Quilgars and Jones, 2010), pointing towards the difficulties in withdrawing equity in a timely and flexible manner.

The more adequate welfare purpose – and in line with the lifecycle hypothesis – is to become an outright owner and live rent-free when household incomes decline due to retirement (Ronald and Doling, 2012). In fact, there is strong evidence for a trade-off between a high ownership rate and a generous public pension system (Castles, 1998; Dewilde and Raeymaeckers, 2008), though with less empirical support for some jurisdictions (such as Ireland; see Fahey, 2003). In other words, the accumulation of housing wealth for a large share of the population compensates for weak public pension benefits; that is, outright ownership increases the disposable income in old age when public pension benefits are low.

With prolonged longevity and declining relevance of family ties, demand for formal long-term care has increased. In a country like the UK with a strong means test for receiving public care support, some households are forced to draw down their housing assets (Fox O'Mahony and Overton, 2015). Evidence from the US, however, shows that take-up of long-term care insurance increased when housing asset thresholds for means-tested benefits were increased through coverage (Greenhalgh-Stanley, 2014). This indicates that housing wealth is traded off against insurance cover and means-tested benefits in households' risk management strategies.

Welfare needs earlier in the life course can be addressed through intergenerational transfers of housing wealth. For instance, instead of saving (or equity borrowing) for their children's higher education expenses, parents can take advantage of interest rates by repaying their mortgage earlier and finance tuition fees with their potentially higher disposable income. Such options are, of course, only available when the mortgage is taken out before the first child is born, considering that typical repayment plans cover 25 years. Hence, most welfare benefits of housing wealth are in the middle to later stages in the life course, though inter-vivo transfers could also contribute to welfare effects earlier in the life course or the acquisition of an owner-occupied home (Heath and Calvert, 2013).

Looking beyond the direct financial benefits of housing wealth, some research claims that there is indeed an association between being a home owner and more tangible welfare effects such as increased wellbeing, human capital investments, political participation and social cohesion (Searle, 2008; Searle et al., 2009; Chen, 2013). However, most longitudinal evidence finds little support for the hypothesis that holding (housing) assets decreases poverty and contributes to higher wellbeing on a number of indicators. Contrary to the effects suggested by the asset-based welfare approach, the effect could well be the other way around; for instance, higher human capital could lead to increased home ownership and higher wealth accumulation (Searle and Köppe, 2014).

In sum, over the life course, housing wealth has a strong income maintenance and consumption-smoothing function – especially in old age, to cover lower disposable incomes in retirement or long-term care expenses. However, equity borrowing to cover other welfare functions and risks in working age is by far the most frequent approach to using housing wealth (Ong et al., 2013); non-welfare usage such as holidays and repaying debt is also common. In the next section, we turn to the risks associated with relying on housing wealth, especially to cover working-age risks.

Risks, Worries and Perpetuation of Inequalities

Despite the clear welfare utility of housing wealth over the life course, there are several shortcomings, risks and welfare trade-offs to consider. We will address two issues in this section. First, we will discuss the apparent dysfunctional usages at each stage and the new social risks (Bonoli, 2005) emerging from them. Little attention has been paid to the effects of individualizing assets and the initially debt-financed asset accumulation, which creates new social risks instead of direct welfare functions. Second, we will discuss the wider welfare trade-offs, such as intragenerational and intergenerational inequalities associated with – and resulting from – a greater reliance on housing wealth at each stage.

In contrast to the security and asset repository later in life, investing in housing wealth exposes individuals and households to new risks in the acquisition and managing stages that are often underestimated, both by first-time buyers fulfilling their dream of owner-occupation and by policy makers promoting home ownership.

Prior to acquiring housing wealth, young adults may decrease their earning potential and individual autonomy. Longitudinal evidence suggests that one route into home ownership is to live longer at the parental home to save for a deposit (Köppe et al., 2013). Prioritizing housing wealth acquisition through this route limits young adults' labour market flexibility by preventing them from moving to prosperous regions with better earnings potential. It also reinforces family ties at a stage when other young adults form independent households, leading to a re-familiarization of welfare. Evidence from UK court cases also indicates that living with parents can lead to enduring conflicts between parents and children (Izuhara and Köppe, 2017).

Once individuals have acquired housing wealth, they are constrained and exposed to new social risks in various dimensions. First, welfare entitlements are increasingly based on the individual instead of households, though family ties remain strong in means-tested programmes and more familiaristic welfare states. When acquiring housing wealth with family support for a deposit, this would strengthen family ties. Housing wealth as a means of social protection depends under these circumstances on much stronger informal family relations than more formal welfare programmes (for example, in East Asia; see Ronald and Doling, 2012). Depending on the conditions of the parental support (interest charged or free loan; gift), children would trade autonomy and independence for acquiring a home. Heath and Calvert (2013) report that first-time buyers who received parental support felt uneasy about receiving money, guilty when they could not pay it back and a loss of autonomy. Thus, the concept of 'my home is my castle' could turn into 'mum and dad's castle' or 'the in-laws' prison'.

Second, owning a property reduces labour market flexibility – considerably so in Britain (Böheim and Taylor, 2002). While renters are relatively flexible in their capacity to move to more prosperous regions, home owners have higher transactions costs when moving home. The problems for home owners are also heightened during recessions, when house prices decline and unemployment rises; should unemployment hit, home owners also face the risk of negative equity. Böheim and Taylor (2002) show that negative equity actually increases the pressure to move to either a cheaper home or better employment prospects, but little is known about the long-term wealth effects of these moves under higher economic pressures.

Third, in the acquisition stage, and even more so throughout the managing stage, home owners are exposed to new risks that are not covered through traditional welfare schemes. Home owners with little net housing wealth turn into risk managers instead of gaining security, as claimed in the asset-based welfare hypothesis (for social risk management, see Holzmann and Jørgensen, 2001). On the one hand, owning involves the risk of losing the acquired property and associated wealth. Managing housing wealth therefore includes the need to protect against physical and social risks that could lead to losing the investment. Environmental risks to the housing stock (for example, flooding or fire) can be covered by home insurances, whereas social risks such as unemployment, ill health, need of care or bereavement can be protected by various schemes or informal arrangements. Though protection against the physical asset loss due to environmental risks has social implications, such as the unequal distribution of risk exposure and implications for socializing some of the risk-protection measures (for example, public goods such as flood defences), we will focus our discussion on the social risks.

Certain social risks do not discriminate between renters and owners, such as unemployment and illness, but the effects on disposable income can vary considerably. While most advanced welfare states have some form of income protection for these working-age risks, usually associated with the managing stage, such welfare benefits are limited in duration (for example, unemployment, sickness, accident insurance and redundancy pay). Moreover, public means-tested benefits typically pay rent allowances but do not cover mortgage repayments.

More specific social protection schemes for mortgage debtors have been developed to meet mortgage payments in various social risk scenarios. A few public schemes help to repay mortgages, or at least the interest due, when standard social risks such as unemployment or sickness strike (for example, Support for Mortgage Interest (UK) and Mortgage Interest Supplement (Ireland); see Searle, 2012). More common are private welfare solutions such as mortgage holidays (often flexible criteria), Mortgage Payment Protection Insurance (MPPI) (more specific criteria such as unemployment and critical illness) (Ford et al., 2004) and life insurances (following the loss of a partner). Other social risks, such as divorce, negatively affect the amount of accumulated housing wealth and have yet remained formally uninsurable (Rowlingson and Joseph, 2010). Mortgage holders are faced with managing and balancing these social risks to a larger degree than outright owners as their housing wealth is financed through debt.[1]

Utilizing housing wealth already at the management stage also reduces long-term asset-building potential and future welfare uses, as suggested by the asset-based welfare approach (see Ronald and Doling, 2012). Though some of the risk associated with the managing stage can be insured privately, risk exposure and insurance take-up is unevenly distributed. While those on higher incomes and in higher occupational groups have a lower likelihood of falling into arrears and facing repossession, they are usually better covered through occupational and private schemes. Low-income households bear larger risks of defaulting due to higher rates of unemployment, worse health and shorter longevity. In addition, their labour-market risks are often uninsurable when in fixed-term employment, zero-hour contracts or self-employment. Research on take-up of private insurances underscores this trend that low-income households are not adequately covered against these working-age risks and would otherwise struggle to repay their mortgage (Ford and Quilgars, 2001; Smith et al., 2002; Clasen and Koslowski, 2013). On top of this, mis-selling of MPPI in the UK particularly affected those households with uninsurable risks while also increasing their monthly costs (FSA, 2009). In sum, low-income households disproportionately shoulder this divide in risk exposure and coverage associated with managing housing wealth, which is in contrast to welfare policies with the aim of reducing inequalities.

Using housing wealth bears far fewer risks than the managing stage, but certain risks associated with assets remain. As previously discussed, the two main welfare purposes of housing wealth in old age are rent-free accommodation to increase the disposable income in retirement and using the asset for long-term care services. The net pension effect of housing wealth is more of a contingency that everyone faces than an unpredictable social risk, but this means the mortgage has to be repaid by retirement age, which some pensioners do not manage to do (Parkinson et al., 2009). Retirement planning also has to account for continued maintenance cost to avoid property depreciation in the context of increasing longevity, which means housing wealth has to last longer. This affects mainly housing-rich income-poor elderly households, which are by and large a minority, although predominantly female and single-person households (Rowlingson and McKay, 2012).

A larger effect on inequalities at the usage stage is the distribution of long-term care needs. While increased longevity means that periods of care needs are also longer, the welfare effects of the unequal risk of needing care are large. About one-fifth of the elderly requires formal care services – sometimes for several years – and women are far more likely to need care in old age (Parker and Schneider, 2007). Thus, some can pass on their housing wealth while others have to use it for their own care needs. This is, of course, more often the case in jurisdictions with a strong means test for access to public long-term care services (such as in the US and the UK). In other countries, housing wealth is more protected (a maximum of 15% property value in Ireland: Considine and Dukelow, 2009, p. 389) or assets are exempt from income tests altogether (such as in Sweden and Australia).

Equity release products that offer an annuity for part or all of the property value have been developed to enable home owners to withdraw equity for consumption (housing-rich, income-poor) or long-term care needs while living in their home. Downsizing (moving into a cheaper property) is also an option for releasing equity. However, evidence from the US shows that downsizing is more likely to be related to life events (such as divorce or disability) than age itself (Morrow-Jones and Wenning, 2005; Painter and Lee, 2009). This finding suggests that weak public welfare schemes are inadequate to support households following life-changing events and that individuals draw from their housing assets instead. Both equity release and downsizing are more likely to be used by low-income households and single women, often to finance consumption in old age

(Painter and Lee, 2009; Overton, 2010). Being housing-rich has positive welfare effects for these people as they are better off than those who are housing- and income-poor, but the risk coverage of income poverty in old age becomes individualized instead of risk pooling through pension insurance. Moreover, longitudinal evidence suggests that these marginal home owners tended to regret their decision, to feel uncomfortable having withdrawn equity and to fear losing the security normally associated with home ownership (Fox O'Mahony and Overton, 2015). In a nutshell, using housing wealth remains a last resort for vulnerable households. Equity withdrawal exposes home owners to new risks instead of providing the security of holding assets and these risks are skewed towards women and low-income households.

Finally, the transfer stage of housing wealth contributes to a perpetuation of the intragenerational inequalities observed above. As noted, inter-vivo transfers can provide welfare benefits to younger generations and parents tend to discriminate towards children in welfare need (for example, hardship or family formation: Cox, 2003). The transfer of housing wealth is different, as it is often transferred as a lump sum rather than a flow of income support. This can take the form of an estate being signed over or support for a deposit. Evidence from European countries indicates that larger parental gifts and transfers are key for children to acquire their first home (Helderman and Mulder, 2007; Heath and Calvert, 2013). Such a perpetuation of wealth inequalities counteracts other welfare aims such as mitigating income inequalities and poverty reduction.

To sum up, all housing wealth stages offer opportunities and risks for personal welfare, especially to smooth consumption and as an emergency buffer against social risks. We will discuss these trade-offs in more detail in the next section, but it seems evident that overall housing wealth contributes to both intergenerational and intragenerational inequalities.

DYSFUNCTIONS OF WEALTH AS WELFARE

Our life-course perspective has revealed the trade-offs of housing wealth as a source of welfare and a new risk for households and individuals. Though our own work has suggested that housing wealth is used as insurance (Searle and Smith, 2010), these new insights into the life-course perspective qualify housing wealth only as a financial buffer. The concept of (social) insurance is based on the key principles of risk pooling, sharing administration cost, annuity of benefits (often indexed), an actuarial benefit formula and often (quasi) compulsory membership (Barr, 2004). Housing wealth lacks these key characteristics and redistributive welfare effects of social insurance. Properties are an individual asset holding and all risks throughout the life course are borne by the individual or household: administration costs (maintenance) are individualized and, although wealth can be liquefied through mortgage equity borrowing or equity release, contributions and benefits are highly volatile (such as interest rates and house prices). Furthermore, once housing wealth is used, it ceases to become a safety net or insurance until the mortgage debt is repaid: 'you can't have your cake and eat it too' (Ronald and Doling, 2012, p. 955).

It becomes apparent that housing wealth can only fulfil the risk protection associated with social insurances through financial vehicles such as annuities, equity release products or additional insurances (such as MPPI). However, the big advantage of housing wealth is that it can be used for multiple purposes over the life course. Equity withdrawal can cover core social risks and services as well as being an asset for any other purpose. Despite being a very illiquid asset, the evidence on mortgage holidays and equity withdrawal has also shown the increased short-term usage of housing wealth.

Housing wealth also creates a dualization of welfare (Emmenegger et al., 2012) between insiders and outsiders; that is, between home owners and renters, respectively. While shorter rental periods earlier in life are part of housing wealth biographies, many renters remain tenants for their entire lives and are permanently excluded from this welfare resource (about 17% in the UK: Köppe et al., 2013).

Research also shows a strong negative relationship between generous public welfare schemes and housing wealth. People only invest heavily in and draw on their housing wealth when public schemes are not adequate to cover social risks, mainly in retirement (Castles, 1998). This also transcends to attitudes towards housing wealth as a piggy bank. Home owners in relatively generous welfare states have no concept of using housing wealth for welfare and instead rely on the mandatory public and occupational schemes available (Doling and Elsinga, 2013). This does not mean they would not withdraw equity as a last resort, but it would not be part of their financial risk management.

From an individual risk management perspective, the 'really big trade-off' (Castles, 1998) seems to be not between housing and pension, but rather between a safety net built on assets and exposure to financial market risks. This tension between relying on housing wealth and financial markets has been revealed in extreme measures through the global financial crisis at the end of the first decade of the 2000s. Subprime lending practices had created housing bubbles in various jurisdictions that relied heavily on asset-based welfare through home ownership. This turn of events exposed just how volatile the system had become, where housing wealth is in fact a debt-financed welfare system (Searle and Köppe, 2017) in the acquisition and management stages until it eventually turns into an asset-based welfare system once mortgage debts are repaid. Risks and welfare effects contradicting social policy objectives, like mitigating inequality and reducing poverty, fundamentally question the welfare function of housing wealth as propagated by the asset-based welfare hypothesis.

CONCLUSIONS

With the gAMUT framework we have presented a conceptual toolkit to analyse housing wealth comprehensively over the life course. The four dimensions — (1) Acquiring; (2) Managing; (3) Using; and (4) Transferring — cover the gamut of housing wealth statuses across different life stages. It should serve as an analytical toolkit that crosses disciplines and can be applied in multiple contexts. The common terminology and methodological openness aims to cover various research approaches under one umbrella, but it is flexible enough to allow for specifying particular research questions. Specifically, it has proved very useful for tracing housing pathways with sequence analysis (Köppe et al., 2013) as well as any other longitudinal inquiry.

We have also stressed that the housing wealth cycle is neither a closed system nor a linear process. Moreover, transitions of housing wealth can occur in any order and potentially overlap between stages. This brings fresh insights into interlinked and overlapping life stages, which have often been studied as single transitions without discussing the wider family, generational and biographical context.

With this lens on housing wealth, we have discussed the opportunities and risk for welfare. Though a mainly theoretical discussion, we have drawn from the UK example that a greater reliance on housing wealth also exposes those risks. The financial crisis was only the tip of the iceberg and has amplified the risks inherent in a move towards debt-financed and individualized welfare through property wealth. In our assessment of the benefits and drawbacks of housing wealth as a financing mechanism for welfare purposes, we have stressed the risks and inequalities related to it, especially as housing wealth is largely debt-financed. In a wider welfare discussion of asset-based welfare as one pillar, beside tax-financed basic protection and earnings-related social insurance, there seems to be only a marginal role for asset-based welfare as a top-up and financial buffer.

NOTES

* This work was supported by the Leverhulme Trust under Grant RP2011–IJ–024 (Mind the (Housing) Wealth Gap).
1. In this context, attrition of housing wealth is more of a future contingency than a potential risk.

REFERENCES

Angel, Jacqueline L. and Stipica Mudrazija (2011), 'Aging, Inheritance, and Gift-Giving', in Robert H. Binstock and Linda K. George (eds.), *Handbook of Aging and the Social Sciences* (7th Edition), San Diego: Academic Press, pp. 163–173.

Barr, Nicholas (2004), *The Economics of the Welfare State*, Oxford: Oxford University Press.

Beer, Andrew, Debbie Faulkner, Chris Paris and Terry Clower (2011), *Housing Transitions Through the Life Course: Aspirations, Needs and Policy*, Bristol: Policy Press.

Böheim, René and Mark P. Taylor (2002), 'Tied Down or Room to Move? Investigating the Relationships Between Housing Tenure, Employment Status and Residential Mobility in Britain', *Scottish Journal of Political Economy*, 49 (4), 369–392.

Bonoli, Giuliano (2005), 'The Politics of the New Social Policies: Providing Coverage Against New Social Risks in Mature Welfare States', *Policy & Politics*, 33 (3), 431–449.

Brannen, Julia and Ann Nilsen (2005), 'Individualisation, Choice and Structure: A Discussion of Current Trends in Sociological Analysis', *Sociological Review*, 53 (3), 412–428.

Castles, Francis G. (1998), 'The Really Big Trade-Off: Home Ownership and the Welfare State in the New World and the Old', *Acta Politica*, 33 (1), 5–19.

Chen, Jie (2013), 'Housing Tenure, Residential Mobility and Adolescents' Education Achievement: Evidence from Sweden', *Annals of Regional Science*, 50 (1), 275–294.

Clapham, David (2002), 'Housing Pathways: A Post Modern Analytical Framework', *Housing, Theory and Society*, 19 (2), 57–68.

Clapham, David (2005), *The Meaning of Housing: A Pathways Approach*, Bristol: Policy Press.

Clapham, David, Peter Mackie, Scott Orford, Kelly Buckley, Ian Thomas, Iain Atherton and Ursula McAnulty (2012), *Housing Options and Solutions for Young People in 2020*, York: Joseph Rowntree Foundation.

Clark, William A. V., Marinus C. Deurloo and Frans M. Dieleman (2003), 'Housing Careers in the United States, 1968–93: Modelling the Sequencing of Housing States', *Urban Studies*, 40 (1), 143–160.

Clarke, John, Nicholas Smith and Elizabeth Vidler (2006), 'The Indeterminacy of Choice: Political, Policy and Organisational Implications', *Social Policy & Society*, 5 (3), 327–336.

Clasen, Jochen and Alison Koslowski (2013), 'Unemployment and Income Protection: How do Better-Earning Households Expect to Manage Financially?', *Journal of Social Policy*, 42 (3), 587–603.

Clasen, Jochen and Nico A. Siegel (eds.) (2007), *Investigating Welfare State Change: The 'Dependent Variable Problem' in Comparative Analysis*, Cheltenham, UK and Northampton, MA, USA: Edward Elgar Publishing.

Considine, Mairéad and Fiona Dukelow (2009), *Irish Social Policy: A Critical Introduction*, Dublin: Gill & Macmillan.

Cox, Donald (2003), 'Private Transfers Within the Family: Mothers, Fathers, Sons and Daughters', in Alicia H. Munnell and Annika Sundén (eds.), *Death and Dollars: The Role of Gifts and Bequests in America*, Washington, DC: Brookings Institution, pp. 168–196.

Dewilde, C. and P. Raeymaeckers (2008), 'The Trade-Off Between Home-Ownership and Pensions: Individual and Institutional Determinants of Old-Age Poverty', *Ageing & Society*, 28, 805–830.

Doepke, Matthias and Martin Schneider (2006), 'Inflation and the Redistribution of Nominal Wealth', *Journal of Political Economy*, 114 (6), 1069–1097.

Doling, John and Maria Elsinga (2013), *Demographic Change and Housing Wealth: Home-Owners, Pensions and Asset-Based Welfare in Europe*, Dordrecht: Springer.

Elder, Glen H. (1994), 'Time, Human Agency, and Social Change: Perspectives on the Life Course', *Social Psychology Quarterly*, 57 (1), 4–15.

Emmenegger, Patrick, Silja Häusermann, Bruno Palier and Martin Seeleib-Kaiser (eds.) (2012), *The Age of Dualization: The Changing Face of Inequality in Deindustrializing Societies*, Oxford: Oxford University Press.

Fahey, Tony (2003), 'Is There a Trade-Off Between Pensions and Home Ownership?: An Exploration of the Irish Case', *Journal of European Social Policy*, 13 (2), 159–173.

Fahey, Tony and Michelle Norris (2010), 'Housing', in Francis G. Castles, Stephan Leibfried, Jane Lewis, Herbert Obinger and Christopher Pierson (eds.), *The Oxford Handbook of the Welfare State*, Oxford: Oxford University Press, pp. 479–493.

Ford, Janet and Deborah Quilgars (2001), 'Failing Home Owners? The Effectiveness of Public and Private Safety-Nets', *Housing Studies*, 16 (2), 147–162.

Ford, Janet, Deborah Quilgars, Roger Burrows and David Rhodes (2004), *Homeowners Risk and Safety-Nets: Mortgage Payment Protection Insurance (MPPI) and Beyond*, London: Office of the Deputy Prime Minister.

Fox O'Mahony, Lorna and Louise Overton (2015), 'Asset-Based Welfare, Equity Release and the Meaning of the Owned Home', *Housing Studies*, 30 (3), 392–412.

FSA (Financial Service Authority) (2009), *MPPI Premium Variation Clauses: Industry-Wide Agreement*. CEO letter, 7 October, London: FSA.

Gerring, John (2001), *Social Science Methodology: A Criterial Framework*, Cambridge: Cambridge University Press.

Greenhalgh-Stanley, Nadia (2014), 'Can the Government Incentivize the Purchase of Private Long-Term Care Insurance? Evidence from the Partnership for Long-Term Care', *Applied Economics Letters*, 21 (8), 541–544.

Hacker, Jacob S. (2006), *The Great Risk Shift: The Assault on American Jobs, Families, Health Care, and Retirement. And How You Can Fight Back*, Oxford: Oxford University Press.

Hareven, Tamara K. (2000), *Families, History, and Social Change: Life Course and Cross-Cultural Perspectives*, Boulder: Westview Press.

Heath, Sue and Emma Calvert (2013), 'Gifts, Loans and Intergenerational Support for Young Adults', *Sociology*, 47 (6), 1120–1135.

Helderman, Amanda and Clara Mulder (2007), 'Intergenerational Transmission of Homeownership: The Roles of Gifts and Continuities in Housing Market Characteristics', *Urban Studies*, 44 (2), 231–247.

Holzmann, Robert and Steen Jørgensen (2001), 'Social Risk Management: A New Conceptual Framework for Social Protection, and Beyond', *International Tax and Public Finance*, 8 (4), 529–556.

Hurst, Erik and Frank Stafford (2004), 'Home is Where the Equity is: Mortgage Refinancing and Household Consumption', *Journal of Money, Credit and Banking*, 36 (6), 985–1014.

Izuhara, Misa and Stephan Köppe (2017), 'Inheritance and Family Conflicts: Exploring Asset Transfers Shaping Intergenerational Relations', *Families, Relationships and Societies* (forthcoming).

Karagiannaki, Eleni (2011), *Recent Trends in the Size and the Distribution of Inherited Wealth in the UK*. CASE Research Paper 146. London: Centre for Analysis of Social Exclusion, London School of Economics.

Kneale, Dylan, Ruth Lupton, Polina Obolenskaya and Richard D. Wiggins (2010), *A Cross-Cohort Description of Young People's Housing Experience in Britain over 30 Years: An Application of Sequence Analysis*. DoQSS Working Paper No. 10–17.

Kohli, Martin (1999), 'Private and Public Transfers Between Generations: Linking the Family and the State', *European Societies*, 1 (1), 81–104.

Köppe, Stephan, Beverley Searle and Duncan Maclennan (2013), 'Idealised Housing Trajectories from Renting via Mortgaging to Ownership? Complex Housing Wealth Transitions between Re-Mortgaging and Downsizing'. Paper presented at ENHR Conference, Taragona.

Le Grand, Julian (2007), *The Other Invisible Hand: Delivering Public Services through Choice and Competition*, Princeton: Princeton University Press.

Lowe, Stuart G., Beverley A. Searle and Susan J. Smith (2012), 'From Housing Wealth to Mortgage Debt: The Emergence of Britain's Asset-Shaped Welfare State', *Social Policy and Society*, 11 (1), 105–116.

Mahoney, James (2000), 'Path Dependence in Historical Sociology', *Theory and Society*, 29 (4), 507–548.

McKee, Kim (2012), 'Young People, Homeownership and Future Welfare', *Housing Studies*, 27 (6), 853–862.

Modigliani, Franco and Richard Brumberg (1954), 'Utility Analysis and the Consumption Function: An Interpretation of Cross-Section Data', in Kenneth K. Kurihara (ed.), *Post Keynesian Economics*, New Brunswick: Rutgers University Press, pp. 388–436.

Morrow-Jones, Hazel A. and Mary V. Wenning (2005), 'The Housing Ladder, the Housing Life-Cycle and the Housing Life-Course: Upward and Downward Movement among Repeat Home-Buyers in a US Metropolitan Housing Market', *Urban Studies*, 42 (10), 1739–1754.

Ong, Rachel, Sharon Parkinson, Beverley A. Searle, Susan J. Smith and Gavin A. Wood (2013), 'Channels from Housing Wealth to Consumption', *Housing Studies*, 28 (7), 1012–1036.

Overton, Louise (2010), *Housing and Finance in Later Life: A Study of UK Equity Release Customers*, London: Age UK.

Painter, Gary and Kwan Ok Lee (2009), 'Housing Tenure Transitions of Older Households: Life Cycle, Demographic, and Familial Factors', *Regional Science and Urban Economics*, 39 (6), 749–760.

Parker, Gillian and Justine Schneider (2007), 'Social Care', in John Baldock, Nick

Manning and Sarah Vickerstaff (eds.), *Social Policy*, Oxford: Oxford University Press, pp. 441–474.

Parkinson, Sharon, Beverley A. Searle, Susan J. Smith, Alice Stoakes and Gavin Wood (2009), 'Mortgage Equity Withdrawal in Australia and Britain: Towards a Wealth-Fare State?', *European Journal of Housing Policy*, 9 (4), 365–389.

Prabhakar, Rajiv (2009), 'The Assets Agenda and Social Policy', *Social Policy & Administration*, 43 (1), 54–69.

Quilgars, Deborah and Anwen Jones (2010), 'Housing Wealth: A Safety Net of Last Resort? Findings from a European Study', in Susan J. Smith and Beverley A. Searle (eds.), *The Blackwell Companion to the Economics of Housing: The Housing Wealth of Nations*, Chichester: Wiley-Blackwell, pp. 295–315.

Ronald, Richard and John Doling (2012), 'Testing Home Ownership as the Cornerstone of Welfare: Lessons from East Asia for the West', *Housing Studies*, 27 (7), 940–961.

Rowlingson, Karen (2009), 'From Cradle to Grave : Social Security and the Life Course', in Jane Millar (ed.), *Understanding Social Security: Issues for Policy and Practice*, Bristol: Policy Press, pp. 133–150.

Rowlingson, Karen and Ricky Joseph (2010), *Assets and Debts within Couples: Ownership and Decision-Making*, Surrey: Friends Provident Foundation.

Rowlingson, Karen and Stephen McKay (2012), *Wealth and the Wealthy: Exploring and Tackling Inequalities between Rich and Poor*, Bristol: Policy Press.

Searle, Beverley A. (2008), *Wellbeing: In Search of a Good Life?*, Bristol: Policy Press.

Searle, Beverley A. (2012), 'Recession, Repossession and Family Welfare', *Child and Family Law Quarterly*, 24 (1), 1–23.

Searle, Beverley A. and Stephan Köppe (2014), *Savings, Assets and Wealth, and Poverty: A Review of Evidence*, Final Report to the Joseph Rowntree Foundation, Bristol: Personal Finance Research Centre.

Searle, Beverley A. and Stephan Köppe (2017), 'Geographies of Debt', in Ron Martin and Jane Pollard (eds.), *Handbook of the Geographies of Money and Finance*, Cheltenham, UK and Northampton, MA, USA: Edward Elgar Publishing.

Searle, Beverley A. and Susan J. Smith (2010), 'Housing Wealth as Insurance: Insights from the UK', in Susan J. Smith and Beverley A. Searle (eds.), *The Blackwell Companion to the Economics of Housing: The Housing Wealth of Nations*, Chichester: Wiley-Blackwell, pp. 339–360.

Searle, Beverley A., Susan J. Smith and Nicole Cook (2009), 'From Housing Wealth to Well-Being?', *Sociology of Health & Illness*, 31 (1), 112–127.

Sherraden, Michael (1990), 'Stakeholding: Notes on a Theory of Welfare Based on Assets', *Social Service Review*, 64 (4), 580–601.

Sherraden, Michael (1991), *Assets and the Poor: A New American Welfare Policy*, New York: M.E. Sharpe.

Smith, Susan J. and Beverley A. Searle (2008), 'Dematerialising Money? Observations on the Flow of Wealth from Housing to Other Things', *Housing Studies*, 23 (1), 21–43.

Smith, Susan, Moira Munro and Janet Ford (2002), *A Review of Flexible Mortgages*, London: Council of Mortgage Lenders.

Thaler, Richard H. and Cass R. Sunstein (2009), *Nudge: Improving Decisions About Health, Wealth and Happiness*, London: Penguin.

Toussaint, Janneke and Marja Elsinga (2009), 'Exploring "Housing Asset-Based Welfare": Can the UK be Held Up as an Example for Europe?', *Housing Studies*, 24 (5), 669–692.

Van Kersbergen, Kees and Anton Hemerijck (2012), 'Two Decades of Change in Europe: The Emergence of the Social Investment State', *Journal of Social Policy*, 41 (3), 475–492.

Vickerstaff, Sarah (2006), 'Life Course, Youth, and Old Age', in Peter Taylor-Gooby and Jens O. Zinn (eds.), *Risk in Social Science*, Oxford: Oxford University Press, pp. 180–201.

Walker, Alan (2012), 'The New Ageism', *The Political Quarterly*, 83 (4), 812–819.

Wood, Gavin, Sharon Parkinson, Beverley Searle and Susan J. Smith (2013), 'Motivations for Equity Borrowing: A Welfare-Switching Effect', *Urban Studies* 50 (12), 2588–2607.

5. Housing wealth and welfare state restructuring: between asset-based welfare and the social investment strategy

Christian Lennartz

INTRODUCTION

More than 30 years ago, in his book *The Myth of Home Ownership*, Jim Kemeny (1981) laid the foundation for housing researchers to understand how private home ownership ties in with the structure and development of the welfare state in economically advanced societies. The original argument of a trade-off between high home ownership rates and small welfare states has come a long way since then. While some studies (for example, Castles, 1998; Delfani et al., 2014; Lennartz, 2011; Malpass, 2008; Schwartz, 2014) have primarily focused on what the trade-off actually implies and how it translates into political practice, others (for example, Ronald and Doling, 2012; Smith and Searle, 2008) have reconsidered the meaning of housing wealth and home ownership as an investment and the risks and benefits this investment entails. Yet another set of studies has concentrated on the neoliberalization and financialization of housing finance and mortgage markets and how these phenomena were key ingredients of the Global Financial Crisis (GFC) in 2008 (for example, Aalbers, 2015; Christophers, 2013). Hence, for a longer period and using various theoretical angles, housing researchers have sought to build a case for the centrality of housing in the transformation processes of welfare capitalism and the welfare state in particular. This contribution does not argue against such ideas; rather, it equally relies on the assumption that housing has gained increasing importance as both a critical resource for the welfare positions of individuals and families and a key determinant of welfare provision and wealth stratification in most western societies.

What I try to achieve here is to give a more nuanced interpretation of the links between the accumulation of housing property wealth on an aggregate level and the direction of welfare state change. The starting point of this chapter is the observation that the conceptualization of welfare state change in housing studies is built on a narrow 'change-as-retrenchment' perspective. This, however, misses the multidimensionality of the transformation processes that welfare states have endured in the past 20 years. Supported by descriptive statistics of national-level aggregate data in 26 Organisation for Economic Co-operation and Development (OECD) countries, the chapter will work towards the argument that, in many countries, the rise of home ownership and the establishment of an asset-based welfare (ABW) approach have not implied the outright dismantling of the postwar welfare model. Rather, these processes may be understood as a necessary condition for the restructuring of the welfare state towards a more productive-[1] and employment-oriented social policy approach: the so-called social investment strategy. Interpreting the links between housing wealth, ABW, and welfare policies in this way, the chapter will further show that these are not universal developments across all advanced economies; rather, they relate primarily to the Northern European and Liberal welfare regimes. Hence, the final argument of this chapter is that, at least before the GFC of 2008, we can observe the emergence of two distinct types of welfare capitalism: an investment-oriented welfare model versus a traditional protectivist approach to welfare capitalism.

HOUSING WEALTH AND ASSET-BASED WELFARE

In the last 10 years, housing researchers have repeatedly pointed out the increased centrality of housing assets in securing the welfare position of individual citizens and families. Indeed, accompanying the demographic change towards ageing societies and the resulting pressure on public resources, an ABW model has emerged on political agendas and in academic debates alike (Ronald et al., 2015). Sparked by the credit and house prices boom that preceded the GFC in 2008, the principle assumption of the concept of ABW is that private households can tap into their property assets – typically an owner-occupied house – at any stage of the life course, but particularly in times of need and in old age. Private housing wealth – which in its simplest form can be understood as the debt-free share of the market value of a property – has been linked to the financing of care needs, the supplementation of public pension entitlements, and financial support for children and other family members (Doling and Elsinga, 2013; Lowe et al., 2012; Ronald and Doling, 2012; Smith and Searle, 2008).

A crucial consideration here is that wealth and income do not necessarily match throughout the life course. It might be true that higher incomes open up more possibilities for accumulating assets, and vice versa; yet, from a dynamic perspective, the appreciation of assets can – at least temporarily – be much more rapid than the growth of real income (see Aalbers and Christophers, 2014; Hamnett, 1999). This potential disconnection means that, in theory, private property wealth can be used as a 'buffer stock' against increased risks of income poverty, where in its most extreme form it implies a shift from 'employment-led' to 'asset-dominated' welfare stratification in western societies (Ansell, 2014; Carroll, 2004). Given the astounding rise of housing wealth in the Eurozone – from €3.7 trillion in 1980 to €13.2 trillion in 1999 and €24.2 trillion in 2006 (ECB, 2009), a period in which income from wages hardly increased at all – the numbers behind this shift seem to support this assessment.

It has been argued that the key to understanding the rise of property ownership and the adherent house prices boom in the western world is the financialization of the banking industry and the adherent (political) liberalization of mortgage markets in what Aalbers (2015) calls the 'flexible neoliberal period' (1985–2007). Although there are different ways through which house purchase can be accomplished, mortgage loans have become the main financing channel in most national housing markets. The growing availability of easy and low-interest credit offered households the possibility to take on large amounts of private debt with the promise that this debt would turn into a valuable and highly tangible asset. Certainly, first-time home owners do not actually have considerable housing equity that they can rely on; to the contrary, they might be facing large amounts of debt that might additionally burden them in times of need. Hence, many (for example, Aalbers and Christophers, 2014; Forrest and Hirayama, 2015; Malpass, 2008; Montgomerie and Büdenbender, 2014; Watson, 2009) have observed that the ABW model can only persist – if it can at all – when property prices continue to rise and housing wealth can be accessed through, for instance, selling the house or withdrawing equity without being left with negative equity. Indeed, where house prices rise quickly and continuously, debt appears to be risk-free.

On the macro level, Crouch (2009) argues that the rise of private mortgage debt became an economic model in itself. Where governments have largely withdrawn from the Keynesian model of using public investment to stimulate economic growth, the primacy of balanced budgets in the Great Moderation period (since the mid 1980s) has implied a shift of such responsibilities to private households. In the era of privatized Keynesianism, private debt is considered as not a problem but a solution to stagnating economic growth; as Aalbers (2015, p. 10) argues: 'Where credit once enabled growth and wealth, it now comes to replace wealth creation in the real economy'. Again, the rise in property prices is a crucial element here. Although rising prices could primarily be seen as the outcome of growing credit availability, they have been used as ex-post justification for mortgage market liberalization and have in fact further stimulated such efforts. Whereas general price inflation is perceived to be counterproductive to long-term economic growth in neoliberal economies, a rise in asset prices is seen as a corresponding rise in their value (and thus as contributing less to general inflation). Consequently, governments have come to support the appreciation of property assets in policy practice, be it through mortgage guarantees, mortgage tax deductibility, the deregulation of credit markets, backing the development and application of innovative financial products, or the dismantling of affordable rental housing to limit tenure choice (Forrest and Hirayama, 2015; Lennartz et al., 2012).

Although the neoliberalization of housing and mortgage markets was widespread across advanced economies, the political implementation of home-ownership access through debt accumulation is far from universal. Indeed, if we look at the development of aggregate outstanding mortgage debt as a percentage of Gross Domestic Product (GDP) across 26 OECD countries in 1995 and 2007 (see Figure 5.1), a general trend towards substantially higher private mortgage debt levels can be observed. Yet, a more thorough analysis of the data reveals that the highest levels (measured by percentages) and the highest increases (measured by percentage-point changes) in the 12-year period can be observed in Northern Europe and the English-speaking liberal countries. In contrast, a large group of countries seems to have retained different home-ownership access modes. Spearheaded by Germany, Finland, Italy, and Japan (and also observable in most Central and Eastern European countries), many states have seen a far less rapid liberalization of mortgage markets and have actually preserved a more family-based approach to property purchase. Indeed, home ownership in these contexts is still largely a matter of support mechanisms in the family (see also Poggio, 2012), including the transfer of land and property entitlements or financial support for down payments (Schwartz and Seabrooke, 2008). Meanwhile, some individual countries – including Spain and Estonia – have recalibrated towards a regime shift, implying a move away from the familialistic model to the individual debt accumulation approach.

A remarkable qualification here concerns the link between easy mortgage credit for households and home-ownership rates on the aggregate level. While it seems logical that the more that younger households qualify for mortgage credit and high loan-to-value ratios, the higher that the share of home owners will become, this association is not backed up by empirical evidence. Particularly in the debt-driven liberal economies of the English-speaking world, decreasing home ownership rates could be observed prior to the crisis and more intensely since then. One reason is that high

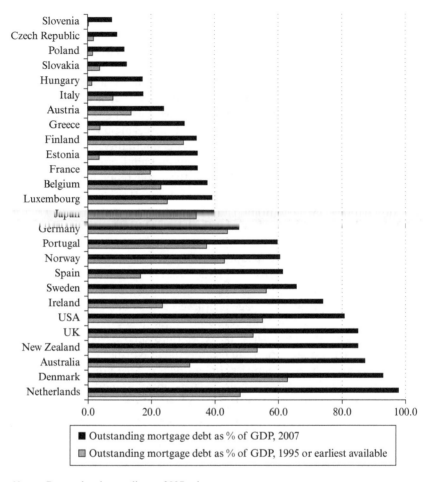

Note: Bars ordered according to 2007 values.

Sources: EMF (2014).

Figure 5.1 Outstanding mortgage debt as percentage of GDP in 26 OECD countries, 1995–2007

mortgage take-up has boosted house prices substantially, making the sector more unaffordable for many households. The fact that ownership rates are still rising in the highly financialized housing markets of the Netherlands, Denmark, and Sweden could then indicate that these countries are at an earlier stage of becoming a stratified home-ownership society (see Aalbers and Christophers (2014) for a similar argument).

I agree with the view (see also Norris in this volume) that the way in which home ownership is accessed has some critical implications for the meaning of housing wealth. Whereas the wealth effect of housing assets in the family-based access model mainly comes from the house's role as a family home that can be shared and transferred between generations, housing wealth in the debt-driven access model is primarily a hypothetical parameter that relies on the tradable or exchange value of the property in the housing market at a particular point in time. One implication of this is that, in the latter model, housing wealth gains are higher when house prices appreciate strongly; but in the same vein, housing wealth can easily turn into a housing burden when market conditions deteriorate – as exemplified by the GFC in 2008.

To conclude, it seems undeniable that housing assets have become a more crucial resource for individual households and families to satisfy their welfare needs (the question is rather: when they have ever not been?). To paraphrase Malpass (2008), housing wealth has become a 'cornerstone' in the welfare equation. Similarly, many political economies have identified and implemented home ownership and the take-up of mortgage debt to gain access to home-ownership markets as a source of economic growth and development. However, the way in which housing property is acquired, what housing wealth means, and how such wealth can be tapped into still differ across groups of countries, implying specific variegations in the way home ownership and housing wealth relate to, and may propel transformations of, contemporary welfare states.

THE REALLY BIG TRADE-OFF AND ITS IMPLICATIONS FOR WELFARE STATE CHANGE

Most studies on the links between home ownership and welfare states are grounded in Kemeny's hypothesis (1981) of a 'trade-off' between owner-occupied residential property and the quantity and quality of public welfare provision. The basic assumption of the trade-off hypothesis is that smaller welfare states help sustain larger home ownership sectors, and vice versa. To simplify a complex story, Kemeny assumes a temporal distribution of housing costs over the life course. Where home owners face a frontloading of housing expenses through mortgage deposit requirements and high transaction costs at an early life stage, renters have more evenly distributed costs. Kemeny then posits that home owners should oppose higher taxes, which are the basis for more generous welfare states, and which is expressed in voting behavior that supports conservative parties and economic liberal parties. Conversely, this implies that, when facing less generous public provision of welfare goods, households are more inclined to invest in private welfare means – most often housing assets – to generate individual welfare and economic security, particularly in later life. In Kemeny's thinking, the home ownership/welfare state trade-off thus links individual preferences with macroeconomic and political outcomes on the national level.

More recently, the debate has regained some scholarly attention. First, there is much to say about the foundational assumptions of the trade-off hypothesis. On the one hand, the frontloading of costs for home owners is a politically designed outcome. Where home ownership is highly subsidized through mortgage-interest tax deductibility, very low down-payment requirements, and macroeconomic policies that aim to keep interest rates at low levels, house purchase may actually be financially more viable and also more rational for younger households (see also Schwartz, 2014). On the other hand, Kemeny presumes that welfare preferences and consequent voting behavior always follow the premise of what could be called 'age-based self-interest' (Goerres and Tepe, 2010). Yet, research shows that such preferences do not have a single origin and may be altered by diverging attitudes towards intergenerational solidarity (Szydlik, 2012). Finally, the logics of welfare state expansion and retrenchment are not necessarily aligned, meaning that generous pension systems are very resilient to retrenchment policies simply because they are highly popular across all households; that is, renters and owners alike (see Delfani et al., 2014). Resistance against pension cuts by most voters might simply make the implementation of a retrenchment trade-off impossible.

A second set of studies elaborates on the links between home ownership and voting behavior. Both Malpass (2008) and Ansell (2014) take a dynamic view on the trade-off mechanisms, claiming that retrenchment policies in mature welfare states are directly affected by changing voting preferences among housing-asset holders. The central notion here is that rising asset values and the duration of house price appreciation, rather than home ownership per se, may bolster households' trust in their means to achieve secure welfare positions (see also André and Dewilde, 2016). Similar to Kemeny's original work, the authors argue that this translates into voting preferences for parties that promise to reduce public welfare expenditure and to achieve balanced budgets.

Third, picking up on Castles' (1998) finding of a negative relationship between home-ownership rates and public pension spending (rather than welfare spending as a whole), Schwartz and Seabrooke (2008) and Schwartz (2012; 2014) have sought to explain political realignment in and around welfare states through the 'home ownership-access lens'; that is, how the structure of national mortgage markets and mortgage finance regulation may impact on welfare policies. In short, where home ownership is accessed almost exclusively through the accumulation of private mortgage debt, privately or publicly funded pension plans are likely to prevail. In countries where home ownership is accessed through other channels (for instance, through family resources) and in countries where large rental sectors exist, public PAYGO (pay-as-you-go)[2] pension systems are dominant (see also Delfani et al., 2014). The trade-off is caused by two different mechanisms. The economic mechanism necessitates the harmonization of all assets with all liabilities of financial institutions. Pension funds have long-term obligations to their customers; these funds tend to buy mortgages as corresponding financial assets off the capital market to guarantee a constant cash flow to serve these liabilities. In contrast, large, unfunded, public PAYGO pension systems maintain their cash flow through pension contributions and tax revenues. The political mechanism is based on state interventions that allow financial institutions, and pension funds in particular, to match their balance sheets. Typically, this is achieved through the deregulation of financial markets to guarantee an unrestricted trade of assets and liabilities. It also involves subsidies and tax breaks to increase mortgage availability for households, as well as the direct provision of housing funds and mortgage guarantee systems that aim to ameliorate the risks of a highly financialized system.

As stated previously, housing researchers are right to claim that the rise of housing assets needs to be accounted for as a crucial dimension of welfare state change. In many developed societies, accessing home ownership at an early life stage has become an important means to secure one's welfare position throughout the life course. What the review of the trade-off debate implies, then, is that individual asset accumulation may be utilized as a political vehicle for welfare state retrenchment, particularly through voters' support for – or at least toleration of – the downsizing of unfunded public pension systems. There are, however, two major concerns with the trade-off debate.

First, the links between voting preferences and house price appreciation, and more broadly home ownership, are in my view not fully convincing – or at least undertheorized (for an exception, see Ansell, 2014). Where housing wealth is highly unequally distributed towards (older) housing market insiders (that is, those who bought before prices became increasingly unaffordable), and where accumulating housing assets has become increasingly difficult for younger generations (market outsiders), it is unclear how home ownership and housing wealth could define voting agendas. For instance, we would expect this growing class of outsiders to vote for parties that promise the continuation of cheap credit flows and home ownership support, but also for parties that accommodate their welfare needs through the continuation or reintroduction of public welfare programs.

Second (and connected), the housing literature has come to understand how housing may impact on welfare state change purely on an expansion–retrenchment continuum. Where the individual and political significance of housing grows, welfare states would move towards more retrenchment. Yet, this view is misleading as it neglects the multidimensional character of welfare state transformation processes and the political repercussions of the implementation of the ABW model herein. In other words, the rise of housing assets as a potential private welfare resource does not necessarily imply a smaller welfare state. Housing assets may merely signify and enable welfare restructuring processes in which new state functions emerge. To sharpen our understanding of these processes, it is useful to look more closely at how and where welfare states have transformed recently.

WELFARE STATE CHANGE AND THE SOCIAL INVESTMENT STRATEGY

Whereas post-World War Two the welfare state primarily addressed the social and economic risks of income loss, the emergence of new social risks – such as in-work poverty, insufficient skill endowment, problems reconciling work with family life, and single parenthood – implied that new state functions had to emerge (Bonoli, 2007; Bonoli and Natali, 2012; Taylor-Gooby, 2008). Taking on all these responsibilities seemed to be too large a burden for European welfare states, leading to the prediction of its demotion towards a more residual, low-expenditure social policy model reminiscent of the United States (Pierson, 1994; 2001). Indeed, retrenchment programs were part of the most salient transformation processes. A first key program was first-pillar pension reforms that included a rollback of early retirement schemes, lower benefits, and more limited eligibility for universal protection. Second- and third-tier pensions have become more prominent, resulting in a rapid shift from defined-benefit to defined-contribution pension plans (van Kersbergen and Hemerijck, 2012). Labor market policies were reoriented towards stronger activation measures and stricter conditionality for unemployment benefits. Furthermore, the introduction of 'flexicurity' policies promoted temporary, de-unionized contracts, particularly in low-skilled, low-income sectors (Emmenegger, 2012; Gilbert, 2002). Meanwhile, on a macroeconomic policy level, governments have followed mainstream economists' belief that balanced budgets, the reduction of public debt, hard currencies, and low inflation are the only way to sustain market economies (Starke et al., 2013).

It is not difficult to imagine where the belief in the housing literature of the dismantling of the welfare state and the dominance of neoliberal retrenchment policies has come from. However, a more careful understanding and empirical investigation of the matter expose the endurance of large welfare states, at least up until the GFC of 2008. Some scholars argue that, if anything, a convergence to the top has taken place; this is underpinned by recent OECD data on the development of social expenditure and welfare generosity indices (see Obinger and Starke, 2014). One explanation for this development has been the emerging restructuring of social policies towards a more 'productive welfare state' (Hudson and Kühner, 2009). Here, social policies are considered an inherent part of wider socioeconomic settlements and may have a supporting role vis-à-vis economic policy.

The key to understanding the multifaceted nature of welfare state change, therefore, is to understand that social policy is not only geared towards income protection and poverty reduction (that is, addressing 'old' social risks), but that it may be equally concerned with economic development and growth in high-quality employment (Bonoli and Natali, 2012). What has been labeled the 'New Welfare State' thus straddles the middle ground between the primarily protectivist approach of the Keynesian industrialist welfare state and the retrenchment primacy that was propagated in the neoliberal period (Hemerijck, 2012). Many prominent social policy scholars have interpreted these changes as the emergence of a social investment strategy (SIS) (for example, Esping-Andersen, 2002; Morel et al., 2012; Vandenbroucke and Vleminckx, 2011). Connecting various new social risk policies, the SIS may be defined as a comprehensive policy approach that seeks to stimulate public and private investments in the current and future employability of risk bearers (Häussermann, 2012). It combines two main goals: first, to endow the (potential) workforce with skills and human capital that can prepare them for the insecurities and constantly changing demands of knowledge-based economies, and second, to provide citizens – particularly women – with opportunities to utilize their human capital in the labor market and maximize their employment efforts (Hemerijck, 2012).

It has been proposed in the literature that, in policy practice, these two goals resulted in growing government social spending on public and publicly subsidized private childcare and elderly care facilities, the implementation of generous family benefits, and investments in education and labor market activation policies (Morel et al., 2012; Nikolai, 2012). Such productive social investment policies are in opposition to the more protective 'old risk' policies, including public spending on old age, unemployment benefits, survivors' pensions, and disability transfers (Hemerijck,

2012). Certainly, this dichotomy is not without problems, as it simplifies the objectives of productive and protective spending. Unemployment benefits, for instance, seek to retain the purchasing power of individuals and the society, particularly in times of mass unemployment. Moreover, generous child benefits and parental leave schemes clearly protect the income of young parents against the risk of having a child, but in effect often discourage mothers from returning to work on short notice rather than support their effort to find a more balanced work–childcare ratio.

Another issue with the approach taken in this chapter – that is, the focus on 'protective' versus 'productive' welfare spending – might be that an analysis focused solely on government outlays inevitably misses the multidimensional character of welfare state change through, for instance, regulatory modifications. Studies on the transformation of the welfare state ideally integrate spending data with measures of welfare generosity, policy stratification, and regulatory change (Seeleib-Kaiser, 2008). Moreover, Adema et al. (2011) have shown that social expenditure is (to put it mildly) an imperfect measure, as it does not incorporate welfare provision through taxation, mandatory private spending, and voluntary private spending. The analysis presented in this chapter would ideally have looked at net public spending for each field of productive and protective social expenditure. However, this was not possible due to data limitations.[3] A final limitation is that public spending is not necessarily the outcome of explicit policy decisions – in our case, a reorientation towards social investment spending – as increases or decreases in public spending might be artifacts of macroeconomic cycles instead, meaning that, in periods of high unemployment, unemployment spending will be higher.

Bearing in mind these potential shortcomings, a useful starting point in empirically tracing the variegations of transformation processes, and where and what kind of shifts can be observed, is the classification of protective and productive welfare policies into a 'directions of change' matrix (see Häussermann, 2012). Where governments have reduced spending on both types of policies, we can speak of a wider *welfare retrenchment* process (see lower-left quadrant in Figure 5.2). Where spending was increased on both policy domains, the direction of change is one of *welfare expansion* (upper-right quadrant). On the other side, *welfare protectionism* (upper-left quadrant) denotes the case of increasing spending on protective policies and decreasing spending on productive policies, while it is vice versa for a *welfare readjustment* (lower-right quadrant) approach in public social spending. Using OECD data on aggregate public spending in 26 countries for the years 1995 and 2007 to fill in the 'matrix of welfare state change' (see Table 5.1 for raw data), the following patterns emerge. First of all, certainly not all OECD countries have experienced a retrenchment

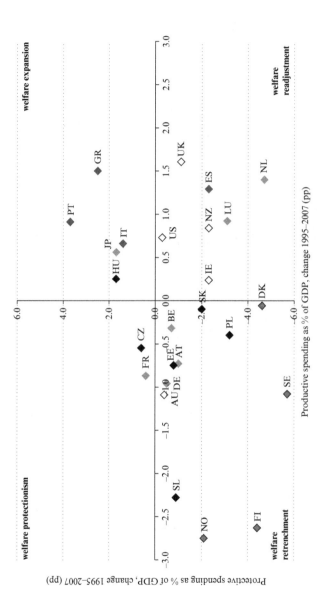

Note: *Retrenchment* = decrease in productive and protective spending; *expansion* = increase in productive and protective spending; *readjustment* = increase in productive and decrease in protective spending; *protectionism* = decrease in productive and increase in protective spending.

Sources: OECD Social Expenditure Database (2014); own calculations.

Figure 5.2   Directions of welfare state change as measured by changes in productive and protective spending, OECD, 1995–2007 (percentage points)

Table 5.1 Public social spending in the OECD, change 1995–2007

	Productive spending as % of GDP, 2007	Productive spending as % of GDP, change 1995–2007 (pp)	Protective spending as % of GDP, 2007	Protective spending as % of GDP, change 1995–2007 (pp)	Relative spending on productive functions of WS, 2007 (%)	Relative spending on productive functions of WS, change 1995–2007 (pp)
Austria	9.3	−0.7	15.5	−1.0	37.4	−0.3
Belgium	10.8	−0.3	14.0	−0.7	43.5	0.5
Germany	8.2	−1.0	13.3	−0.5	38.3	−1.7
France	10.8	−0.9	15.9	0.4	40.5	−2.5
Japan	5.4	0.6	9.1	1.7	37.1	−2.2
Luxembourg	8.0	0.9	9.3	−3.1	46.3	9.9
Netherlands	9.4	1.4	9.1	−4.7	50.8	14.1
Denmark	15.2	−0.1	11.0	−4.6	58.1	8.6
Finland	11.4	−2.6	13.4	−4.4	45.9	1.9
Norway	11.7	−2.8	10.1	−2.1	53.6	−0.6
Sweden	14.4	−1.1	10.7	−5.7	57.4	8.8
Australia	8.0	−1.1	7.0	−0.4	53.4	−1.8
Ireland	9.1	0.2	6.6	−2.3	58.1	8.1
New Zealand	9.9	0.8	7.2	−2.3	58.0	9.1
UK	10.2	1.6	8.2	−1.1	55.5	7.4
US	6.5	0.7	7.6	−0.3	46.2	3.9
Greece	5.6	1.5	13.4	2.5	29.5	2.1
Italy	6.9	0.7	15.2	1.4	31.1	0.1

Spain	7.1	1.3	12.5	-2.3	34.4	8.0
Portugal	7.4	0.9	14.1	3.7	36.2	-4.0
Czech Republic	6.8	-0.6	9.6	0.6	41.3	-3.5
Estonia	7.0	-0.8	6.9	-0.8	50.2	0.2
Hungary	9.9	0.3	12.9	1.7	43.3	-2.9
Poland	6.8	-0.4	13.3	-3.2	33.8	3.5
Slovakia	6.1	-2.3	7.9	-0.9	43.7	-5.2
Slovenia	7.1	-0.1	11.9	-2.0	37.4	3.2
OECD average	8.8	-0.1	11.0	-1.2	44.6	2.5

Notes: *Productive spending* = public expenditure on active labor market policies (ALMP), education (all levels), family spending, incapacity-related in-kind transfers, childcare, and pre-schooling; *protective spending* = public expenditure on old age, unemployment, survivor pensions, disability pension, and paid sick leave; *relative spending on capacitating functions of welfare state* = (productive spending ÷ productive + protective spending as % of GDP) × 100.

Sources: OECD Social Expenditure Database (2014); own calculations.

trajectory; rather, it is evident that welfare state change has been varied, with numerous cases signifying expansion and readjustment processes. Most strikingly, it is the Nordic countries that have undergone the most profound retrenchment processes, whereas the Southern European countries (with the exception of Spain) have seen an expansion of welfare state spending. Furthermore, most liberal English-speaking nations are clear cases of the welfare readjustment model. Central and Eastern European countries show a less clear direction of change, yet a majority are located in the retrenchment quadrant. The development towards welfare protectionism has generally been weak and is only exemplified by France and the Czech Republic.

Again, understanding welfare state change in this framework is helpful in that it highlights the variegations of social policy development at the turn of the century. However, a more careful reading of the data tells a slightly different story. If we do not look at absolute levels of public spending on protective and productive spending, but investigate their relative shares and the development thereof in the 1995 to 2007 period (see columns 5 and 6 in Table 5.1), there is a clearer case for a welfare restructuring process towards new social policy priorities; that is, a more pronounced position of the productive functions of the welfare state. Indeed, within the OECD as a whole we can see that, in relative terms, a minor shift towards productive-oriented social investment spending occurred. Yet, this was not necessarily instigated through higher public expenditure on productive social policies, but may also be the result of lower spending on traditional welfare policies.

Depicting the country-specific differences, there appears to be substantial divergence within and between different types of welfare regimes. Generally, most conservative continental countries, Central, Eastern, and particularly Southern European nations have retained a prevalence of their traditional old-risk social policy model. By contrast, the already social investment-oriented Northern European nations, as well as English-speaking liberal states, the Netherlands, Luxembourg, and Spain, have restructured their social policies, fostering a more employment- and new-risk-oriented approach. Overall, thinking more in terms of changing policy priorities, a social investment agenda clearly exists – but it is certainly not universal. The questions, then, remain: why is the social investment strategy limited to these countries, and how exactly do the rise in home ownership, easy credit, and importance of housing wealth tie into these (variegated) welfare state transformation processes?

SOCIAL INVESTMENT AND ASSET-BASED WELFARE: TWO SIDES OF THE SAME COIN?

Integrating my observations on the increasing significance of housing property wealth and the variegations of transformations in the welfare state across the OECD, it becomes apparent that the rise of the former does not necessarily imply the dismantling of the latter – as is suggested by the debate on ABW state restructuring. Rather, the (political) implementation of the ABW approach may be better understood as part of a welfare restructuring process towards a more productive welfare state. Where citizens have experienced an increased ability and willingness to invest into housing property assets and to use these as a private safety net against income loss, governments were enabled to redirect public resources to other welfare dimensions, which were often those that address the emergence of new social risks. And indeed, from an empirical viewpoint, there is a clear positive association between the two variables. Nations with a relatively high share of productive social investment spending in 2007 also had relatively high amounts of private outstanding mortgage debt in the same year (Pearson's correlation coefficient is 0.69, with a statistical significance of $p<0.01$). Similarly, countries that have reoriented their spending capacities towards SIS policies in the period 1995 to 2007 more strongly also tended to have the largest increases in private mortgage debt in the same period (Pearson's correlation coefficient is 0.48 at $p<0.01$). This is the case for the liberal English-speaking countries, the Northern European nations (excluding Finland but including the Netherlands), and Spain. Here, income protection is to an increasing extent achieved through the accumulation of private debt that eventually amortizes into asset wealth, which in turn may enable governments to reorient the welfare state increasingly towards the social investment strategy. In contrast, we can see that the continental regime, the Central and Eastern European nations, and most Southern European countries combine a persisting orientation towards the more protective functions of the welfare state with a more traditional, less financialized approach to home-ownership access. Here, we can see the fortification of a more protectivist form of welfare capitalism, in which social policy still primarily addresses old social risks and aims to preserve a familialistic model. The financialization of housing markets and easy access to cheap (mortgage) credit as alternative sources of welfare security are less pressing and imminent issues here.

Of course, it could be argued that we are dealing with the empirical contingency that debt-driven home ownership access and relatively high social investment spending levels may correlate but have little to do with each other conceptually. Indeed, it seems highly unlikely that governments have such a precise understanding of how different policy dimensions could be integrated into one coherent policy model, or that they would engage in the meticulous and far-sighted planning that the productive welfare capitalism approach would require. I would contend, however, that there are various reasons to consider them as interspersed, compatible social policy approaches.

First, even though politicians are often more inclined to strive for short-term electoral success than long-term policy ideas and outcomes, there is still a political argument for the compatibility thesis. Since the late 1980s, combining robust economic growth with the ideal of balanced government budgets has been an increasingly successful tactic for being reelected (Taylor-Gooby, 2008). In this context, it is a dilemma that public welfare provision is still highly popular in most western democracies and often guarantees electoral winnings (Vis et al., 2011). Governments in Northern Europe and the liberal welfare states have seemingly found a balance between these opposing matters by using private debt for economic growth while redirecting freed-up public money to widely supported, but essentially cheaper, employment- and employability-oriented social policies (see also Hay, 2011; 2013). In contrast, a different growth model is operated in protectivist European welfare states. Since the male breadwinner model still has a much stronger footing here, the orientation of public policies towards protection from old risks and conservation of traditional family models remains highly popular. Here, governments have tended to focus on high private savings rates and increasing productivity through real wage stagnation rather than through better education, skill deployment, and innovations.

Second, I would argue that the compatibility of the SIS and ABW approaches is grounded in how labor markets are structured in the Nordic and liberal welfare states. On the one hand, the tertiarization of national economies has led to a meaningful rise in female labor participation. Dual-income couples and families have attained a stronger market position and may cope better with high levels of private debt, as they are more capable to satisfy monthly mortgage repayments in housing markets that are characterized by high and increasing prices. Conversely, this means that those who are burdened by high levels of mortgage debt need to maximize their employment efforts permanently. Again, from an empirical viewpoint, there is a clear positive association between these two variables. We see that countries with a high female employment rate tend to have higher amounts of private outstanding mortgage debt (Pearson's correlation coefficient for 2007 is 0.45, with a statistical significance of $p<0.01$). Hence, to sustain their dual-income position, younger couples and families are likely to support political parties and policies that ensure

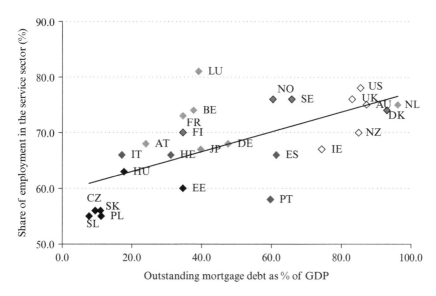

Note: R² of relationship is 0.44, significant at p<0.05 (one-tailed).

Sources: EMF (2014); World Bank (2014).

Figure 5.3   *Mortgage debt as percentage of GDP vs. share of employment in the service sector in the OECD, 2007*

employment maximization through widely available and relatively cheap care facilities (see also Schwartz and Seabrooke, 2008). On the other hand, these economies – arguably, this is more so the case in liberal nations – are marked by a relatively high share of employment in the service sector, implying a relatively high share of low-paid, low-skilled jobs. The relatively low tax returns that follow from such a labor market structure, as well as the relatively low average salaries, may then result in stronger political pressure to implement policies that support the abundance of mortgage credit (see Figure 5.3 for an empirical visualization of this relation).

Third, a conceptual argument is that both the SIS and the ABW approaches take a life-course perspective on the manifestation of social problems and their solution. Poverty, social exclusion, and inequality are primarily defined as individual rather than collective problems. In this context, individual responsibility, risk-taking behavior, and long-term financial planning have, in the eyes of policy makers, become key ingredients in securing one's own welfare position. Social policy in this framework is reduced to the function of adapting people to the needs of the market instead of diminishing their dependency on it (see also Crouch, 2009). As a result of this embedded market logic, both policy approaches share the same fundamental limitations. Employment- and human-capital-oriented spending, as well as policies that support home ownership, are oriented towards the needs of middle-income groups and are also taken up more by those who need them less. Indeed, many studies have shown that opportunities to gain access to high-quality education and to accumulate housing wealth are highly unequal (for example, Dewilde and Lancee, 2013; Vandenbroucke and Vleminckx, 2011). There is thus no definite solution to the question of how to include the 'unproductive class' (labeled 'housing market outsiders' earlier); that is, those who lack the means for investing in education and vocational training on the one hand, and in property assets on the other. Hence, given the significance of family background to invest in human capital and assets alike, both policy approaches appear to reinforce rather than limit the intergenerational transmission of poverty risks and life chances (see also Cantillon and van Lancker, 2013; Nolan, 2013).

PRODUCTIVE WELFARE CAPITALISM AFTER THE CRISIS

Welfare states in western societies are not on the retreat, but they have taken different forms through various transformation processes in the past two decades. Some policy dimensions – most notably public pension systems and labor protection – were targeted by retrenchment and deregulation, while other dimensions have been expanded, including, inter alia, family policies and the provision of care services. However, the restructuring process towards a more productive social policy approach has been far from universal. Rather, this study has illustrated the divergence of welfare policy priorities across the OECD, in which the Northern European and liberal English-speaking nations in particular have moved towards a policy approach that predominantly aims for human capital formation and employment maximization. In contrast, most continental, Southern, Central, and Eastern European countries have retained a welfare model that primarily aims to protect and stratify income. Bringing the notion of ABW and the significance of private housing wealth into the equation of welfare state change, this chapter has put forward the idea that the divergence of these two welfare approaches might be explained through the rise of home ownership and property wealth, and how individuals and families access these. Where governments enabled citizens to take up large amount of debts to purchase housing property, the accumulation of such assets could increasingly serve as a private source of income protection and welfare security, which in turn facilitated the rechanneling of public resources to new welfare state functions. Ergo, the implementation of an ABW approach – the accumulation of housing wealth to satisfy private welfare needs – did not lead to the demise of the welfare state; on the contrary, it might be considered as a necessary condition for the restructuring of social policy towards a welfare state that builds on a comprehensive social investment strategy.

As this chapter mainly relied on data from the pre-crisis period (that is, pre-2007), the question of whether the described developments are still apparent after the GFC of 2008 remains. Indeed, post-recession welfare policies in Europe, particularly since 2010, have been geared more strongly towards welfare state retrenchment. Here, austerity measures have not only targeted income protection policies, but also revoked various social investment policies, including care expenditure and education spending (Farnsworth and Irving, 2011). An interesting observation is that it was exactly the housing market meltdown of 2007, instigated by exuberant mortgage lending and resulting in programs to save indebted banks and consequently in skyrocketing government debt, which gave momentum to these retrenchment policies. This could imply that the causal context of changes in housing instigating welfare state restructuring that was proposed – yet not evidenced – has radically shifted after the crisis.

Furthermore, it has become apparent in many contexts that human capital investments do not necessarily guarantee secure and well-paid jobs. Quite contrarily, unemployment and precarious employment have become pressing issues not only for low-skilled individuals but also for well-educated employees (Bell and Blanchflower, 2011). In a similar vein, the housing market crash has unmasked the fragility of the ABW approach and the whole economic growth model that stands behind it. Where house prices are stagnating or even falling, the promise of debt turning into wealth has become a particularly bogus idea.

Finally, the conditions for accessing the home ownership market have deteriorated significantly since 2008. Primarily through the tightening of mortgage credit and political measures that aim to stabilize the (housing) finance industry, younger adults have been facing increasing difficulties in stepping onto and moving up the housing ladder, leading to a widening intergenerational gap between housing-wealthy older people and a housing-poor younger generation (Forrest and Yip, 2012; Lennartz et al., 2015). In short, the GFC has made it clear that having a good education and owning a (heavily indebted) house is not necessarily enough to satisfy all welfare needs, hence questioning the stability and durability of the productive, investment-oriented welfare model.

Be that as it may, however, it was recently pointed out that although social policy austerity is still a primary political goal on the European continent, retrenchment is not the only game left in town (van Kersbergen et al., 2014). Indeed, many countries – as well as the European Commission – have discussed or even implemented the renunciation of budgetary restraints, putting skill-oriented and employment-maximization policies in place instead. Similarly, even though access to home ownership has become more difficult in practice, the political rhetoric around the primacy of housing property ownership has been unchanged – and indeed, house prices are almost back to pre-crisis levels in many places. The fact that these recent developments are often found in countries marked by the clearest shift towards a 'productive welfare capitalism' model before the crisis might suggest the persistence of the divergence between the more protective and the more productive regimes even after the crisis.

NOTES

1. The meaning of 'productive' in this context is not to be understood in a normative way and will be defined more accurately later on.
2. In more detail, an unfunded PAYGO pension system means that no assets are set aside but current pension benefits are paid by the contributions of the current workforce, often complemented through state contributions out of tax income. In many countries, however, a hybrid pension system with partial funding exists. Hence, a clear-cut distinction between the two approaches is often not possible, making Schwartz's balance sheet approach more of a bipolar theoretical model.
3. Unfortunately, net public spending data are only published for total public spending and retirement spending. To make the empirical analysis more robust, I tested all available spending measures for all different policy domains, in all countries, for the whole period. To deal with potential problems of timing (the use of selected years), I compared the different measures for different starting and ending years, and used 3-year as well as 5-year averages rather than the 1995–2007 change measure. The results for all these different approaches were very similar to the approach presented here and differences between approaches were not statistically significant (data are available on request).

REFERENCES

Aalbers, M.B. (2015), 'The Great Moderation, the Great Excess and the global housing crisis', *International Journal of Housing Policy*, **15** (1), 43–60.
Aalbers, M.B. and B. Christophers (2014), 'Centering housing in political economy', *Housing, Theory and Society*, **31** (4), 1–22.
Adema, W., P. Fron and M. Ladaique (2011), *Is the European Welfare State Really More Expensive? Indicators on Social Spending, 1980–2012; and a Manual to the OECD Social Expenditure Database (SOCX)*, OECD Social, Employment and Migration Working Papers No. 124, Paris: OECD Publishing.
André, S. and C. Dewilde (2016), 'Home ownership and support for government redistribution', *Comparative European Politics*, **14** (3), 319–348.

Ansell, B. (2014), 'The political economy of ownership: housing markets and the welfare state', *American Political Science Review*, **108** (2), 383–402.

Bell, D.N. and D.G. Blanchflower (2011), 'Young people and the Great Recession', *Oxford Review of Economic Policy*, **27** (2), 241–267.

Bonoli, G. (2007), 'Time matters: postindustrialization, new social risks, and welfare state adaptation in advanced industrial democracies', *Comparative Political Studies*, **40** (5), 495–520.

Bonoli, G. and D. Natali (eds) (2012), *The Politics of the New Welfare State*, Oxford: Oxford University Press.

Cantillon, B. and W. Van Lancker (2013), 'Three shortcomings of the social investment perspective', *Social Policy and Society*, **12** (4), 553–564.

Carroll, C. (2004), *Theoretical Foundations of Buffer Stock Saving*, Working Paper 10867, Cambridge, MA: National Bureau of Economic Research.

Castles, F.G. (1998), 'The really big trade-off: home ownership and the welfare state in the new world and the old', *Acta Politica*, **33**, 5–19.

Christophers, B. (2013), 'A monstrous hybrid: the political economy of housing in early twenty-first century Sweden', *New Political Economy*, **18** (6), 885–911.

Crouch, C. (2009), 'Privatised Keynesianism: an unacknowledged policy regime', *The British Journal of Politics and International Relations*, **11** (3), 382–399.

Delfani, N., J. De Deken and C. Dewilde (2014), 'Home-ownership and pensions: negative correlation, but no trade-off', *Housing Studies*, **29** (5), 657–676.

Dewilde, C. and B. Lancee (2013), 'Income inequality and access to housing in Europe', *European Sociological Review*, **29** (6), 1189–1200.

Doling, J. and M. Elsinga (eds) (2013), *Demographic Change and Housing Wealth: Homeowners, Pensions and Asset-Based Welfare in Europe*, Dordrecht: Springer.

ECB (European Central Bank) (2009), *Housing Wealth and Private Consumption in the EURO Area*, Monthly Bulletin, January, Frankfurt: ECB.

EMF (European Mortgage Federation) (2014), *Hypostat 2013*, Brussels: EMF.

Emmenegger, P. (ed) (2012), *The Age of Dualization: The Changing Face of Inequality in Deindustrializing Societies*, Oxford: Oxford University Press.

Esping-Andersen, G. (ed) (2002), *Why We Need a New Welfare State*, Oxford: Oxford University Press.

Farnsworth, K. and Z.M. Irving (eds) (2011), *Social Policy in Challenging Times: Economic Crisis and Welfare Systems*, Bristol: Policy Press.

Forrest, R. and Y. Hirayama (2015), 'The financialisation of the social project: embedded liberalism, neoliberalism and home ownership', *Urban Studies*, **52** (2), 233–244.

Forrest, R. and N.M. Yip (eds) (2012), *Young People and Housing: Transitions, Trajectories and Generational Fractures*, London: Routledge.

Gilbert, N. (2002), *Transformation of the Welfare State: The Silent Surrender of Public Responsibility*, Oxford: Oxford University Press.

Goerres, A. and M. Tepe (2010), 'Age-based self-interest, intergenerational solidarity and the welfare state: a comparative analysis of older people's attitudes towards public childcare in 12 OECD countries', *European Journal of Political Research*, **49** (6), 818–851.

Hamnett, C. (1999), *Winners and Losers: The Home Ownership Market in Modern Britain*, London: Routledge.

Häussermann, S. (2012), 'The politics of old and new social policies', in G. Bonoli and D. Natali (eds), *The Politics of the New Welfare State*, Oxford: Oxford University Press, pp. 111–134.

Hay, C. (2011), 'Pathology without crisis? The strange demise of the Anglo–liberal growth model', *Government and Opposition*, **46** (1), 1–31.

Hay, C. (2013), 'Treating the symptom not the condition: crisis definition, deficit reduction and the search for a new British growth model', *The British Journal of Politics and International Relations*, **15** (1), 23–37.

Hemerijck, A. (2012), *Changing Welfare States*, Oxford: Oxford University Press.

Hudson, J. and S. Kühner (2009), 'Towards productive welfare? A comparative analysis of 23 OECD countries', *Journal of European Social Policy*, **19** (1), 34–46.

Kemeny, J. (1981), *The Myth of Home Ownership*, London: Routledge.

Lennartz, C. (2011), 'Power structures and privatization across integrated rental markets: exploring the cleavage between typologies of welfare regimes and housing systems', *Housing, Theory and Society*, **28** (4), 342–359.

Lennartz, C., R. Arundel and R. Ronald (2015), 'Younger adults and homeownership in Europe through the Global Financial Crisis', *Population, Space and Place* (Early View).

Lennartz, C., M. Haffner and M. Oxley (2012), 'Competition between social and market renting: a theoretical application of the structure-conduct-performance paradigm', *Journal of Housing and the Built Environment*, **27** (4), 453–471.

Lowe, S.G., B.A. Searle and S.J. Smith (2012), 'From housing wealth to mortgage debt: the emergence of Britain's asset-shaped welfare state', *Social Policy and Society*, **11** (1), 105–116.

Malpass, P. (2008), 'Housing and the new welfare state: wobbly pillar or cornerstone?', *Housing Studies*, **23** (1), 1–19.

Montgomerie, J. and M. Büdenbender (2014), 'Round the houses: homeownership and failures of asset-based welfare in the United Kingdom', *New Political Economy*, **20** (3), 1–20.

Morel, N., B. Palier and J. Palme (eds) (2012), *Towards a Social Investment Welfare State? Ideas, Policies and Challenges*, Bristol: Policy Press.

Nikolai, R. (2012), 'Towards social investment? Patterns of public policy in the OECD world', in N. Morel, B. Palier and J. Palme (eds), *Towards a Social Investment Welfare State? Ideas, Policies and Challenges*, Bristol: Policy Press, pp. 91–115.

Nolan, B. (2013), 'What use is "social investment"?', *Journal of European Social Policy*, **23** (5), 459–468.

Obinger, H. and P. Starke (2014), *Welfare State Transformation: Convergence and the Rise of the Supply Side Model*, TranState Working Papers No. 180, Bremen: University of Bremen.

OECD (Organisation for Economic Co-operation and Development) (2014), *Social Expenditure Database*, Paris: OECD.

Pierson, P. (1994), *Dismantling the Welfare State? Reagan, Thatcher, and the Politics of Retrenchment*, Cambridge: Cambridge University Press.

Pierson, P. (ed) (2001), *The New Politics of the Welfare State*, Oxford: Oxford University Press.

Poggio, T. (2012), 'The housing pillar of the Mediterranean welfare regime: relations between home ownership and other dimensions of welfare in Italy', in R. Ronald and M. Elsinga (eds), *Beyond Home Ownership: Housing, Welfare and Society*, London: Routledge, pp. 51–67.

Ronald, R. and J. Doling (2012), 'Testing home ownership as the cornerstone of welfare: lessons from East Asia for the West', *Housing Studies*, **27** (7), 940–961.

Ronald, R., J. Kadi and C. Lennartz (2015), 'Homeownership-based welfare in transition', *Critical Housing Analysis*, **2** (1), 52–64.

Schwartz, H. (2012), 'Housing, the welfare state, and the Global Financial Crisis: what is the connection?', *Politics & Society*, **40** (1), 35–58.

Schwartz, H. (2014), *Is There a Really Big Trade-Off? Housing, Welfare and Pensions Reconsidered from a Balance Sheet Perspective*, Working Paper, accessed 15 October 2016 at http://people.virginia.edu/~hms2f/trade-off.pdf.

Schwartz, H. and L. Seabrooke (2008), 'Varieties of residential capitalism in the international political economy: old welfare states and the new politics of housing', *Comparative European Politics*, **6** (3), 237–261.

Seeleib-Kaiser, M. (ed) (2008), *Welfare State Transformations: Comparative Perspectives*, London: Palgrave Macmillan.

Smith, S.J. and B.A. Searle (2008), 'Dematerialising money? Observations on the flow of wealth from housing to other things', *Housing Studies*, **23** (1), 21–43.

Starke, P., A. Kaasch and F. Van Hooren (2013), *The Welfare State as Crisis Manager: Explaining the Diversity of Policy Responses to Economic Crisis*, London: Palgrave Macmillan.

Szydlik, M. (2012), 'Generations: connections across the life course', *Advances in Life Course Research,* **17** (3), 100–111.

Taylor-Gooby, P. (2008), 'The new welfare state settlement in Europe', *European Societies*, **10** (1), 3–24.

van Kersbergen, K. and A. Hemerijck (2012), 'Two decades of change in Europe: the emergence of the social investment state', *Journal of Social Policy*, **41** (3), 475–492.

van Kersbergen, K., B. Vis and A. Hemerijck (2014), 'The Great Recession and welfare state reform: is retrenchment really the only game left in town?', *Social Policy & Administration*, **48** (7), 883–902.

Vandenbroucke, F. and K. Vleminckx (2011), 'Disappointing poverty trends: is the social investment state to blame?', *Journal of European Social Policy*, **21** (5), 450–471.

Vis, B., K. van Kersbergen and T. Hylands (2011), 'To what extent did the financial crisis intensify the pressure to reform the welfare state?', *Social Policy & Administration*, **45** (4), 338–353.

Watson, M. (2009), 'Planning for a future of asset-based welfare? New labour, financialized economic agency and the housing market', *Planning, Practice & Research*, **24** (1), 41–56.

World Bank (2014), *Employment in Services (%)*, accessed 12 February 2015 at http://data.worldbank.org/indicator/SL.SRV.EMPL.ZS.

PART II

Institutional variegations of the relationship between housing, welfare provision and inequality

6. Financial resilience and security: the impacts of the housing market downturn on low-income home owners in Northern Ireland

Alison Wallace

INTRODUCTION

> The state can shape markets to help build assets and resources for us and our families over our lives, so they are there when we need them, and build emotional and financial resilience regardless of the circumstances of birth.
>
> (Kitty Usher, 2012)

The above quote from a former United Kingdom (UK) Treasury Minister under the previous New Labour Government (1997–2010) argues that the role of states, even after the financial crisis, was to prompt markets into helping even low-income households build assets and increase their financial capacity. This reflects a burgeoning interest in ideas of resilience across different disciplines and fields, which examine ways to reinforce individuals', regions' or systems' ability to recover from exogenous shocks, preferably by their own resources and tenacity. This chapter examines to what extent the idea of asset-based welfare dovetails with these sentiments and whether housing assets strengthen home owners' resilience, specifically their capacity to manage market downturns. It reports on research that considered the impact of the loss of housing wealth on low-income home owners in the extreme housing market conditions of Northern Ireland, a devolved region of the UK. The decline in house prices in Northern Ireland exceeded 50 per cent between 2007 and 2013, and at Q1–2015 remained 1 per cent below 2005 values. As housing wealth has been positioned as a significant welfare resource to home owners, Northern Ireland provides a pertinent case study to examine the impact of the loss of housing assets and the role home equity played in supporting people during a recessionary period. The chapter explores whether housing assets have augmented home owners' capacity to manage the economic downturn and what the removal of this resource in the falling housing market meant for low-income home owners.

Given the importance that the existing evidence base places on asset accumulation and home ownership, it was anticipated that the falling housing market would adversely affect households' feelings of financial security and their ability to get by in a crisis. Certainly, this study found a minority of home owners profoundly affected in this way by negative equity, the prospect of debt and limited residential mobility. Critically, however, the dominant narrative was of home owners receiving great succour during a period of market turmoil – not from using their housing assets to tide them over depleted household income, but by having adopted a conservative approach to the financialization of the home. The home owners impervious to feeling undermined or disorientated by the loss of housing wealth, regardless of the sums involved, were those who implicitly rejected the private asset model of welfare and prioritized the use-value of the home over the asset-value. Resistance to, rather than engagement with, contemporary home economics increased low-income home owners' resilience in a turbulent market.

This chapter first considers the concept of resilience, the synergies between this and asset-based welfare and the place of home ownership therein. The Northern Ireland housing market is then documented, showing the impact of the financial crisis on the region. Home owners' perceptions of the loss of housing equity are considered. This is followed by a discussion of the implications of the research findings for applying the concept of resilience to housing and personal finance in a post-financial-crisis context in which the pursuance of asset-based welfare centred on housing assets remains prominent.

RESILIENCE, ASSET-BASED WELFARE AND HOME OWNERSHIP

The concept of resilience is widely deployed in a range of policy contexts, but its meaning is malleable, enabling it to transcend different domains (Davoudi, 2012; MacKinnon and Derickson, 2012; Walker and Cooper, 2011). Resilience is commonly used to encapsulate qualities within complex systems, organizations and communities – or even households and individuals – that can resist, rebound, adapt or recover from significant exogenous shocks, and it reflects contemporary concerns with insecurity and uncertainty (Christopherson et al., 2010). The concept of resilience accentuates agency in the face of change; however, individuals and communities may lack resources or power to secure their future independently in the face of, for example, globalization and economic change (Ben-Galim and Lanning, 2010; Harrison, 2013). Nonetheless, other conceptualizations of resilience reflect a wider interpretation, involving actions at different levels (Cardenas and Lopez, 2010) and multiple actors and agencies (Davoudi, 2012), as well as emphasizing a collective response to identify, anticipate and mitigate stresses (Pendall et al., 2012).

The idea of resilience has been infrequently applied to personal financial management or housing, but clearly there are similarities between this and asset-based welfare, which within housing studies more typically frames ideas of an individual's preparedness to resist or recover from crises independently. Asset accumulation is said to increase self-reliance and the ability to smooth income shocks, provide a financial cushion for households, increase self-efficacy and control and stimulate the growth of other assets, such as social and human capital (Sherraden, 1991). Some are explicit about the link between the concept of asset holding and resilience. For example, Dolphin (2012) finds that creating opportunities for asset accumulation for lower-income young people secured their financial resilience. Asset-based welfare approaches make individuals responsible for their own financial risk in society. Rowlingson and McKay (2011) note that this shift towards personal assets and away from collective welfare began in the 1980s and appeals to a wide political spectrum by seemingly simultaneously addressing inequality and making poorer people self-reliant.

The UK's 1997–2010 Labour Government introduced saving vehicles for adults and children to encourage the accumulation of financial assets among lower-income households (Prabkahar, 2009). These were explicit asset-based welfare policies; however, de facto asset-based welfare policies were also associated with the promotion of home ownership, which provided subsidized access to home ownership – in part and explicitly – to extend the opportunities for asset accumulation to lower-income groups (ODPM, 2005). Arguably, these interventions to support home ownership operated on a much wider scale than the other savings initiatives. Although the 2010–2015 Coalition Government abolished these savings schemes, policy support for home ownership in Westminster and the devolved jurisdictions of the UK remains strong (DCLG, 2011; Semple, 2007). Debates on home ownership and housing wealth have become increasingly important in many other countries as well; as Forrest (2008, p. 172) notes, these are associated with good economic citizenship, as housing assets can supplement earned income and help owners 'weather adverse economic circumstances'.

What McKnight (2011) called an 'asset-effect' is evident, as savings in early adulthood have an independent and positive influence on earnings and employment later in life, after controlling for possible confounders.

The mechanism by which assets have a positive impact is uncertain, however, as it was beyond the scope of this study to explain the process of accumulation or how assets should be spent to achieve more positive outcomes (ibid.). But while financial assets are the most unequally distributed, housing assets are more widely held and represent a greater share of all wealth (Bastagli, 2012). However, to what extent *housing* assets, as opposed to *financial* assets, augment life chances in the UK is underexplored. There are some positive associations between home ownership and educational attainment (Bramley and Karley, 2007), but methodological problems – including selection effects, the direction of causality and unobserved mediating variables – challenge research in this field (Brook Lyndhurst, 2006; O'Sullivan and Gibb, 2012; Turner and Luea, 2009).

Prior to the financial crisis, UK home owners undoubtedly accrued significant sums of housing equity. Housing equity is often low income home owners' only form of wealth (Rowlingson and McKay, 2011), leaving them with a highly undiversified wealth portfolio (Stegman et al., 2007). Home owners became increasingly financialized and aware of the fungibility of housing assets, making homes important components of financial planning during the life course (Smith et al., 2009; Watson, 2009). In the UK and other English-speaking countries, home owners can withdraw equity from their homes in various ways (Reinold, 2011). Prior to the financial crash, remortgaging in situ comprised a substantial part of the mortgage market (Smith, 2004). This housing equity withdrawal occurred at times of critical life events, more usually associated with welfare needs (Ong et al., 2013; Parkinson et al., 2009).

There are downside risks to utilizing home equity in this way, however, as remortgaging was also associated with an increased risk of repossession (Searle, 2012). Indeed, equity withdrawal formed an important component of lower-income UK home owners' biographies when exiting home ownership with mortgage arrears (Ford et al., 2010; Wallace et al., 2011; Wilcox et al., 2010). Moreover, housing equity remains highly unevenly distributed by age, region and social class, potentially undermining the utility of its welfare role (Bastagli, 2012; Burbidge, 2000; Hamnett, 1999; Hills et al., 2013; Montgomerie and Büdenbender, 2015; Searle, 2014). Therefore, the loss of housing equity has been identified as a new risk to contemporary home ownership (Smith et al., 2009). Yet, the empirical examination of the impact of significant house price falls arising from the financial crisis on home owners is limited. This chapter reports on a study that sought to address these issues in the context of a severe housing market downturn in Northern Ireland. The chapter continues by outlining the research and reporting its findings on the impact of the crisis on local home owners and their perceptions of the loss of housing equity.

THE RESEARCH

The study was funded by the Northern Ireland Office of the First Minister and Deputy First Minister (OFMDFM). The core component comprised in-depth telephone interviews with a total of 51 home owners. Of these, 11 were higher-income home owners, 6 were home owners who had used low-cost home ownership initiatives and 34 were low-income home owners, defined by their household income being at or below 60 per cent of the equivalized median income identified in the UK Family Resources Survey (FRS) for 2010/11. The home owners were drawn from across Northern Ireland, comprised a balanced religious profile and were recruited by a local market research agency. This qualitative work was supported by administrative data and the analysis of time-series FRS data. FRS data were pooled for the period 2002/3 to 2004/5 to reflect the period of the rising market, for the years 2005/6 to 2007/8 for the market peak and for the years 2008/9 to 2010/11 for the period of the falling housing market. This provided contextual data about how Northern Ireland's housing market and home owners differed from those found across the UK and allowed for the identification of changes across the whole housing market cycle, particularly following the financial crisis.

NORTHERN IRELAND'S HOUSING MARKET

Until the global financial crisis, Northern Ireland had not experienced housing market volatility, as the legacy of conflict meant a lack of investor confidence in the region's housing market (Adair et al., 1998). During the first decade of the millennium, however, volatility was extraordinarily pronounced (Figure 6.1). With an average loss of £106,641 per property – or 53 per cent of house price values – from peak to trough, the sums lost to the housing market downturn are significant.

Various reasons are advanced for this volatility, which remain contested. While a 'peace dividend' was evident as house prices shifted slightly upwards following the ceasefires of the mid 1990s, the economic patterns of cheap credit, inward migration and spill-over effects from the Celtic Tiger south of the border were more important than the cessation of violent hostilities (Adair et al., 1998; Besley and Mueller, 2011; Gibb et al., 2007). While cross-border housing market activities between Northern Ireland and the Republic of Ireland are often emphasized, McCord et al. (2011) found few interconnections between the two housing markets. Frey (2008) therefore suggested that similar market conditions were as much a response to the same global trends as they were caused by direct

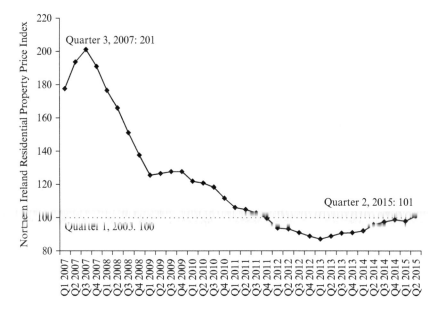

Source: Northern Ireland Research and Statistics Agency (NISRA) Residential Property
Price Index (RPPI).

Figure 6.1   Standardized price by property type, Q1–2005 to Q2–2015

transactional links. Caution was expressed on the upswing, but the local
construction and housing market industries were myopic and unable to
restrain their activities (Frey and Gray, 2010). Bridle (2008, p. 1) therefore
suggested that the 'upswing was marked by exuberance, some might say
hubris'.

What is clear is that a number of factors combined to produce a series
of unprecedented housing market outcomes. The scale of the slump in
house prices is illustrated in Figures 6.2 and 6.3. Only in the Republic of
Ireland was the housing market downturn so deep, compared with leading
European countries and the United States (although individual states may
have been more affected). Housing affordability improved for younger
cohorts, but Northern Ireland's existing home owners experienced a range
of negative impacts of the market downturn.

First, Northern Ireland had the highest level of negative equity in the
UK. By 2012, this was 28–37 per cent of mortgage loans advanced since
2005 (FSA, 2012); by 2013, it was 41 per cent of loans advanced since
2005, compared to only 8 per cent of these loans across the UK (HML,
2014). Negative equity has mixed consequences. There is no real impact if

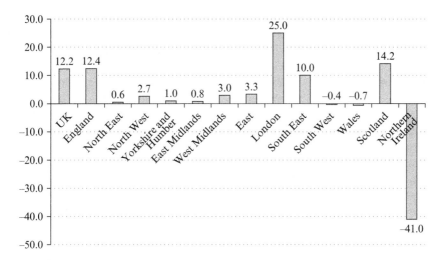

Source: ONS (2015), Table 29, Housing market: simple average house prices all dwellings.

Figure 6.2   *Percentage change simple average house prices for UK regions and devolved countries, 2007–2013*

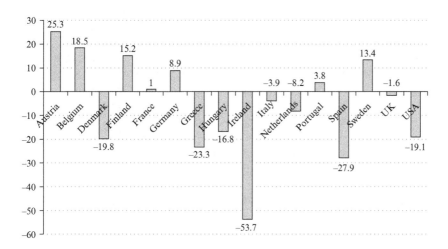

Sources: EMF (2013).

Figure 6.3   *Percentage changes in Hypostat house price index, 2007–2012*

owners are not looking to move or refinance and can sustain their repayments (Tatch, 2009). Problems occur when people want or need to move and residential mobility is constrained (Hellebrandt et al., 2009).

Second, Northern Ireland also displays stubbornly high levels of households struggling with mortgage debt. UK regional data for mortgage repossessions is publicly unavailable, but major differences in lenders' court applications to repossess mortgaged homes are apparent (Ministry of Justice, 2014; NICTS, 2012). While possession orders declined rapidly across the whole of the UK, possession orders in Northern Ireland remained high, reducing only during 2014, due to improving market conditions. The UK literature has always resisted a relationship between negative equity and mortgage arrears (Tatch, 2009), noting that the incidence of mortgage arrears turns on labour market disruption, relationship breakdown and ill health (Ford et al., 2001). Owners' attachment to their home and their often-strident attempts to maintain payments to save the home are emphasized (Nettleton et al., 1999; Wallace et al., 2011). Classical economics, however, rejects subjective assessments of behaviour and asserts that owners will disinvest from poor investments, although Forrest and Kennet (1996) found no evidence of strategic default in their 1990s study of negative equity in the UK. Critical life events remain important triggers to mortgage default, but underlying causes also include high loan-to-values and financially overstretched borrowers (FSA, 2012). Several studies associate negative equity with repossessions and multiple adverse circumstances, particularly when the magnitude of negative equity is high (Aron and Muellbauer, 2010; Bhutta et al., 2010; Gerardi et al., 2013). UK studies point to the importance of voluntary sales to home owners who are self-managing mortgage arrears. Stagnating housing markets and negative equity, however, hamper this household economic strategy because of the potential for large shortfall debts (Ford et al., 2010; Wallace et al., 2011).

Indeed, a third characteristic of the Northern Ireland market is that the volume of property transactions contracted almost twice as much (63 per cent) as the market across the whole of the UK (36 per cent) between 2006 and 2013 (HMRC, 2013). This exerted a break on residential mobility and severed an important route towards arrears resolution, leading struggling borrowers to legal repossession. Thus, negative equity indirectly influences formal repossession data.

A fourth important facet of the local housing market downturn relates to the mortgage market. Cautious lending and tighter mortgage market regulation means that Northern Ireland's home owners had the highest levels of borrowers – dubbed 'mortgage prisoners' – unable to switch to competitive mortgage deals (FSA, 2012). During 2012, between 60 and 70 per cent of home owners in Northern Ireland were estimated to be unable to remortgage, compared to 45 per cent in northern England and 35 per cent in the south of England.

Finally, the local economy and workforce were hit hard. In Northern Ireland, productivity declined by almost twice as much as other UK regions (Plunkett et al., 2014), real household incomes fell the furthest (New Policy Institute, 2014) and the recovery is anticipated to take longer (Murphy and Scott, 2013). Moreover, Northern Ireland has the greatest pool of financially stressed borrowers, who are indebted and unable to cope with any mooted mortgage interest rate rises (Whittaker and Blacklock, 2014). The local rate of personal insolvencies increased significantly up to 2015, while the rate decreased elsewhere in the UK, indicating that the crisis of unsustainable debt remains unresolved (Insolvency Service, 2016).

In combination, these factors have limited the opportunities for existing home owners and produced a highly dysfunctional housing market (DSD, 2014). This chapter goes on to consider who Northern Ireland's home owners are, and evaluates their changing approach to housing finance during the last housing market cycle.

HOUSING EQUITY, HOME OWNERS AND MORTGAGES

Northern Ireland's negative equity is the key outcome of the long tail of damage left by the financial crisis. Using the Halifax House Price Index and Family Resources Survey (FRS) data, it was estimated that 14 per cent of all Northern Ireland's mortgagors carried negative equity during 2010/11, roughly 50 per cent more than the 9.5 per cent of mortgaged home owners across the UK (Table 6.1). Both the incidence and magnitude of negative equity were greater in Northern Ireland than in the UK as a whole, with the sums involved during 2010/11 broadly double that of the UK.

By April 2014, housing markets across the UK in all but a few places in

Table 6.1   Estimates of negative equity 2010/11, Northern Ireland and the UK

		Northern Ireland	UK
In negative equity	Count (weighted)	29,593	782,711
	Within region	14.0%	9.5%
	Mean negative equity	£35,162	£17,485
	Median negative equity	£18,942	£10,173

Source: Family Resources Survey.

the north of England improved significantly, exceeding values of 2007 in many places, especially the south of England and London, where house values were nearly one-third above their level in January 2008 (ONS, 2015). In contrast, Northern Ireland's housing market continued to fall until 2014, when house prices remained 49.6 per cent below the 2008 level. The incidence of negative equity and the values attached to it therefore became greater than observed within the 2010/11 FRS data. An earlier life stage and higher occupational class indicated an increased incidence of negative equity, but the greatest estimated value of negative equity was found among the bottom-income quintile (£72,379), twice the average value of negative equity for all home owners.

Northern Ireland's home owners are also in more vulnerable labour market positions than those in the UK. UK rates of home ownership have fallen, with a notable shift from routine and manual occupational classes towards professional and/or managerial owners. This is less apparent in Northern Ireland, where home owners had lower median incomes than their counterparts across the UK and were more likely to have been self-employed (17.1 per cent compared to 10.3 per cent in the rest of the UK) and to be in lower-grade employment. Self-employed owners hold a precarious position in the labour market and have difficulties with accessing mortgage safety nets; the FRS data reveal that 39 per cent of them were in the bottom income quintile during 2010/11.

The FRS data shows Northern Ireland's home owners, especially lower-income home owners, to be more financially conservative than those across the UK. Lower-income home owners engaged less frequently with financial instruments than higher-income owners, with some notable and risky exceptions. Interest-only mortgages hold the risk of non-repayment if repayment plans are absent at term and negative equity will not reduce unless house prices move (FSA, 2012). Northern Ireland home owners used interest-only loans less frequently than their UK counterparts and reduced their use as the market peaked, more so than borrowers in the UK as a whole. However, low-income home owners in Northern Ireland reverted from interest-only to repayment loans less frequently than higher-income borrowers, producing a pool of poorer home owners in Northern Ireland who remain on loans where – in the context of widespread negative equity and low inflation – their debt burden is not reducing. A social gradient to the use of interest-only loans was also apparent, which, except for the most affluent owners, was steeper in Northern Ireland than across the UK. Northern Ireland's home owners also lagged behind the UK in their use of remortgaging and did so for reasons less associated with consumption spending and more frequently for home improvements. Northern Ireland home owners also remortgaged for better interest rates less frequently than UK home owners, indicating a less savvy approach to home finance. In addition, Keasey and Veronesi (2012) found Northern Ireland to be in the midrange of exposure to sub-prime lending compared to similar areas in England, where the incidence of subprime loans was higher. Given the volume of self-employed home owners in Northern Ireland, a higher rate of subprime loans would be expected.

Hellebrandt et al. (2009) posit that during a downturn, home owners switch investment behaviour from housing to other assets. The FRS data showed that Northern Ireland's home owners continued to have fewer bank current accounts and savings accounts – notably modern tax-free individual savings accounts (ISAs) – than those across the UK, with no increase during the downturn. Credit unions – community mutual savings and loans organizations – are popular in Ireland and Northern Ireland, but the 9 per cent of households holding credit union accounts during 2012/13 (DSD, 2014) is insufficient to bridge the gap between the one-fifth of households holding ISAs or savings accounts in Northern Ireland and the two-fifths to one-half of households in the UK. Furthermore, between 2008 and 2010, Northern Ireland had lower spending on pension contributions than Scotland, Wales or England (DETI, 2013). Thus, investments had not switched from housing to this asset class. Across the piece, these factors reinforce the view that Northern Ireland home owners engage less frequently with the products of financialization than home owners across the UK.

Concluding, although home owners in Northern Ireland exercised greater caution towards the use of riskier home finance – subprime, interest-only and remortgaging products – than those across the UK as a whole, the region nonetheless experienced the greatest incidence and magnitude of negative equity. By and large, Northern Ireland home owners' attitudes toward home finance lagged behind those across the UK. Coming late to the opportunities of home finance left some low-income owners in vulnerable positions, but protected others who engaged less frequently with the possibilities and risks of home finance. This is explored in the next section.

ATTITUDES TOWARDS THE LOSS OF HOUSING EQUITY

The home owner interviews confirmed this moderate approach to the financialization of the home and demonstrated that adopting such a framework provided greater succour or a protective quality in the face of market collapse. So rather than utilizing housing equity to support them over the downturn, as suggested in the literature, it was other attributes of home ownership – of control and independence in the home – that bolstered home owners' resilience, even when in a vulnerable financial position. A portion of home owners understandably reflected profound anxieties about the house price falls. Home owners risked incurring large shortfall debts if they defaulted on their loans in the recession or due to an inability to move or extricate themselves from homes bought with others, and thus were living with greater costs, complexity and uncertainty in their lives. Notwithstanding these home owners' precarity, a key narrative viewed the spending of the home as anathema and asserted the use-value of the home rather than its asset-value. This section explores these perceptions of the market downturn and how home owners had been affected.

Home owners reported mixed responses regarding whether the market collapse had affected them. The interviewees acknowledged the impacts on their lack of mobility and on those with mortgage debts. However, regardless of the losses involved, a majority were largely impervious to the market adjustment.

> Not affected in anyway, we weren't looking to sell or buy a second house to rent out. (Home owner no.32)

> I just feel luck that I didn't dip into it because a lot of people did. (Home owner no.57)

Conversely, a minority of interviewees felt profoundly affected by the market downturn, aggrieved and angry at the turn of events.

> We always thought whenever we were going to buy it that it was going to make us money . . . whereas now if we wanted to sell it'd lose money. (Home owner no.58)

> I was going to sell the house and use it for retirement, get a wee flat. But can't do anything now, can't even change the mortgage, they wouldn't give me a better deal. (Home owner no.60)

> I haven't been able to pay one penny towards my daughter going to college, not a penny. She's going to be up to her eyes in debt and I won't be able to do it for the second one either. (Home owner no.23)

Ronald et al. (2015) noted that home owners adopted passive and active approaches to the incorporation of home equity into personal financial planning. The current study highlighted a third category of home owner:

those who wholly rejected the fungibility of home equity. Home owners' attitudes to the market downturn influenced their view of financialization, and whether they viewed the property as:

- a home: they asserted the use-value of the property and, in rejecting the asset-value of the homes, did not recognize their home as a source of finance;
- a financial security: they recognized the home was an asset over the long term but prioritized the use-value, adopting a passive approach to using home equity; or
- an investment: they were conscious of the asset-value of the property in the short term and were active in incorporating their housing equity into their financial plans.

A key finding of the study was that perceiving property as primarily a home and prioritizing its use-value rather than asset-value engendered feelings of security and protection from the market downturn. Despite suffering large house price falls, people who could sustain their mortgage payments continued to enjoy their home as originally intended and their home or financial security had not been threatened. Importantly, they were still receiving the qualities or housing services from their home that they had sought at the outset of their purchase. Toussaint (2011) notes the cultural dimensions to the use of housing equity in financial planning, and in Northern Ireland a strong attachment to the concept of a family home was evident. Rather than the home bequest representing a financial resource, there was a strong expectation that the property would also remain a family home in which one of the children's families would actually reside. This was particularly the case for rural home owners, who had inherited property or land on family farms. The thought of tapping into equity in the home was incomprehensible to these home owners regardless of age, as this could jeopardize the property. These home owners could barely conceptualize the home as having any financial value, let alone one that could be utilized.

> I know we'll never sell it, so I don't know how to answer. (Home owner no.63, when asked the value of the home)

> Once we get the big family home we'd keep it. I'd rather spend my days in it and pass it on. That's how it is over here. That's what my parents would do and what my grandparents would've done. (Home owner no.58)

> We're not planning on selling, it's a home home, for the next generation, when it's their turn they can have it. (Home owner no.65)

The second set of intermediate owners valued their home for the services received but acknowledged that the home had an asset-value that could be drawn upon in an emergency. However, not one of these owners (or indeed the next group of owners) had attempted to do so during the recession, despite experiencing unemployment or financial difficulties.

> Always at the back of my mind, we always had it there if you need it. I wouldn't like to go down that road if anything did happen [though] as you have to pay it back. (Home owner no.26)

Those home owners who felt most let down by the market downturn conceptualized the home as a financial asset and had explicitly incorporated their housing equity into their financial planning. They had thus suffered a significant economic — and frequently emotional — blow. The gap between their beliefs in homes as investments and their contrasting experiences of the market decline fuelled these home owners' anxieties.

> I felt financial secure and I felt that I could retire early and that I would have enough money to live on, but now I came completely the opposite way. I am skint and I feel like I am going to have to work until I die and my children are going to be worse off. (Home owner no.23)

> The mortgage advisor made it sound so easy to get the money, but it was the worst thing I could've done . . . with hindsight, I could've done without it, but they made it so easy. Taking money out for not much more in repayments, too good to be true. (Home owner no.62)

We conclude that, contrary to the view that cashing in housing equity to cover shortfalls in income increased resilience and the ability to cope in a recession, the evidence suggests that it was other attributes of home ownership that grounded people and helped them to cope with the market turbulence.

MANAGING MARKET DECLINE

Stagnating local housing markets exerted great pressure on those who wished to move or sell property without incurring a large shortfall debt. Higher-income owners were able to overpay their mortgage to reduce negative equity, to take higher-paid employment opportunities in London and to rent out their home to pay down the mortgage. Lower-income owners were more limited in their options, with siblings and former partners being unable to buy each other out of their shares of the properties when their co-owner had met other people. Higher-earning co-owners were left to pay two lots of housing costs rather than leave their siblings or former partners homeless. Higher earners were more likely to report that they had three months or more savings, which they could use to bridge financial gaps should they become unemployed or require emergency funds for unexpected bills; lower-income owners felt insecure and fearful of attracting large debts, fearing that their homes could be repossessed.

> We haven't got enough savings to buy our way out, or to move on. (Home owner no.75)

Ratcliffe (2010) noted that wealth effects increase people's propensity to spend in the wider economy and found that wealth reductions undermined both confidence in the wider economy and wellbeing. Home owners interviewed felt vulnerable as their finances were restricted by lower incomes and higher living costs during the recession. It is, however, a challenge to disentangle the effects of the wider recession from that of the loss of equity, but owners who recognized the value in their homes certainly felt exposed.

> There's no money to spend. People aren't going out, they're afraid to spend, as the house prices have dropped so much. Everyday living costs have gone up and everyone is cautious as there is no security in the house, like there was a few years ago. You can't fall back on money. (Home owner no.26)

Other home owners described poor household finances, but valued their home as a haven.

> It did feel good, that I managed to do it with all the recession and I've paid and held on to my home. (Home owner no.56)

The shared owners – those who had used the part-rent, part-buy co-ownership housing scheme in Northern Ireland – were less exposed to the market downturn, as they had also benefited less from the buoyant market prior to the crash. One owner had regrettably bought more shares at the market peak. Another shared owner misunderstood the terms of her lease and was anxious that she not only would owe the negative equity on her share but also the 50 per cent share the co-ownership agency had paid to acquire her home. Although not immune to negative equity on their shares, the size of the potential shortfalls was reduced for these owners.

Where negative equity or immobility had become problematic, lower-income home owners held fewer resources to remedy their situation and those with reduced incomes were struggling with payments. These households looked for external support to strengthen their ability to get by. Many home owners felt the government or banks were culpable in constantly promoting additional mortgage lending and should take action, although many also cited individual profligacy and personal responsibility for borrowing and expenditure.

GOVERNMENT RESPONSES TO THE HOUSING MARKET DOWNTURN

The devolved administration in Northern Ireland was slow to respond to the market downturn, resisting calls for mortgage rescue support for the high number of defaulting borrowers (Shapiro, 2012). While profession-als from the housing and debt advice sectors supported calls for public intervention, other market intermediaries and lenders were initially less convinced due to concerns about moral hazard.

> There was a sharp up, now there's a sharp down. Dry your eyes, get over it. (Market intermediary 1)

> Unless we have government intervention and lender support about how to help people in negative equity, this market will not function for a generation. (Market intermediary 2)

The government set up a Housing Repossessions Taskforce in 2014, prompted by the persistence of negative equity, mortgage default and lower transactions in the context of a fragile economic recovery and the potential risk of rising Bank of England base rates. The Taskforce exam-ined the local evidence and held a conference to 'help home owners help themselves' (DSD, 2014). Its final report called on lenders to do more to support home owners who could not swap mortgage deals or move home or who were struggling with repayments, called for additional funds for mortgage advice services for home owners, asked the Behavioural Insight Team – a former government research unit set up to consider 'nudge' techniques in policymaking (Thaler and Sunstein, 2009) – to consider how lenders could better engage borrowers and suggested a feasibility study on a local mortgage rescue scheme (BIT, 2015; DSD, 2015). While housing and debt advice funding increased, the feasibility report on mortgage rescue has failed to emerge and the market-based strategies of bolster-ing self-help solutions have not changed the narrative of experiences in the region where negative equity, interest-only loans and mortgage debt remain a live issue for a significant minority. Moreover, private firms have emerged – providing unregulated solutions and using delayed completions and lease-style arrangements – to fill this policy gap. This increases the vulnerability of struggling home owners.

So while the state may assist people to accumulate assets – Northern Ireland has a popular equity-sharing scheme to support access to home ownership – its capacity to shield people from market volatility or to support people in overcoming adverse housing market consequences is more limited, due to constrained public finances and concerns about moral hazard. The local Northern Ireland administration has also been limited in its ability to leverage attention for its small population in the face of a larger national lending industry. Moreover, the region is faced with a national UK government intent on further reducing help for struggling borrowers to pay their mortgage (Pawson and Wilcox, 2012). Changes include restricting qualification, lengthening the waiting period before any payment is made and placing an equity charge on borrowers' homes so that any funds advanced are repaid on sale of the property. Making explicit the link between self-reliance and using assets to fund welfare in this way will, however, undermine lender forbearance and decrease the capacity of home owners to sustain their home (Ford et al., 2011).

CONCLUSION

Existing evidence proposed that the loss of housing equity was a new risk to home ownership because home owners had drawn upon housing assets to boost household finances. This chapter has outlined the findings of a study that examined this risk in the context of Northern Ireland and considers whether or how home owners used home equity to boost their resilience during the financial crisis.

Following a peak-to-trough decline in house prices of around 50 per cent as a consequence of the financial crisis, home owners in Northern Ireland experienced the greatest incidence and magnitude of negative equity across the UK. Survey data and in-depth interviews showed a greater conservatism among Northern Ireland home owners in respect of the financialization of the home compared to the UK. Prior to the financial crisis, home owners in Northern Ireland engaged less frequently with innovative products in the mortgage market than their counterparts in the UK. When they did engage, they did so later in the housing market cycle and, in the case of remortgaging and interest-only loans, were vulnerable in the falling market.

The interviews reflected this limited engagement with housing assets, which was to the owners' advantage. During the longest and deepest market downturn in the postwar period, this study found little evidence that low-income home owners in Northern Ireland used their homes to smooth income and manage external shocks to their household finances. Nonetheless, home ownership did offer security and control through the market turmoil, when the use-value of the home was prioritized above the asset-value. Although the personal impact of the housing market downturn was less than anticipated at the outset of the study, there were households who had been adversely affected by the market fall. The ramifications of the market downturn on residential mobility, negative equity and mortgage arrears or possession were deeply felt by a minority and were viewed as critical issues by professionals. In these circumstances, the loss of housing assets threatened the financial security and resilience of some home owners. As Montgomerie and Büdenbender (2015) note, shifting towards an asset-based welfare housing culture undermines the maxim 'safe as houses'.

Smith (2015, p. 62) captures the multiple attributes of home ownership in terms of 'a spatial and a financial paradox that allows people to be and to feel, not just at home but positively sheltered, in the uncomfortable hybrid of money, meanings and materials which constitutes owner occupation today'. These ensemble characteristics of home ownership – representing a risk as well as a safety net (Elsinga and Hoekstra, 2015) or ontological security (Colic-Peisker and Johnson, 2010) – were reflected in the interviews. However, less prominence was afforded to housing assets than the qualities of familial associations, control and security enjoyed by owners. This group of owners were unconcerned about a limited investment portfolio as their home was largely a 'home home' (home owner no.65) rather than a financial asset. However, the 'investor figure' or the 'financialized citizen', who actively involves housing assets in his financial planning (Smith, 2015), was evident among the research participants. These owners were most aggrieved by the downturn and were undergoing difficult emotional adjustments to the new market conditions. Other studies acknowledge a diversity of approaches to home economics among owners (Smith, 2015; Toussaint, 2011), but it was striking that, regardless of sums lost and even the presence of negative equity, a key point from this Northern Ireland study must be in reasserting the use-value of home ownership rather than further fostering the investment potential of housing, however structured. The extent to which global trends towards the financialization of housing can be reversed is, however, a moot point. Further encouraging a climate of risk-taking to somehow bolster resilience, secure self-reliance and shift perceptions of the home from a residence to a financial cash cow is unwise, particularly without adequate safety nets.

Aalbers (2015) argues for a return to decommodified housing and to resist the financialization of the owner-occupied home in global economies, which would certainly make for a more resilient housing system. But can contemporary home ownership exist without financialization? Pursuing marginal home ownership may be misguided, but can motivations for home purchase be shifted from capital gains to the housing services offered? Fahey and Norris (2011) note that home ownership in Ireland was rarely developed as a personalized investment vehicle but rather reflected the importance of owning land in the context of historic sovereignty disputes and conflict, as well as a way of protecting tenants from the vagaries of the private rental market. The narratives in this chapter also echo the findings of Murphy and Scott (2013), who found that, prior to the financial crisis, rural home owners in the Republic of Ireland were more conservative and less engaged in the exuberance of the housing market than city dwellers, who were harder hit after 2008. There were clear parallels in Northern Ireland, where a portion of home owners displayed strong cultural attachment to the land and adopted familial mechanisms of support, buying the home for the housing services obtained rather than for its investment qualities. But this was not a universal position, and a proportion of home owners had embraced the new financial possibilities of home finance.

How, then, to reverse these fierce trends towards foundational goods as significant investment vehicles? Such an undertaking is likely to require a range of interventions to make the housing system more resilient to shocks and to temper volatility in housing and mortgage markets. This includes land taxation or capital gains tax to capture the untaxed wealth stored in homes in a progressive and equitable manner, rendering it capable of being redistributed and deployed in support of welfare-associated services (O'Sullivan and Gibb, 2012). Such moves would also reduce the emotional demands associated with tapping into housing wealth (Fox O'Mahony and Overton, 2015), would not undermine the security offered by the home and would be sensitive to the spatial and temporal unevenness that limits the outcomes of this tacit acceptance of asset-based welfare in the context of welfare retrenchment.

This study shows that the impacts of the housing market downturn in Northern Ireland were indeed profound for those who had incorporated housing assets into their financial planning, but that the primacy of housing services over financial assets mitigated any dislocation felt by home owners and strengthened their ability to manage adversity. Were it not for the resistance to the use of housing assets in contemporary financial planning, the impact of the housing market downturn in Northern Ireland may have been even more profound. It is not anticipated that the results are directly transferable outside Northern Ireland or perhaps the Republic of Ireland, but the takeaway point is applicable. The study indicates that further policy drift towards asset-based welfare undermines rather than supports home owners' resilience to market fluctuations, as it destabilizes owners who value the security and control derived from their home.

REFERENCES

Aalbers, M. (2015), 'The Great Moderation, the Great Excess and the global housing crisis', International Journal of Housing Policy, **15** (1), 43–60.

Adair, A., J. Berry and S. McGreal (1998), 'Assessing influences upon the market in Northern Ireland', Journal of Property Research, **15** (2), 121–134.

Aron, J. and J. Muellbauer (2010), Modelling and Forecasting UK Mortgage Arrears and Possessions, London: Department of Communities and Local Government.

Bastagli, F. (2012), Wealth Accumulation in Great Britain: The Role of House Prices and the Life Cycle, London: CASE London School of Economics.

Ben-Galim, D. and T. Lanning (2010), Strength against Shocks: Low-Income Families and Debt, London: Institute for Public Policy Research.

Besley, T. and H. Mueller (2011), 'Estimating the peace dividend: the impact of violence on house prices in Northern Ireland', American Economic Association, **102** (2), 810–833.

Bhutta, N., J. Dokko and H. Shan (2010), The Depth of Negative Equity and Mortgage Default Decisions. Finance and Economics Discussion Series, Washington, DC: Federal Reserve Board.

BIT (Behavioural Insights Team) (2015), Applying Behavioural Insights to Encourage Earlier Engagement from Borrowers in Mortgage Arrears, London: BIT.

Bramley, G. and N. Karley (2007), 'Homeownership, poverty and educational achievement: school effects as neighbourhood effects', Housing Studies, **22** (5), 693–722.

Bridle, A. (2008), 'A journey through the unknown', in NIHE (Northern Ireland Housing Executive), Northern Ireland Quarterly House Price Index Q2–2008, Belfast: University of Ulster and Bank of Ireland.

Brook Lyndhurst (2006), Social Mobility and Homeownership: A Risk Assessment, London: Communities and Local Government.

Burbidge, A. (2000), 'Capital gains, homeownership and economic inequality', Housing Studies, **15** (2), 259–280.

Cardenas, A. and L. Lopez (2010), 'Analysis matrix of resilience in the face of disability, old age and poverty', International Journal of Disability, Development and Education, **57** (2), 175–189.

Christopherson, S., J. Machie and P. Tyler (2010), 'Regional resilience: theoretical and empirical perspectives', Cambridge Journal of Regions, Economy and Society, **3** (1), 3–10.

Colic-Peisker, V. and G. Johnson (2010), 'Security and anxiety of homeownership: perceptions of middle-class Australians at different stages of their housing careers', Housing, Theory and Society, **27** (4), 351–371.

Davoudi, S. (2012), 'Resilience: a bridging concept or a dead-end?', Planning Theory and Practice, **13** (2), 299–333.

DCLG (Department of Communities and Local Government) (2011), Laying the Foundations: A Housing Strategy for England, London: DCLG.

DETI (Department of Enterprise, Trade and Investment) (2013), Financial Capability in Northern Ireland 2012, Belfast: DETI.

Dolphin, T. (2012), Saving and Asset Building in Low Income Households, London: Institute for Public Policy Research.

DSD (Department for Social Development) (2014), Repossessions Taskforce Initial Evidence Paper: Negative Equity, Arrears and Possessions in Northern Ireland, Belfast: DSD.

DSD (2015), Housing Repossessions Taskforce: Final Report, Belfast: DSD.

Elsinga, M. and J. Hoekstra (2015), 'The Janus face of homeownership-based welfare', Critical Housing Analysis, **2** (1), 32–41.

EMF (European Mortgage Federation) (2013) Hypostat 2013: A Review of Europe's Mortgage and Housing Markets, Brussels: EMF.

Fahey, T. and M. Norris (2011), 'From asset based welfare to welfare housing? The changing function of social housing in Ireland', Housing Studies, **26** (3), 459–469.

Ford, J., J. Bretherton, A. Jones and D. Rhodes (2010), Giving up Home Ownership: A Qualitative Study of Voluntary Possession and Selling because of Financial Difficulties, London: Communities and Local Government.

Ford, J., R. Burrows and S. Nettleton (2001), Homeownership in a Risk Society: A Social Analysis of Mortgage Arrears and Possessions, Bristol: Policy Press.

Ford, J., A. Wallace, M. Munro, N. Sprigings and S. Smith (2011), An Evaluation of the January 2009 and October 2010 Arrangements for Support for Mortgage Interest: The Role of Lenders, Money Advice Services, Jobcentre Plus and Policy Stakeholders, London: Department for Work and Pensions.

Forrest, R. (2008), 'Globalization and the housing asset rich: geographies, demographies and policy convoys', Global Social Policy, **8** (2), 167–187.

Forrest, R. and P. Kennet (1996), 'Coping strategies, housing careers and households with negative equity', Journal of Social Policy, **25** (3) 369–394.

Fox O'Mahony, L. and L. Overton (2015), 'Asset-based welfare, equity release and the meaning of the owned home', Housing Studies, **30** (3), 392–412.

Frey, J. (2008), 'A challenging time – but also one of opportunity', in NIHE (Northern Ireland Housing Executive), Northern Ireland Quarterly House Price Index Q2–2008, Belfast: University of Ulster and Bank of Ireland.

Frey, J. and P. Gray (2010), 'Northern Ireland's housing market: prospects for recovery, the role of mortgage markets and the perspective in an era of public expenditure constraint', Housing Finance International, Summer 2010. Available from the International Union for Housing Finance.

FSA (Financial Services Authority) (2012), Mortgage Market Review Data Pack: Supplement to PS12/16, London: FSA.

Gerardi, K., K. Herkenhoff, L. Ohanian and P. Willen (2013), Unemployment, Negative Equity and Strategic Default, Working Paper, Atlanta: Federal Reserve Bank of Atlanta.

Gibb, K., M. Livingston, V. Williams, J. Berry, L. Brown and S. McGreal (2007), The Northern Ireland Housing Market: Drivers and Policies, Belfast: Northern Ireland Housing Executive.

0# 156

0*Housing wealth and welfare*

Hamnett, C. (1999), Winners and Losers: Home Ownership in Modern Britain, London: Routledge.

Harrison, E. (2013), 'Bouncing back? Recession, resilience and everyday lives', Critical Social Policy, **33** (1), 97–113.

Hellebrandt, T., S. Kawar and M. Waldron (2009), 'The economics and estimation of negative equity', Quarterly Bulletin 2009 Q2, London: Bank of England.

Hills, J., J. Bastagli, F. Cowell, E. Karagiannaki, H. Glennerster and A. McKnight (2013), Wealth in the UK: Distribution, Accumulation and Policy, Oxford: Oxford University Press.

HML (2014), BBC Negative Equity Report, accessed on 16 February 2015 at http://www.hml.co.uk/latest-thinking/2014/03/bbc-negative-equity-report/.

HMRC (Her Majesty's Revenue and Customs) (2013), UK Property Transaction Statistics, London: HMRC.

Insolvency Service (2016), Insolvency Statistics January–March 2016: Tables 4b and 14, London: The Insolvency Service.

Keasey, K. and G. Veronesi (2012), 'The significance and implications of being a subprime homeowner in the UK', Environment and Planning A, **44** (6), 1502–1522.

MacKinnon, D. and K. Derickson (2012), 'From resilience to resourcefulness: a critique of resilience policy and activism', Progress in Human Geography, **37** (2), 253–270.

McCord, M., D. McIlhatton and S. McGreal (2011), 'The Northern Ireland housing market and interconnections with the UK and Irish housing markets', Housing Finance International, Autumn 2011. Available from the International Union for Housing Finance.

McKnight, A. (2011), 'Estimates of the asset-effect: the search for a causal effect of assets on adult health and employment outcomes', CASE Paper 149, London School of Economics.

Ministry of Justice (2014), Mortgage and Landlord Possession Statistics Quarterly October to December 2013, London: Ministry of Justice.

Montgomerie, J. and M. Büdenbender (2015), 'Round the houses: homeownership and failures of asset-based welfare in the United Kingdom', New Political Economy, **20** (3), 386–405.

Murphy, E. and M. Scott (2013), 'Mortgage-related issues in a crisis economy: evidence from rural households in Ireland', Geoforum, **46**, 34–44.

Nettleton, S., R. Burrows, J. England and J. Seavers (1999), Losing the Family Home: Understanding the Social Consequences of Mortgage Repossession, York: Joseph Rowntree Foundation.

New Policy Institute (2014), Monitoring Poverty and Social Exclusion in Northern Ireland 2014, York: Joseph Rowntree Foundation.

NICTS (Northern Ireland Courts and Tribunal Service) (2012), Statistical Press Release – Mortgages: Actions for Possession April–June 2012, Belfast: NICTS.

NISRA (Northern Ireland Statistics and Research Agency) (2015), Residential Property Price Index (RPPI): Detailed Statistics Q2–2015, Belfast: NISRA.

ODPM (Office of the Deputy Prime Minister) (2005), Homebuy: Expanding the Opportunity to Own, London: ODPM.

Ong, R., S. Parkinson, B. Searle, S. Smith and G. Wood (2013), 'Channels from housing wealth to consumption', Housing Studies, **28** (30), 1012–1036.

ONS (Office of National Statistics) (2015), Comparison of Regional House Price Indices Before and After the Financial Crisis, London: ONS.

O'Sullivan, A. and K. Gibb (2012), 'Housing taxation and the economic benefits of homeownership', Housing Studies, **27** (2), 267–279.

Parkinson, S., B.A. Searle, S.J. Smith, A. Stoakes and G. Wood (2009), 'Mortgage equity withdrawal in Australia and Britain: towards a wealth-fare state?', European Journal of Housing Policy, **9** (4), 363–387.

Pawson, H. and S. Wilcox (2012), UK Housing Review Briefing Paper, Coventry: Chartered Institute of Housing.

Pendall, R., B. Theodos and K. Franks (2012), 'Vulnerable people, precarious housing, and regional resilience: an exploratory analysis', Housing Policy Debate, **22** (2), 271–296.

Plunkett, J., A. Hurrell and M. Whittaker (2014), The State of Living Standards: The Resolution Foundation's Annual Audit of Living Standards in Britain, London: Resolution Foundation.

Prabkahar, R. (2009), The Assets Agenda, London: Palgrave Macmillan.

Ratcliffe, A. (2010), 'Housing wealth or economic climate: why do house prices matter for well-being?', Working Paper No. 10/234, Bristol: Centre for Market and Public Organisation.

Reinold, K. (2011), 'Housing equity withdrawal since the financial crisis', Bank of England Quarterly Bulletin 2011 Q2.

Ronald, R., J. Kadi and C. Lennartz (2015), 'Homeownership-based welfare in transition', Critical Housing Analysis, **2** (1), 52–64.

Rowlingson, K. and S. McKay (2011), Wealth and the Wealthy: Exploring and Tackling Inequalities between Rich and Poor, Bristol: Policy Press.

Searle, B. (2012), 'Recession, repossession and family welfare', Child and Family Law Quarterly, **24** (1), 1–23.

Searle, B. (2014), 'Who owns all the housing wealth? Patterns of inequality in England', Mind the Wealth Gap Briefing No. 3, accessed on 16 February 2015 at http://wealthgap.wp.st-andrews.ac.uk/files/2013/02/WealthGap_No_03_Housing_wealth_inequalities.pdf.

Semple, J. (2007), Review into Affordable Housing: Final Report, Belfast: Northern Ireland Department for Social Development.

Shapiro, Y. (2012), 'DSD has no plans to introduce mortgage rescue scheme', BBC News Online, 4 March. Accessed 13 October 2016 at http://www.bbc.co.uk/news/uk-northern-ireland-17250424.

Sherraden, M. (1991), Assets and the Poor: The New American Welfare Policy, New York: Sharpe Inc.

Smith, J. (2004), 'Mortgage equity withdrawal and remortgaging activity', Housing Finance (Autumn), London: Council of Mortgage Lenders.

Smith, S. (2015), 'Owner occupation: at home in a spatial, financial paradox', International Journal of Housing Policy, **15** (1), 61–83.

Smith, S., B. Searle and N. Cooke (2009), 'Rethinking the risks to homeownership', Journal of Social Policy, **38** (1), 83–102.

Stegman, M., R. Quercia and W. Davis (2007), 'The wealth-creating potential of homeownership', in W. Rohe and H. Watson (eds), Chasing the American Dream: New Perspectives on Affordable Homeownership, Ithaca and London: Cornell University Press, pp. 271–292.

Tatch, J. (2009), 'Homeowner housing equity through the downturn', Housing Finance (1), London: Council of Mortgage Lenders.

Thaler, R. and C. Sunstein (2009), Nudge: Improving Decisions about Health, Wealth, and Happiness, New Haven: Yale University Press.

Toussaint, J. (2011), 'Housing assets as a potential solution for financial hardship: households' mental accounts of housing wealth in three European countries', Housing, Theory and Society, **28** (4), 320–341.

Turner, T. and H. Luea (2009), 'Homeownership, asset accumulation and income status', Journal of Housing Economics, **18** (2), 104–114.

Usher, K. (2012), 'Taking the long view of welfare', in J. Denham (ed.), The Shape of Things to Come, London and Brussels: Fabian Society and the Foundation for European Progressive Studies, pp. 55–64.

Walker, J. and M. Cooper (2011), 'Genealogies of resilience: From systems ecology to the political economy of crisis adaptation', Security Dialogue, **42** (2), 143–160.

Wallace, A., D. Quilgars and J. Ford (2011), Exiting Unsustainable Homeownership: Understanding Current Practice and the Potential of Assisted Voluntary Sales, London: Shelter.

Watson, M. (2009), 'Planning for a future of asset-based welfare? New Labour, financialized economic agency and the housing market', Planning Practice & Research, **24** (1), 41–56.

Whittaker, M. and K. Blacklock (2014), Hangover Cure: Dealing with the Household Debt Overhang as Interest Rates Rise, London: Resolution Foundation.

Wilcox, S., A. Wallace, G. Bramley, J. Morgan, F. Sosenko and J. Ford (2010), Evaluation of the Mortgage Rescue Scheme and Homeowners Mortgage Support, London: DCLG.

7. Trends in social inequalities regarding home ownership: a comparison of East and West Germany

Kathrin Kolb and Sandra Buchholz

INTRODUCTION

Numerous studies have shown that home ownership is the most important route to wealth accumulation (Brandolini et al., 2004; Grabka and Westermeier, 2014; Kolb, 2013; Sierminska et al., 2007; Skopek et al., 2012). Simultaneously, home ownership seems to have a positive effect on reducing social inequalities within the home-ownership segment, as housing wealth tends to be more equally distributed than financial wealth (Skopek et al., 2012). Certainly, there is also a 'contrary' trend toward increasing risks, growing debts, speculative price bubbles and more limited access to home ownership for young and low-income households due to market liberalization (see, for example, Dreger and Kholodilin, 2013; Kurz, 2000). Germany offers a particularly interesting case, allowing for a differentiated analysis of the distribution of owner-occupied housing. Even 25 years after reunification, noticeable differences can still be observed regarding the home-ownership situation in East and West Germany (Grabka and Frick, 2007), although relatively little is known about the underlying dynamics and mechanisms or the social inequality structures. Therefore, this chapter focuses on housing market changes and the development of social inequality in home ownership by means of an inner-German comparison. We pay special attention to how unequal access to home ownership and differences in the value of housing affect social inequality. More specifically, we investigate the influence of central socioeconomic characteristics from a longitudinal perspective on the likelihood of being a home owner, the value of residential real estate and the access to home ownership in East and West Germany. The empirical analyses are based on data from the German Socio-Economic Panel (GSOEP, 2013). Its longitudinal data structure is particularly suitable for our research questions because it offers detailed information over time on household characteristics and the home ownership situation in East and West Germany.

This chapter is structured as follows. We start with an overview of the home ownership situation in East and West Germany since 1945. After that, we draw on the state of research on social inequality to formulate hypotheses on access to housing, the chance of being a home owner and residential real-estate values in East and West Germany. Then – after describing the data used – we test our hypotheses in the empirical part of the chapter. The most striking findings are the remarkable differences regarding home-ownership rates and housing values between East and West Germany, even 25 years after reunification. However, the current transition rates to home ownership of the youngest cohort are similar for East and West Germans, which could lead to an increasing convergence of home-ownership rates in future. We then summarize the main findings on home ownership in East and West Germany before finally discussing them critically.

LIVING IN GERMANY: HISTORICAL DEVELOPMENT AND INNER-GERMAN DIFFERENCES

Home Ownership: the Central Wealth Component

Various studies have revealed that residential property is an essential factor for wealth accumulation, although home-ownership rates as well as the value of housing vary significantly between countries (see Brandolini et al., 2004; Grabka and Westermeier, 2014; Sierminska et al., 2007; Skopek et al., 2012). In particular, residential property is of immense importance for the lower-income quartiles. Although it is also essential for the top-income quartile, the wealth portfolio of the income-rich is much broader and therefore less susceptible to risks (for example, inflation and housing crises) (Skopek et al., 2012). It is notable that the value of home ownership depends significantly on the size, location and amenities of the real estate (Handelsblatt, 2011). This makes it necessary to treat the rate and the value of housing as two distinct dimensions of housing inequality (Kolb et al., 2012). Against the background of a growing demand for private welfare arrangements, the effect of home ownership on social inequality is particularly interesting. In an international comparison of 13 industrialized countries, Skopek et al. (2012) demonstrated that home ownership contributes to a reduction in wealth inequality. In light of the earlier political and economic differences between East and West Germany, it is particularly important to perform a differentiated analysis of the real-estate market in the two formerly separated parts of the country.

Home Ownership in East and West Germany since 1945

After the enormous destruction of living accommodation during World War II, the post-war period was characterized by strong state promotion of house building in West Germany (the Federal Republic of Germany (FRG)). In the immediate post-war period, social housing and the building of private rental apartments were promoted to create housing space for refugees and displaced persons (IW Köln, 2009). Owner-occupied residential property also became more important after World War II. This was the result of a combination of several processes. First, there were various state programmes to support home ownership. Especially in the years of the economic miracle, this was a way to gain citizens' permanent commitment to the capitalist labour market and economic system (Häußermann and Siebel, 2000; Kurz, 2012). Second, the favourable labour market situation from the 1950s to the 1970s, accompanied by almost full employment and secure employment relationships, facilitated long-term planning and the financing of home ownership. A third aspect promoting home ownership in West Germany was the withdrawal into the private protected area of the nuclear family after strong state interference during the Nazi dictatorship (Häußermann and Petrowsky, 1990). All these aspects led to a significant increase in the home-ownership rate: from 27 per cent in 1950 to 41 per cent in 1993 (Wagner and Mulder, 2000). Nevertheless, international comparisons reveal that the home-ownership rate in Germany is still at a low level. Principal reasons for this are the good protection of tenants, the orientation of rents to a local rent index and the high quality of rental apartments. Thus, rental apartments are an attractive alternative to home ownership in Germany (Tegeder and Helbrecht, 2007; Voigtländer, 2006).

However, in East Germany – the German Democratic Republic (GDR) – home ownership was largely prevented by the Government because it ran counter to Socialist ideology and the general idea of a centrally planned economy (Häußermann and Siebel, 2000). The housing market was centralized and strongly regulated by the state. This led to low rental rates and high protection against eviction (Schulz, 2010). In particular, so-called Plattenbau – prefabricated housing characterized by uniform and cost-effective construction – was built on the outskirts of towns from the 1970s onwards (Schulz, 2010). Despite this housing programme, the accommodation situation in the GDR remained difficult due to a lack of maintenance, which was hard to finance with low rents and resulted in a deterioration of the housing stock (Schneider and Spellerberg, 1999). In addition, the construction of single-family homes was partially tolerated in the beginning of the GDR but was not supported by the state. By providing cost-effective building materials, the state finally promoted home ownership for specific groups, such as families with many children, to alleviate the housing shortage from the beginning of the 1970s. As a result, between 1971 and 1989, approximately 200,000 homes were erected (Hannemann, 2000). Nonetheless, despite some new building activities, most houses were built before World War II. In the first years of the GDR, hardly any class distinctions could be observed regarding access to home ownership; they found expression in the quality and amenities of the owner-occupied apartments and houses (for example, central heating) (Diewald and Solga, 1995). Due to their simple design, the quality of building materials and the location, most houses were of low value. Overall, home ownership was the exception (Hannemann, 2000) and declined dramatically in the GDR (Bartholmai and Melzer, 1991).

The differences in home ownership between East and West Germany become even more apparent when we look at the home-ownership rates in the year of reunification, when they varied by almost 20 points between the two regions (45.4 vs. 28.5 per cent[1]).

Value of Housing in East and West Germany

For a long time, the high purchase price of real estate in Germany in international comparison was regarded as an explanation for the relatively low home-ownership rate (for example, Kurz, 2012; Wagner and Mulder, 2000). In fact, however, no increase in real-estate prices can be observed since the 1980s (Kholodilin et al., 2008), although there are strong regional variations (Handelsblatt, 2011). This can be explained by the rather 'conservative' nature of the German mortgage market. For instance, mortgages were rare in the subprime segment and the possibility of increasing short-term loans (as in the United States) did not exist in Germany. Subsequently, neither massive price increases before the real-estate crisis nor strong price erosions caused by the crisis could be observed in Germany (Blomert, 2008). Moreover, a mixture of other macroeconomic, demographic and institutional factors secured a general stability of real-estate prices. The weak growth of real per-capita income; low population growth; stagnating level of urbanization; well-developed rental sector, high equity needed to buy property and low mobility due to high transaction costs have all created a situation on the real-estate market in Germany since the 1980s that reveals almost no serious price fluctuations (Kholodilin et al,. 2008; Nguyen and Shlomo, 2009). Because of this stability, the purchase price in Germany is now in a middle position compared to the rest of Europe. However, special attention should be drawn to the inner-German situation; in 2012, the average net real-estate value in West Germany was 151,356 Euros, whereas it was only 87,338 Euros in East Germany (Grabka and Westermeier, 2014).

This brief overview reveals some first trends in the distribution of home ownership, as well as of housing values, in Germany. Up to now, there have been no detailed multivariate analyses taking into account the influence of central socioeconomic variables on both the home-ownership rate and housing values. This indicates that there is no adequate understanding of social inequality in housing in East and West Germany and how this has developed over time. This chapter will close this research gap.

HYPOTHESES

We shall now present hypotheses on the influence of socioeconomic household characteristics on the chances of being a home owner and on the value of housing. Furthermore, we will formulate hypotheses on the transition to home ownership.

A Comparison of Home Ownership in East and West Germany: Convergence Over Time?

Households in the GDR – in contrast to those in West Germany – were unable to profit from the economic miracle from the 1950s to the 1970s. The planned economic system tended to prevent access to home ownership and any accumulation of assets in general. In addition, the chance of inheriting and the amount inherited and gifted are still much lower for young people in East Germany compared to their Western German counterparts because, as mentioned, their (grand)parents were unable to accumulate much wealth (Szydlik and Schupp, 2004). In addition, the labour market situation is still comparatively unfavourable in East Germany since the fall of Communism: average income is lower than in West Germany and the unemployment rate is quite high. This situation is accompanied by strong migration (Blien et al., 2010; Solga et al., 2000). Because of these factors:

Both the home-ownership rate (Hypothesis 1a) and housing value (Hypothesis 1b) should be on a lower level than West Germany.

However, there are also some aspects that reinforce the home-ownership rate in East Germany. First, younger generations started their working

life in an open-market economy and therefore have had better chances
of earning a higher income on the labour market and generating wealth.
Besides, they have not been confronted with limited access to private
property. This situation may lead to an increased probability of transition to home ownership. Second, after reunification two trends regarding
home ownership could be observed: there was a trend of privatization of
Socialist housing (although not that pronounced compared with other
post-Socialist countries, such as Poland; see Stephens et al., 2015), as well
as construction of new private housing promoted by state subsidies for
owner-occupied homes. We therefore hypothesize that:

*There should be a trend towards alignment over time; however, the home-
ownership rate in East Germany should be still remarkably lower than in
West Germany (Hypothesis 1e).*

Are Higher-Status Households Also Privileged Regarding Home Ownership?

Various studies have demonstrated that persons with a higher educational
and occupational status are particularly successful in realizing home ownership as well as valuable property (Kurz and Blossfeld, 2004; Lewin-Epstein
et al., 1997; Statistisches Bundesamt, 2009). These results should also be
examined in the following analyses while taking Germany-specific characteristics into account. A typical result for Germany is that the working class
– despite a relatively low level of income – is quite successful in realizing home
ownership. However, there are large differences within this class (Kurz, 2012;
Petrowsky, 1993). Skilled workers and master craftpersons are as successful
as civil servants in realizing home ownership. Unskilled and semi-skilled
workers, in contrast, have by far the worst chances of owning residential
property (Kurz, 2000). It is also likely that the self-employed will own property because their regional ties are usually close. In addition, this profession
is used to managing larger amounts of money and the self-employed often
already own company property (Kurz and Blossfeld, 2004; Mulder and Smits,
1999). Home ownership should be particularly widespread among farmers.

*We expect to find similar patterns for educational (Hypothesis 2a) and
occupational (Hypothesis 2b) status on home ownership in our analyses.*

Finally, we assume that:

*The importance of educational and occupational status (Hypothesis 3a) as
well as income for becoming and being a home owner (Hypothesis 3c) and*

housing value (Hypothesis 3b) have increased over time (Buchholz and Kolb, 2011; Kurz and Blossfeld, 2004).

This assumption is based on the following developments. The educational expansion since the 1950s has led to an upgrading of skills in large parts of the population. Technical progress and the fast pace of technological change in the labour market have also increased the demand for highly skilled workers. However, in many cases, routine activities are being replaced increasingly by machines or being relocated abroad. This has worsened the labour market situation for unskilled and semi-skilled workers, who originally benefited from well-paid and protected jobs (Blossfeld et al., 2005, 2006, 2008; Buchholz, 2008; Buchholz and Kurz, 2008). This development means that unskilled and semi-skilled workers should experience growing difficulties in generating a sufficiently solid income to avoid poverty and to accumulate wealth through, for example, home ownership (Blossfeld et al., 2006). In addition, the growing equality of educational qualifications between the sexes has increased educational homogamy. This means that people with the same social status have become more likely to marry each other; this in turn leads to a pooling of either resources or disadvantages (Blossfeld, 2007; Blossfeld and Buchholz, 2009; Blossfeld and Timm, 2003). Finally, the abolition of the *Eigenheimzulage* in 2006 – an important state support system for access to owner-occupied housing – impacted particularly on low-earning households.

Influence of Further Socioeconomic Factors

Hypotheses on the influence of further socioeconomic household characteristics are as follows.

The distribution of home ownership by age should follow a curvilinear form in West Germany – similar to the lifecycle hypotheses of Modigliani and Brumberg (1954). For East Germany, we should observe a flatter curve, because the middle and older age groups had only low chances to accumulate private wealth during the Socialist regime (Hypothesis 4a).

Of course, this should be more of a cohort than an age effect (Blossfeld, 1985). In addition, no significant differences between age groups should be found regarding house values, because real-estate prices remained largely constant over the last decades (Hypothesis 4b).

Finally, we know from past research that there is no typical age but more an age span at transition to home ownership; people are most likely to realize home ownership in the age span between 25 and 44 years (Wagner and Mulder, 2000) (Hypothesis 4c).

We assume that single-person households less frequently possess (valuable) owner-occupied housing compared to all other types of household because of their higher mobility and their lower available resources (Andreß et al,. 2003; Engelbrech and Jungkunst, 2001) (Hypotheses 5a/5b).

The transition to home ownership should be realized mainly by couples (Hypothesis 5c).

Households benefiting from inheritances and gifts should more often be home owners (Hypothesis 6a) and should own more valuable housing (Hypothesis 6b), because intergenerational transfers strengthen the wealth position (Kohli et al., 2006; Mulder and Smits, 1999; Szydlik and Schupp, 2004).

Inheriting owner-occupied housing should be a relatively common option to realize home ownership (Hypothesis 6c).

Finally, we expect the following pattern regarding the residential area:

Home ownership should be less widespread in urban areas because of higher land and property prices (Hypothesis 7a).

This should also be expressed in a lower transition rate (Hypothesis 7c).

But, in case of home ownership, the property value should increase with rising population size of the residential area (Hypothesis 7b).

DATA AND METHODS

Data

We used data from the GSOEP (2013) to study the distribution of home ownership and the value of housing in Germany. The GSOEP is an annual, representative, longitudinal study of private households carried out in West Germany since 1984 and in Eastern Germany since 1990. In 2012, the sample contained approximately 15,000 households containing more than 25,000 people. Central topics are household composition, occupational biographies, employment and earnings.

For the subsequent analyses, we used data on the household level from

1990 to 2013. The household questionnaire includes questions about the housing situation and household wealth and income, as well as financial transfers. It is usually answered by the head of the household (Erler, 1996). In addition to the regular annual topics, there are also annually changing themes. In the years 2002, 2007 and 2012, the focus was on personal wealth (Grabka and Frick, 2007). In this context, more information was also gathered on the value of housing and on mortgages. The use of three periods allows an insight into the development of social inequalities in housing value over time – although, due to the time-series nature of these data, no conclusions on causal relationships are permissible.

Analysis and Research Issues

The unit of analysis is the household because most residential property is owned jointly by couples. In addition, it can be assumed that the construction or purchase of residential property depends more on the socioeconomic composition of the household than on characteristics of the individual.

The first research question concerned the influence of socioeconomic household characteristics on the chance of home ownership. This took the entire population into account. The starting population consisted of 4,098 households. More precisely, we analysed the housing situation of 2,371 West and 1,727 East German households. To reflect historical facts, we created the following two periods:

1. The 1990s (1990–99) covers a period in which a short phase of economic recovery after reunification was followed by increasing labour market turbulences and therefore a shift in long-term binding decisions (Blossfeld et al., 2005; Buchholz, 2008).
2. The period 2000–2013, which was characterized by an increasing convergence of living conditions in East and West Germany. In addition, an increasing part of the East German population grew up in the free, social market economy.

For the second research question, we focused solely on the group of home owners, because only these could answer the question on housing value.[2] In the empirical analyses, we studied 1,822 (2002), 1,780 (2007) and 1,268 (2012) households.[3] Financial value stands for the subjective market value estimated by the respondent, without considering mortgages and debts.[4]

In the third step, we analysed the transition to home ownership. Previous studies have revealed that the transition takes place mainly within the age span of 25 to 45 years (see Kurz, 2012; Wagner and Mulder, 2000).

Descriptive analyses with the GSOEP (2013) also confirm this trend. Because of this knowledge, we included only households meeting the following criteria in the analyses. First, all households that were home owners at the time of their interview were excluded because they had already made the transition to (first) home ownership. In addition, households with a household head older than 25 years when the investigation started were not integrated because of the increased risk that they had owned residential property before. The period of observation ends at the age of 45, because we assumed that few further events can be observed at this age. The analyses included a total of 1,277 households (West: 753, East: 524). In the empirical analysis, we differentiated between two cohorts: Cohort 1970 (1965 to 1974) and Cohort 1980 (1975 to 1987). The East German cohort born between 1965 and 1974 spent their school and training period still largely in GDR society. Accordingly, their occupational status as well as their wealth accumulation should be shaped by the Socialist regime and should differ from the situation in West Germany. Finally, the recent East German cohort (born between 1975 and 1985) started their working life in the market economy system.

Variables

The socioeconomic household characteristics in Table 7.1 were used as covariates in the analyses.

RESULTS OF THE EMPIRICAL ANALYSES

Home-Ownership Rate in East and West Germany

Figure 7.1 presents the home-ownership rates in East and West Germany from 1990 to 2012. The home-ownership rate has increased steadily: from 45.4 per cent in 1990 up to 53.3 per cent in 2012 in West Germany. The home-ownership rate in East Germany increased from 28.5 per cent in 1990 to 42.4 per cent in 2012. Therefore, despite a major catching-up process over the last 20 years, the home-ownership rate in East Germany is – as expected – still about 10 percentage points below that of West Germany (Hypothesis 1a). However, only the transition-rate models presented in the last step of our analyses will be able to reveal whether or not patterns of home ownership still differ in post-unification cohorts.

Table 7.1 *Covariates for the analyses of the real-estate market in Germany*[a]

Origin	East German vs. West German (ref.)
Periods	1990–99, 2000–2012
Birth cohorts	1956–1964, 1965–1974, 1975–1987
	Home ownership/real-estate value
	Below 25, 25–34, 35–44, 45–54 (ref.), 55–64, 65-plus
Age	*Transition to home ownership*
	Birth cohort 1959–1964/1965–1974
	25–29 years, 30–34 years, 35–39 years (ref.), 40–44 years
	Birth cohort 1975–87
	25–29 years, 30–34 years, 35–37 years (ref.)
Type of household	Single person (ref.), one-parent family, couple without children, couple with child(ren), multi-generational family, other
Qualification	Based on CASMIN classification (Brauns and Steinmann, 1997; Shavit and Müller, 1998)
Occupational class	Based on classification of Erikson and Goldthorpe (1992)
Income	Annual net household income, post-government (metric variable); adjusted for inflation
Intergenerational transfers	Binary variable; yes ($=1$) vs. no ($=0$)
Residential area	Village (up to 20,000 inhabitants), small town (20,001–100,000 inhabitants), large city (100,001–500,000 inhabitants), metropolis (more than 500,000 inhabitants)

Note: a. Additionally, we controlled for gender. As the household is the unit of interest, we decided not to present the (non-significant) individual effect of gender.

Influence of Socioeconomic Factors on Home Ownership

In the next step, we analysed the influence of (further) socioeconomic factors on home ownership by running logistic regression models for two time periods (see Agresti, 1990) (see Table 7.2). In addition, we examined their influence for East and West Germany in separate models (see Table 7.3). Compared to the reference group (aged 45–54), the three youngest age groups are home owners significantly less often. This is in line with our expectations (Hypothesis 4a). Also, the lower chances of home ownership for the aged are as expected. The hypothesis that East Germans would be home owners significantly less often (even after taking social status and financial resources into account) is also confirmed by the analyses reported

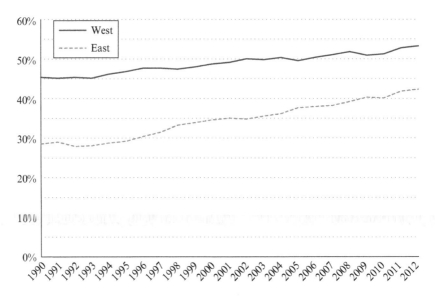

Source: GSOEP (2013) (weighted); own calculations.

Figure 7.1   Home-ownership rate in East and West Germany, 1990–2012

in Table 7.2. The effect of household composition is stable over the years
and shows a higher likelihood of home ownership for all household types
in comparison to the reference category 'single persons' (Hypothesis 5a).
A higher educational and occupational status, as well as a higher income,
tends to promote home ownership in both periods (Kurz and Blossfeld,
2004; Lewin-Epstein et al., 1997). In line with Hypothesis 2a, compared
to unskilled and semi-skilled workers, all other occupations are more frequently home owners. For the unemployed, who did not differ from the
unskilled and semi-skilled workers in the first period, chances are significantly lower than the reference category in the last period under study.

Separate models provide interesting results for the two population
groups (see Table 7.3). Especially for West Germans, having a higher
occupational status than being an unskilled or semi-skilled worker seems
to be central for home ownership. In East Germany, in contrast, the occupational status is not that important for all classes – only the high-ranked
occupational classes like the high service class and the self-employed
(including farmers) are better off than all other occupational classes.
This may be a consequence of past Socialist policies. The result for the
unemployed is also quite interesting in East Germany. Unemployment
has a significant negative influence on home ownership, compared with

Table 7.2   Chance of home ownership by period

	Period 1990–99		Period 2000–2012	
	Model 1	Model 2	Model 1	Model 2
Age				
Below 25	−2.01**	−1.79**	−3.35**	−2.65**
25–34	−0.30**	−0.28**	−1.21**	−1.31**
35–44	0.48	0.35**	−0.05	−0.37**
45–54 (ref.)	–	–	–	–
55–64	−0.78**	−0.26**	−0.51**	0.05
65-plus	−1.50**	−0.28**	−1.58**	−0.41**
Origin				
West German (ref.)	–	–	–	–
East German	−1.17**	−1.19**	−0.44**	−0.52**
Type of household				
Single person (ref.)	–	–	–	–
Couple without children		0.55**		0.47**
One-parent family		0.39**		0.31**
Couple with child(ren)		1.12**		1.26**
Multi-generational family		1.29**		0.81**
Other		1.26**		1.10**
Qualification (CASMIN)				
Lower secondary degree without occupational qualifications		−0.64**		−0.55**
Lower secondary degree with occupational qualifications		−0.15*		−0.30**
Upper secondary degree without occupational qualifications		−0.07		0.04
Upper secondary degree with occupational qualifications		0.11*		0.04
College/university degree (ref.)		–		–
Occupational class (EGP)				
Higher service class		0.54**		0.40**
Lower service class		0.41**		0.30**
Routine non-manual		0.14+		0.28**
Self-employed		0.46**		0.33**
Skilled manual		0.26**		0.20**
Farmer		1.64**		1.23**
Un-/semi-skilled (ref.)		–		–
Unemployed		0.06		−0.18*
Retiree		0.29**		0.25**

Table 7.2 (continued)

	Period 1990–99		Period 2000–2012	
	Model 1	Model 2	Model 1	Model 2
Income		0.57**		0.60**
Intergenerational transfers = yes		−0.16		0.37**
Residential area				
Village		1.67**		1.65**
Small town		1.02**		1.02**
City		0.37**		0.34**
Metropolis (ref.)		–		–
Constant	−1.60**	−5.24**	−0.33**	−4.61**
Pseudo R^2	0.07	0.21	0.07	0.25
N#	32,246	32,246	38,582	38,582

Notes:
Logistic regression models. Controlled for gender and missing values.
Household: years of observation.
** Significant at $\alpha \geq 0.01$.
* Significant at $\alpha \geq 0.05$.
+ Significant at $\alpha \geq 0.1$.

Sources: GSOEP (2013); own calculations.

unskilled and semi-skilled workers. This result is of concern in light of the difficult labour market situation and high unemployment rate in the East. Hence, unemployed people seem to be especially unsuccessful in protecting themselves financially and building up some private wealth. A higher income and intergenerational transfers (only for West Germany[5]) have a significant positive effect on home ownership due to the higher resource endowment of these households (Hypothesis 6a). The influence of intergenerational transfers gains in importance over time and is perhaps an expression of the declining reliability of labour market income. This trend could further intensify already-increasing social inequalities. Finally, the size of the community shows the expected effect: the more densely populated the residential area, the lower the chances of home ownership (Hypothesis 7a).

The results of the empirical analyses on the influence of socioeconomic household characteristics are largely in line with previous research and our expectations. It is remarkable that East Germans are still disadvantaged in comparison to West Germans on the housing market. In spite of the

Table 7.3   Chance of home ownership by population (1990–2012)

	West	East
Periods		
1990–99 (ref.)	–	–
2000–2012	0.27**	0.96**
Age		
Below 25	−2.40**	−2.20**
25–34	−0.97**	−0.82**
35–44	−0.14**	−0.15**
45–54 (ref.)	–	–
55–64	−0.00**	−0.05
65-plus	−0.30**	−0.44**
Type of household		
Single person (ref.)	–	–
Couple without children	0.52**	0.45**
One-parent family	0.24**	0.47**
Couple with child(ren)	1.27**	1.01**
Multi-generational family	1.37**	0.34
Other	1.25**	1.18**
Qualification (CASMIN)		
Lower secondary degree without occupational qualification	−0.55**	−0.34**
Lower secondary degree with occupational qualification	−0.26**	−0.13+
Upper secondary degree without occupational qualification	0.02	0.14
Upper secondary degree with occupational qualification	0.03	0.04
College/University degree (ref.)	–	–
Occupational class (EGP)		
Higher service class	0.56**	0.35**
Lower service class	0.48**	0.12
Routine non-manual	0.36**	0.14
Self-employed	0.40**	0.54**
Skilled manual	0.36**	0.09
Farmer	1.26**	2.82**
Unskilled/semi-skilled (ref.)	–	–
Unemployed	−0.06	−0.24**
Retiree	0.36**	−0.01
Income	0.58**	0.62**
Intergenerational transfers = yes	0.31**	−0.02

Table 7.3   (continued)

	West	East
Residential area		
Village	1.39	2.39**
Small town	1.05	1.12**
City	0.26	0.80**
Metropolis (ref.)	–	–
Constant	−4.85**	−6.44**
Pseudo R²	0.24	0.27
N#	39,156	24,254

Notes:
Linear regression models. Controlled for gender and missing values.
Household: years of observation.
** Significant at $\alpha \geq 0.01$.
* Significant at $\alpha \geq 0.05$.
+ Significant at $\alpha \geq 0.1$.

Sources: GSOEP (2013); own calculations.

significant increase in the home-ownership rate for the East German population, an identical home-ownership situation still cannot be observed.
The results stress that residential property is affected more and more by
labour-market status, particularly unemployment. This is a noteworthy
result, particularly in times of growing demand for more privatized forms
of welfare provision. In a contribution-based welfare system like Germany,
pensions are linked to employment and unemployment spells lead to
pension shortfalls.

Value of Housing

Table 7.4 shows the average and median value of housing in 2002, 2007
and 2012. The values vary clearly between East and West Germany: the
mean value in West Germany is around 80,000 Euros higher than that
in East Germany in 2002 and around 100,000 Euros higher in 2007/2012
(Hypothesis 1b). Hence, the value differences between East and West
Germany have increased even further over time. Moreover, the Gini coefficient (see Table 7.4) indicates that property values are distributed quite
unequally. Inequality even increases over time. A comparison of the Gini
coefficients reveals an interesting result: the real-estate value is distributed
more unequally in East than in West Germany, which could reinforce

Table 7.4   *Value of housing (mean, median and Gini) by population (2002, 2007 and 2012)*

		All	West Germany	East Germany
Mean	2002	EUR 210,938	EUR 232,666	EUR 152,261
	2007	EUR 224,548	EUR 252,362	EUR 158,964
	2012	EUR 242,893	EUR 278,197	EUR 171,777
Median	2002	EUR 200,000	EUR 200,000	EUR 150,000
	2007	EUR 203,300	EUR 214,000	EUR 139,100
	2012	EUR 216,450	EUR 234,000	EUR 155,025
Gini	2002	0.314	0.290	0.314
	2007	0.330	0.317	0.332
	2012	0.322	0.288	0.338

Sources: GSOEP (2013) (weighted, corrected for inflation); own calculations.

existing income inequalities and therefore overall social inequality in East Germany even more. Only a relatively small group of people are able to provide themselves with sufficient financial security via home ownership.

What Socioeconomic Factors Influence the Value of the Real Estate?

We applied linear regression models (see Long, 2011) to examine the influence of socioeconomic characteristics on housing values in order to learn more about the underlying mechanisms (see Table 7.5). Our aim was to work out the development of social inequalities over time (2002, 2007 and 2012).

For all years under study, the results show a significant East German disadvantage in housing value (Model 1) (Hypothesis 1b). This negative effect for East Germans is still highly significant after taking educational and occupational status into account in Model 2. The disadvantage of the East German population thus seems to go beyond differences in socioeconomic status. It can hence be concluded that East Germans are disadvantaged on both dimensions: access to home ownership and value of real estate. In line with our expectations (Hypothesis 4b), results for age reveal almost no noticeable effect on the value of housing. Interestingly, in comparison with the age group of 45–54-year-olds, the two oldest age groups hold lower real-estate values. As expected, compared to single-person households, all other household types own more valuable housing (Hypothesis 5b). In particular, couples without children own significantly more valuable housing, due to their lower financial resources and smaller space requirements.

Table 7.5 Value of the owner-occupied property, 2002, 2007 and 2012 (linear regression)

	2002		2007		2012	
	Model 1	Model 2	Model 1	Model 2	Model 1	Model 2
Age						
Below 25	-0.04	0.03	-0.38	-0.34	-0.17	-0.10
25–34	-0.00	0.01	-0.00	0.02	0.00	-0.01
35–44	-0.01	-0.01	0.01	0.01	0.04	0.04
45–54 (ref.)	–	–	–	–	–	–
55–64	0.06	0.12*	-0.04	0.00	-0.03	0.02
65-plus	-0.02	0.13	-0.05	0.14+	-0.03	0.17**
Origin						
West German (ref.)	–		–		–	
East German	-0.48**	-0.42**	-0.55**	-0.51**	-0.55**	-0.51**
Type of household						
Single person (ref.)	–		–		–	
Couple without children	0.23**	0.08	0.30**	0.17**	0.28**	0.17**
One-parent family	0.22*	0.11	0.17+	0.09	0.16+	0.08
Couple with child(ren)	0.37**	0.14*	0.37**	0.22**	0.40**	0.23**
Multi-generational family	0.21	-0.02	0.40*	0.25	0.21	0.21
Other	0.35*	0.08	0.10	0.09	0.03	0.04
Qualification (CASMIN)						
Lower secondary degree without occupational qualifications		-0.12		-0.28**		-0.21**
Lower secondary degree with occupational qualifications		-0.08		-0.12*		-0.10*
Upper secondary degree without occupational qualifications		-0.02		-0.04		-0.19**

	(1)	(2)	(3)	(4)	(5)	(6)
Upper secondary degree with occupational qualifications			-0.01	-0.12*		-0.07*
College/university degree (ref.)			–	–		–
Occupational class (EGP)						
Higher service class			0.14+	0.24**		0.34**
Lower service class			0.04	0.18*		0.20**
Routine non-manual			-0.05	0.07		0.14*
Self-employed			0.24**	0.22*		0.29**
Skilled manual			0.00	0.06		0.16*
Farmer			0.22	0.30		0.65**
Un-/semi-skilled (ref.)			–	–		–
Unemployed			-0.02	0.02		-0.21+
Retiree			0.05	0.03		-0.00
Income			0.17**	0.09**		0.10**
Intergenerational transfers = yes			0.08*	0.10**		0.04**
Residential area						
Village			-0.01	0.01		-0.15**
Small town			0.04	-0.05		-0.09*
City			0.06	0.07		-0.05
Metropolis (ref.)			–	–		–
Constant	11.90**	11.92**	10.88**	11.5**	11.9**	11.9**
R^2	0.12	0.15	0.18	0.20	0.18	0.25
N	1,822	1,780	1,822	1,780	1,268	1,268

Notes:
Linear regression models. Controlled for gender and missing values.
** Significant at $\alpha \geq 0.01$.
* Significant at $\alpha \geq 0.05$.
+ Significant at $\alpha \geq 0.1$.

Sources: GSOEP (2013); own calculations.

The empirical analyses show – as hypothesized – that households with higher educational and occupational status are privileged regarding housing value (Hypothesis 2b). These effects become significant for almost all occupational classes in the last year under study; this was not the case in 2002, when occupational class did not seem to matter very much for housing value. The result could indicate an increase in social inequalities over time, confirming Hypothesis 3b. Further analyses reveal that social status seems to be especially important for West Germans. When studying the influence of occupational status, it becomes clear that unskilled and semi-skilled workers hold less valuable real estate in all years under study. As expected, a higher income has a significantly positive effect on the value of residential real estate. This effect remains stable and highly significant in all models. As already noted with regard to access to owner-occupied housing, inheritance has a positive influence on the value of housing in each of the investigated periods (Hypothesis 6b). The size of residential area has the expected impact on the value of the real estate (Hypothesis 7b), even if it is only statistically significant in 2012.

As well as the chance of being a home owner, the value of housing indicates a remarkable disadvantage for East Germans and shows the increasing importance of educational and occupational status. Considering that private wealth is becoming increasingly important and that more and more households with lower social status are excluded from accumulating wealth via home ownership, these are worrying findings.

The Transition to Owning One's Own Home from a Longitudinal Perspective

Has access to home ownership changed over cohorts? Are there differences in transition patterns between East and West Germans? Figure 7.2 presents the results of the Kaplan–Meier estimations, which show the duration of the transition to home ownership for Cohort 1970 (1965–1974) and Cohort 1980 (1975–1987). It is evident that the transition to home ownership is quite rare up to the age of 30 in both birth cohorts and both groups. For the younger cohorts, the transition to home ownership takes place less frequently than in the previous birth cohorts. About 40 per cent of the older cohort became home owners by the age of 35, compared to only about 30 per cent of the 1980 cohort in West Germany.

Nonetheless, it is possible that home ownership is realized later in life because of a prolonged educational phase as well as more difficulties in becoming established in the labour market. Therefore, we may observe a catch-up effect that could lead to a convergence of the transition rates between cohorts (Blossfeld et al., 2005, 2008; Buchholz and Kurz, 2008).

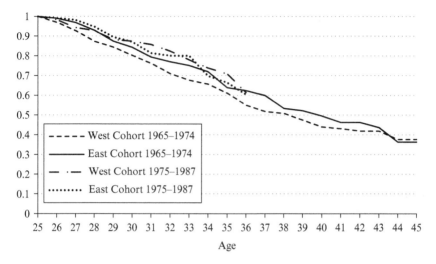

Source: GSOEP (2013) (weighted); own calculations.

Figure 7.2   *Transition to home ownership for different birth cohorts*
              (survival function) in East and West Germany

When considering the survivor function for East German households, the situation of the 1980 cohort is especially noteworthy: East Germans realize home ownership before the age of 35 years even more frequently than West Germans. This development may lead to a merging of the home-ownership rates in East and West Germany over time.

Table 7.6 presents the results of the non-parametric survival model for the transition probability to home ownership (Blossfeld and Rohwer, 2001). It shows that the transition probability for the most recent cohort is lower than for the 1970 cohort. However, this coefficient should be interpreted with caution, because this cohort has not yet completed the transition to home ownership. This assumption is confirmed by the reduction of the highly significant negative effect of birth cohort after controlling for age in Model 2.

The multivariate analysis of the age effect in Table 7.7 seems to confirm the results of the descriptive analyses (a growing probability of home ownership up to the age of retirement), which contradicts Hypothesis 4c. The results show a (significantly) lower transition rate for the 25–29 and 30–34 age groups than the 35–39 age group. On the other hand, the oldest age group (40–44) in Cohort 1970 seems to be less successful than the reference group in realizing home ownership. This result can be explained by the fact that it is not the chances of home ownership that are being

Table 7.6   Transition to home ownership

	Cohort 1965–1987	
	Model 1	Model 2
Constant	−3.64**	−2.90**
Age		
25–29		−0.94**
30–34		−0.43**
35–39 (ref.)		−
40–44		−0.63*
Origin		
West German (ref.)		
East German	−0.13	−0.13
Cohort		
Cohort 1970	0.49**	0.29*
Cohort 1980 (ref.)	−	−
Events	343	343
Total episodes	1,267	1,267
Censored episodes	924	924
LL	−824.8	−803.6

Notes:
Logistic regression models. Controlled for gender and missing values.
** Significant at $\alpha \geq 0.01$.
* Significant at $\alpha \geq 0.05$.
+ Significant at $\alpha \geq 0.1$.

Sources: GSOEP (2013); own calculations.

considered but rather the time at which the home is purchased. With increasing age, more and more households are able to realize home ownership. However, for a large part of the population the transition takes place during the mid-career and family period. That the youngest age group is comparatively unsuccessful in realizing home ownership is probably due to its ongoing establishment on the labour market, as well as its lower inheritances chances. This assumption seems to be confirmed when income and inheritance are considered; the chances of becoming a home owner then no longer differ significantly between the age groups. The results for East Germany largely confirm Hypothesis 1c. Despite the overall much lower home-ownership rate in East Germany, the East German transition rate is not significantly lower than that of the reference group (West Germans) for the last cohort under study. One possible explanation is that the younger

Table 7.7 *Transition to home ownership, by cohort*

	Cohort 1965–1974			Cohort 1975–1987		
	Model 1	Model 2	Model 3	Model 1	Model 2	Model 3
Constant	-3.93**	-5.93**	-7.13**	-3.67***	-6.25**	-7.50**
Age						
25–29	-0.74**	-0.37*	-0.31+	-1.06**	-0.72+	-0.56
30–34	-0.34*	-0.22	-0.20	-0.73+	-0.68	-0.51
35–39 (ref.)	–	–	–	–	–	–
40–44	-0.57*	-0.71**	-0.67*	n.i.	n.i.	n.i.
Origin						
West German (ref.)	–	–	–	–	–	–
East German	-0.27*	-0.01	-0.26+	-0.09	0.15	0.11
Type of household						
Single person (ref.)	–		–	–		–
Couple without children	1.29**		0.17	0.89		-0.23
One-parent family	-0.43		-0.14	0.52		0.64
Couple with child(ren)	1.74**		0.72*	1.30**		0.11
Multi-generational family	-8.96		-10.28	n.i.		n.i.
Other	1.19*		0.66	-12.74		-12.58
Qualification (CASMIN)						
Lower secondary degree without occupational qualifications		-0.34	-0.79*		-0.67	-0.75
Lower secondary degree with occupational qualifications		-0.01	-0.45+		0.79+	0.44
Upper secondary degree without occupational qualifications		-0.07	-0.09		-0.87	-0.77
Upper secondary degree with occupational qualifications		0.17	-0.11		0.44	0.18
College/university degree (ref.)		–	–		–	–
Occupational class (EGP)						
Higher service class		-0.06	0.22		0.36	0.54
Lower service class		-0.23	-0.13		0.27	0.22

Table 7.7 (continued)

	Cohort 1965–1974			Cohort 1975–1987		
	Model 1	Model 2	Model 3	Model 1	Model 2	Model 3
Routine non-manual		-0.01	0.13		0.19	0.23
Self-employed		-0.23	-0.05		0.98+	0.84
Skilled manual		0.29	0.29		0.44	0.51
Farmer		1.51	1.36		0.00	0.00
Un-/semi-skilled (ref.)		–	–		–	–
Unemployed		-0.09	-0.18		-0.16	-0.44
Income		0.75**	0.61**		0.66**	0.66**
Intergenerational transfers = yes			0.05			0.11
Residential area						
Village			1.79**			1.55**
Small town			1.52**			1.49**
City			0.75			0.39
Metropolis (ref.)			–			–
Events	271	271	271	72	72	72
Total episodes	712	712	712	555	555	555
Censored episodes	441	441	441	483	483	483
LL	-542.3	-522.5	-474.4	-206.2	-188.9	-175.8

Notes:
Logistic regression models. Controlled for gender and missing values. Low case number for the cohort 1975–1987 due to right-censoring.
** Significant at $\alpha \geq 0.01$.
* Significant at $\alpha \geq 0.05$.
+ Significant at $\alpha \geq 0.1$.
° n.i. = no information.

Sources: GSOEP (2013); own calculations.

182

generation in East Germany already grew up in the market economy. If the comparable transition rates of the various population groups also continue in this way in the future, this could lead to an increasing convergence of the home-ownership rate. As expected, single households purchase a home especially rarely due to their limited financial resources and their greater mobility (Häußermann and Siebel, 2000). In particular (and as expected), couples take the step into home ownership significantly more often than the reference group (Hypothesis 5c).

Furthermore, the results confirm the hypothesis that the transition to home ownership is stratified by education. In the step-by-step model for the two older cohorts (not presented here), it becomes clear that, in comparison to persons with a college or university degree, all other educational levels have a lower probability of obtaining residential property. The significant effect disappears when controlling for household income as well as inheritance. For the youngest cohort we do not find the expected effect; this might be due to the prolonged educational phase of people with a college or university degree, which leads to belated establishment on the housing market. Surprisingly, we do not find the hypothesized result for occupational class; in our data, the occupational class had no effect. However, as hypothesized, a higher income increases the transition rate. Income seems to be even more important than educational and occupational status. This effect is significant in all models and robust for all birth cohorts (Hypothesis 3c). Surprisingly, households that have received gifts or inheritances do not realize residential property significantly more frequently, contradicting Hypothesis 6c. The reason for this finding can be found in the low inheritance chances of younger people (Szydlik and Schupp, 2004). Finally, as expected, the transition rate is much higher in rural areas than in more densely populated residential areas, confirming Hypothesis 7c.

CONCLUSION

The aim of this chapter was to analyse social inequalities in home ownership as an aspect of welfare provision by means of an inner-German, as well as historical, comparison. In times of less generous state security accompanied by demographic ageing, private assets – and particularly residential property – are becoming more and more important for the financial wellbeing of the population. Even if home ownership is not the essential source for private pension provision in Germany, nonetheless it can provide a not-negligible income source for elderly home owners (Delfani et al., 2014; Doling and Ronald, 2010; Ronald et al., 2015). Therefore, when evaluating the socioeconomic position of households it is important to consider not only income but also assets, with a special focus on home ownership as the central wealth component (Modigliani and Brumberg, 1954).

Analysing the real-estate market in Germany is especially interesting because of the differences in the past political and economic history of the FRG and the GDR. West Germans are at an advantage regarding home ownership as well as the value of housing, which promotes sufficient private financial security. East Germans perform worse in both aspects; they are not only disadvantaged on the labour market, but also regarding wealth and therefore private welfare. The empirical results on housing emphasize the strong influence of socioeconomic characteristics (in particular educational and occupational status). Notably, educational and occupational status is central in West Germany. As hypothesized, the influence of these factors even increases over time – especially for the housing value. So it becomes more and more difficult for lower social classes to protect themselves financially via home ownership, which is especially disadvantageous with regard to welfare provision in later life. This means that social inequality is increasing in not only the labour market (see Blossfeld et al., 2005, 2006; Buchholz, 2008) but also the real-estate market. However, it is notable that only those highly ranked on the occupational scale seem to be privileged in terms of housing in East Germany. More precisely, the Socialist policy of the GDR still seems to influence the home-ownership situation.

Analyses of the transition to home ownership reveal remarkable results: the current transition rates to home ownership are similar for both East and West Germans. This result indicates that the East German disadvantage on the real-estate market is a cohort effect. The present-day differences in home-ownership rates are obviously mainly due to differences in the economic and political past of the two regions rather than general, persistent disadvantages. Hence, it can be expected that the home-ownership rates in East and West Germany will become increasingly similar over time. But it has to be taken into account that first, the West German population is still privileged regarding inheritance and endowments (Szydlik and Schupp, 2004), and second, the East German labour market situation is still more precarious than that in the West. These conditions could be strengthening the West German population's advantageous position on the real-estate market regarding both home ownership and housing value and therefore also their advantage in private welfare provision more generally.

NOTES

1. Results are based on own analyses with data from the GSOEP (2013).
2. As we were interested in the housing values of households that actually own a home, we restricted our sample to home owners and did not run a Heckman selection model or a Tobit regression. These models would create a very specific and hypothetical choice situation (Heckman, 1979). For the purposes of this chapter, we are not interested in this hypothetical decision.
3. These were composed of 1,308 (2002), 1,230 (2007) and 855 (2012) West German and 514 (2002), 550 (2007) and 413 (2012) East German households.
4. The exact question in the questionnaire was: 'If you were to sell it today, how much would you receive for your house/apartment including land?'
5. For East Germany, the effect becomes insignificant when controlling for income.

REFERENCES

Agresti, A. (ed.) (1990), Categorical Data Analysis, New York, Chichester and Brisbane: Wiley.
Andreß, H.-J., B. Borgloh, M. Güllner and K. Wilking (eds) (2003), Wenn aus Liebe rote Zahlen werden: Über die wirtschaftlichen Folgen von Trennung und Scheidung, Wiesbaden: Westdeutscher Verlag.
Bartholmai, B. and M. Melzer (eds) (1991), Künftige Perspektiven des Wohnungsbaus und der Wohnungsbaufinanzierung für das Gebiet der neuen Länder, Berlin: Duncker & Humblot.
Blien, U., J. Fuchs and V. Phan thi Hong (2010), 'Arbeitsmarktentwicklung in ostdeutschen Regionen', Informationen zur Raumentwicklung, **10/11**, 773–785.
Blomert, R. (2008), 'Die Subprime-Krise oder: Wie aus einer Immobilienkrise eine handfeste Wirtschaftskrise wurde', in S.A. Jansen, E. Schröter and N. Stehr (eds), Mehrwertiger Kapitalismus: Multidisziplinäre Beiträge zu Formen des Kapitalismus und seiner Kapitalien, Wiesbaden: VS Verlag für Sozialwissenschaften, pp. 129–147.
Blossfeld, H.-P. (1985), 'Berufseintritt und Berufsverlauf: Eine Kohortenanalyse über die Bedeutung des ersten Berufs in der Erwerbsbiographie', Mitteilungen aus der Arbeitsmarkt- und Berufsforschung, **18** (2), 177–197.
Blossfeld, H.-P. (2007), 'Linked lives in modern societies: the impact on social inequality of increasing educational homogamy and the shift towards dual-earner couples', in S. Scherer, R. Pollak, G. Otte and M. Gangl (eds), From Origin to Destination: Trends and Mechanisms in Social Stratification Research, Frankfurt am Main and New York: Campus, pp. 275–291.
Blossfeld, H.-P. and S. Buchholz (2009), 'Increasing resource inequality among families in modern societies: the mechanisms of growing educational homogamy, changes in the division of work in the family and the decline of the male bread-winner model', Journal of Comparative Family Studies, **40** (4), 601–616.
Blossfeld, H.-P. and G. Rohwer (eds) (2001), Techniques of Event History Modeling: New Approaches to Causal Analysis (2nd edition), Hillsdale, NJ: Lawrence Erlbaum Associates.
Blossfeld, H.-P. and A. Timm (eds) (2003), Who Marries Whom? Educational

Systems as Marriage Markets in Modern Societies, Dordrecht (Netherlands): Kluwer Academic Publishers.

Blossfeld, H.-P., E. Klijzing, M. Mills and K. Kurz (eds) (2005), Globalization, Uncertainty and Youth in Society, London and New York: Routledge.

Blossfeld, H.-P., K. Kurz, S. Buchholz and E. Bukodi (eds) (2008), Young Workers, Globalization and the Labor Market: Comparing Early Working Life in Eleven Countries, Cheltenham, UK and Northampton, MA, USA: Edward Elgar Publishing.

Blossfeld, H.-P., M. Mills and F. Bernardi (eds) (2006), Globalization, Uncertainty and Men's Careers: An International Comparison, Cheltenham, UK and Northampton, MA, USA: Edward Elgar Publishing.

Brandolini, A., L. Cannari, G. D'Alessio and I. Faiella (2004), 'Household wealth distribution in Italy in the 1990s', Temi di discussione [Economic working paper] 530, Rome: Bank of Italy Economic Research Department.

Brauns, H. and S. Steinmann (1997), 'Education reform in France, West-Germany, the United Kingdom and Hungary: updating the CASMIN Educational Classification', MZES Arbeitspapier Nr. 21, Mannheim: Mannheimer Zentrum für Europäische Sozialforschung.

Buchholz, S. (ed.) (2008), Die Flexibilisierung des Erwerbsverlaufs: Eine Analyse von Einstiegs- und Ausstiegsprozessen in Ost- und Westdeutschland, Wiesbaden: VS Verlag für Sozialwissenschaften.

Buchholz, S. and K. Kolb (2011), 'Selective flexibilization and deregulation of the labour market: the German answer to increased needs for employment flexibility and its consequences for social inequalities', in H.-P. Blossfeld, S. Buchholz, D. Hofäcker and K. Kolb (eds), Globalized Labour Markets and Social Inequality in Europe, Basingstoke, UK: Palgrave Macmillan, pp. 25–45.

Buchholz, S. and K. Kurz (2008), 'A new mobility regime in Germany? Young people's labour market entry and phase of establishment since the mid-1980s', in H.-P. Blossfeld, S. Buchholz, E. Bukodi and K. Kurz (eds), Young Workers, Globalization and the Labor Market: Comparing Early Working Life in Eleven Countries, Cheltenham, UK and Northampton, MA, USA: Edward Elgar Publishing, pp. 51–75.

Delfani, N., J. De Deken and C. Dewilde (2014), 'Home-ownership and pensions: negative correlation but no trade-off: why asset-based welfare only fits specific institutional settings', Housing Studies, **25** (5), 657–676.

Diewald, M. and H. Solga (1995), 'Soziale Ungleichheit in der DDR: Die feinen, aber deutlichen Unterschiede am Vorabend der Wende', in J. Huinink and K.U. Mayer (eds), Kollektiv und Eigensinn, Berlin: Akademie Verlag, pp. 261–305.

Doling, J. and R. Ronald (2010), 'Property-based welfare and European home-owners: how would housing perform as a pension?', Journal of Housing and the Built Environment, **25** (2), 227–241.

Dreger, C. and K.A. Kholodilin (2013), 'Zwischen Immobilienboom und Preisblasen: was kann Deutschland von anderen Ländern lernen?', DIW Wochenbericht, **80** (17), 3–10.

Engelbrech, G. and M. Jungkunst (2001), Alleinerziehende Frauen haben besondere Beschäftigungsprobleme. Im Vergleich zu Frauen mit Partner sind sie öfter erwerbslos und nehmen schlechtere Arbeitsbedingungen in Kauf, Herausgegeben von Bundesanstalt für Arbeit, Nürnberg: IAB–Kurzbericht.

Erikson, R. and J.H. Goldthorpe (eds) (1992), The Constant Flux: A Study of Class Mobility in Industrial Societies, Oxford: Clarendon Press.

Erler, M. (ed.) (1996), Die Dynamik der modernen Familie: Empirische Untersuchung zum Wandel der Familienformen in Deutschland, Weinheim and München: Juventa-Verlag.

Grabka, M.M. and J.R. Frick (2007), 'Vermögen in Deutschland wesentlich ungleicher verteilt als Einkommen', DIW Wochenbericht, **74** (45), 665–672.

Grabka, M.M. and C. Westermeier (2014), 'Anhaltend hohe Vermögensungleichheit in Deutschland', DIW Wochenbericht, **9** (81), 151–165.

GSOEP (German Socio-Economic Panel) (2013), Data for Years 1984–2012, version 29, DOI: 10.5684/soep.v29.

Handelsblatt (2011), 'Eigenheim als Geldanlage: Was Wohnhäuser in Deutschland kosten', Handelsblatt, **189**, 40–41.

Hannemann, C. (ed.) (2000), Historischer Abriss zu wesentlichen Entwicklungslinien städtischen Wohnens in Deutschland seit 1945, Berlin: Humboldt-Universität.

Häußermann, H. and W. Petrowsky (1990), 'Lebenszyklus, Arbeitslosigkeit und Hauseigentum', in L. Bertls and U. Herlyn (eds), Lebenslauf und Raumerfahrung, Opladen: Leske + Budrich, pp. 103–122.

Häußermann, H. and W. Siebel (eds) (2000), Soziologie des Wohnens: Eine Einführung im Wandel und Ausdifferenzierung des Wohnens (2nd revised edition), Weinheim and München: Juventa Verlag.

Heckman, J. (1979), 'Sample selection bias as a specification error', Econometrica, **47** (1), 153–161.

IW Köln (2009), 'Wohngebäude schützen vor Inflation', Immobilien Monitor, 1/2009, Köln: Institut der deutschen Wirtschaft.

Kholodilin, K.K., J-O. Menz and B. Siliverstovs (2008), 'Immobilienkrise? Warum in Deutschland die Preise seit Jahrzehnten stagnieren', DIW Wochenbericht, **75** (17), 214–220.

Kohli, M., H. Künemund, A. Schäfer, J. Schupp and C. Vogel (2006), 'Erbschaften und ihr Einfluss auf die Vermögensverteilung', Vierteljahrshefte zur Wirtschaftsforschung, **75** (1), 58–76.

Kolb, K. (2013), Soziale Ungleichheiten beim Vermögen und Immobilienbesitz: Eine Analyse von Vermögens- und Wohneigentumsungleichheiten im internationalen, innerdeutschen sowie historischen Vergleich, Bamberg: University of Bamberg Press.

Kolb, K., N. Skopek and H.-P. Blossfeld (2012), 'The two dimensions of housing inequality in Europe – Are high home ownership rates an indicator for low housing values?', Comparative Population Studies, **38** (4), 1041–1076.

Kurz, K. (2000), 'Soziale Ungleichheit beim Übergang zu Wohneigentum', Zeitschrift für Soziologie, **29** (1), 27–43.

Kurz, K. (ed.) (2012), Beschäftigungsunsicherheiten und langfristige Bindungen: Analysen zu Partnerschaftsverhalten, Familiengründung und zum Erwerb von Wohneigentum, Wiesbaden: VS Verlag für Sozialwissenschaften.

Kurz, K. and H.-P. Blossfeld (eds) (2004), Home Ownership and Social Inequality in Comparative Perspective, Stanford, CA: Stanford University Press.

Lewin-Epstein, N., Y. Elmelech and M. Semyonov (1997), 'Ethnic inequality in home ownership and the value of housing: the case of immigrants in Israel', Social Forces, **75** (4), 1439–1462.

Long, J.S. (ed.) (2011), Regression Models for Categorical and Limited Dependent Variables, Thousand Oaks, CA: Sage Publications.

Modigliani, F. and R. Brumberg (1954), 'Utility analysis and the consumption function: an interpretation of cross-section data', in K.K. Kurihara (ed.), Post-Keynesian Economics, London: Routledge, pp. 383–436.

Mulder, C.H. and J. Smits (1999), 'First-time home-ownership of couples: the effect of inter-generational transmission', European Sociological Review, **15** (3), 323–337.

Nguyen, T. and J.B. Shlomo (2009), 'Determinanten der Wohneigentumsquote: Eine internationale empirische Studie', Zeitschrift für immobilienwirtschaftliche Forschung und Praxis, **13**, 2–11.

Petrowsky, W. (ed.) (1993), Arbeiterhaushalte mit Wohneigentum: Die Bedeutung des Erbes bei der Eigentumsbildung, Bremen: Universität Bremen.

Ronald, R., J. Kadi and C. Lennartz (2015), 'Homeownership-based welfare in transition', Critical Housing Analysis, **2** (1), 52–64.

Schneider, N. and A. Spellerberg (eds) (1999), Lebensstile, Wohnbedürfnisse und räumliche Mobilität, Opladen: Leske + Budrich.

Schulz, M. (2010), 'Wohnen und Fertilitätsverhalten in der DDR', in D. Reuschke (ed.), Wohnen und Gender: Theoretische, politische, soziale und räumliche Aspekte, Wiesbaden: VS Verlag für Sozialwissenschaften, pp. 117–128.

Shavit, Y. and W. Müller (eds) (1998) From School to Work: A Comparative Study of Educational Qualifications and Occupational Destinations, Oxford: Clarendon Press.

Sierminska, E., A. Brandolini and T.M. Smeeding (eds) (2007), Cross-National Comparison of Income and Wealth Status in Retirement: First Results from the Luxembourg Wealth Study (LWS), Chestnut Hill, MA: Center for Retirement Research at Boston College.

Skopek, N., K. Kolb, S. Buchholz and H.-P. Blossfeld (2012), 'Einkommensreich – Vermögensarm? Die Zusammensetzung von Vermögen und die Bedeutung einzelner Vermögenskomponenten im europäischen Vergleich', Berliner Journal für Soziologie, **22** (2), 163–187.

Solga, H., M. Diewald and A. Goedicke (2000), 'Arbeitsmarktmobilität und die Umstrukturierung des ostdeutschen Beschäftigungssystems', Mitteilungen aus der Arbeitsmarkt- und Berufsforschung, **33**, 242–260.

Statistisches Bundesamt (2009), Zuhause in Deutschland: Ausstattung und Wohnsituation privater Haushalte, Wiesbaden.

Stephens, M., M. Lux and P. Sunega (2015), 'Post-socialist housing systems in Europe: housing welfare regimes by default?', Housing Studies, 1–25.

Szydlik, M. and J. Schupp (2004), 'Wer erbt mehr? Erbschaften, Sozialstruktur und Alterssicherung', Kölner Zeitschrift für Soziologie und Sozialpsychologie, **56** (4), 609–629.

Tegeder, G. and I. Helbrecht (2007), 'Germany: home ownership, a Janus-faced advantage in time of welfare restructuring', in M. Elsinga, P. De Decker, N. Teller and J. Toussaint (eds), Home Ownership beyond Asset and Security: Perceptions of Housing-Related Security and Insecurity in Eight European Countries, Amsterdam: IOS Press BV, pp. 101–131.

Voigtländer, M. (ed.) (2006), Mietwohnungsmarkt und Wohneigentum: Zwei Seiten einer Medaille, Berlin: Gutachten für den Verband deutscher Pfandbriefbanken.

Wagner, M. and C.H. Mulder (2000), 'Wohneigentum im Lebenslauf: Kohortendynamik, Familiengründung und sozioökonomische Ressourcen', Zeitschrift für Soziologie, **29** (1), 44–59.

8. Home ownership in post-socialist countries: the negative impact of the transition period on old-age welfare

Srna Mandič and Maja Mrzel*

INTRODUCTION

This chapter focuses on the role of housing for the welfare of older people in post-socialist countries. During the transition period in the 1990s, the housing domain was employed in an instrumental way to back up market reforms and budgetary cuts. Today, it seems that housing is again relevant, this time to help pay for old-age care as welfare state arrangements have not yet been modernized in order to adequately respond to demographic ageing. In post-socialist countries, there is a structural 'old-age welfare gap' in terms of the underdeveloped system of old-age provisions, especially in comparison with other European countries. Housing can be a relevant resource to compensate for this old-age welfare gap in different ways, including the informal role of the family in financing and providing care services, and the co-residence of parents and adult children. The aim of this chapter is thus to gain an insight into the situation in post-socialist countries by way of comparison, particularly with the Southern European countries. Unlike the post-socialist countries, the Southern European countries have been relatively well theorized and empirically explored as a welfare and housing regime cluster (Allen et al., 2004; Esping-Andersen, 2009; Saraceno, 2010). With regard to the provision of welfare in later life, these countries share some characteristics with post-socialist countries – most notably a significant role for the family as welfare provider, combined with relatively weak welfare state services. In developing this analysis, it is also important to recognize that the relationship between home ownership and welfare in later life has been discussed in previous research (see Doling and Ronald, 2010; Ronald and Elsinga, 2012; Doling and Elsinga, 2013). The possibility that housing equity is used to generate additional financial resources to pay for increasing welfare needs in old age, an approach related to the notion of asset-based welfare, may be relevant for the post-socialist countries. In this chapter, services and support in the context of old-age care – including informal provision – are also considered, as well as the quality of housing in view of 'ageing at home', all representing elements of old-age welfare.

We explore the role of housing in old-age welfare in a comparative way, by contrasting the situation in post-socialist countries with other European countries and country groups. This is achieved first by discussing some of the main developmental issues of old-age care in general, followed by an evaluation of the situation in post-socialist countries. In these countries, the entire welfare system was affected by the social cost of the transition, undermining the ability of societies to deal with long-term social challenges such as demographic ageing. Second, the chapter examines a number of system-level indicators of the level of old-age care services, the financing of these services by public versus private funding, and general population attitudes regarding the availability of old-age services and the responsibility for its provision and funding, including the family and the use of housing wealth for care needs. After exploring the institutional context and attitudes towards old-age care, the chapter considers the housing situation of the elderly and evaluates its potential to meet the needs of ageing owners in terms of housing quality for ageing at home, the need for care, and as a wealth resource to finance old-age care. For the analysis, data from various sources, including the fourth wave of the Survey of Health, Ageing and Retirement in Europe (SHARE, 2011), are combined.

IMPORTANT ISSUES IN WELFARE AND CARE PROVISION IN LATER LIFE

In ageing societies, the provision of welfare for older people is an increasingly important issue. As the balance between the economically active and those over 65 years of age is changing, policy makers are considering ways to not only provide adequate services for the aged but also ensure the financial sustainability of public systems – particularly pension, health insurance, and long-term care systems, all of which require a higher financial input. Demographic ageing also implies that the growing number of older people in need of support and care is accompanied by a shrinking pool of potential family carers. During the last three decades, Europe has witnessed a drastic decline in 'the caring capacity', defined as the ratio between the number of women between 45 and 69 years of age as traditional carers, and the population older than 69. As a result, and also due to women's rising employment, active generations are facing increasing difficulties in combining working life with obligations to their (aged) relatives who need support. This work/life balance issue is well recognized by both European policy makers and academic researchers (Armingeon, 2006; Bonoli, 2006; EC, 2007; Saraceno, 2008).

Recent discussions of welfare provision for older people have been influenced considerably by Esping-Andersen's concept of defamilialization. Having defined diverse welfare regimes according to 'the way in which welfare is produced and allocated between state, market and family' (Esping-Andersen, 1999, pp. 34–5), he examined their impact on demographic trends, and particularly on the patterns that have developed with regard to old-age care across Europe. While for most retired people 'welfare comes inevitably from the combination of family, market and government inputs', he emphasized the specificity of care for older people, and the significance of these services being 'defamilialized' (Esping-Andersen, 2009, p. 79). He argues that in modern societies, the externalization of care services (such as universal day care) is needed to make potential care obligations manageable and to give families realistic options. Care for frail older persons represents a specific type of social need to which neither markets nor families are able to respond. Commercial services are extremely expensive, while 'the traditional caring reservoir of non-employed older daughters is disappearing' (Esping-Andersen, 2009, p. 81), resulting in a crucial role for the welfare state. Most other post-war welfare states focused on income maintenance while relying on familialism for most care obligations; however, as early as the 1970s, the Scandinavian welfare states were already focusing much more on family services, both for child care and old-age care, thereby creating more employment opportunities for women. In other European countries, familialism was not questioned so much, least of all in Southern European countries. Taking the coverage of older persons by home-based support services as one of the key indicators of familialism, Esping-Andersen (1999) identified large variations across Europe, ranging from 19 per cent in social-democratic countries to 4 per cent in continental and liberal countries and as low as 1 per cent in Southern European countries.

In addition to developments in defamilialization, welfare of older people has also been located within the paradigm of 'new social risks' (Armingeon and Bonoli, 2006; Morel, 2006). According to this paradigm, old-age care is one of the new social risks that is not yet recognized and hence not sufficiently included in welfare state programmes. New social risks are defined as novel situations in which people experience a deficiency in their wellbeing that is not compensated for by traditional welfare state arrangements. These situations are typical for post-industrial societies characterized by the destabilization of family structures, mass employment of women, and flexibilization of labour. The variety of risks caused by the post-industrial destabilization of traditional social structures and of the relationship between work, welfare, and home ownership has been discussed in terms of the 'weak globalisation thesis' (Doling et al., 2003). Under these new circumstances, a number of new risks are appearing that affect various groups – particularly those who experience new forms of poverty, the vulnerable, and those in need of care and support. According to Morel (2006), old-age and long-term care are such new social risks. Due to demographic ageing, changed models of family living and women's participation in the labour market, the existing welfare programmes are often insufficient and the responsibility for caring for frail older persons may need to be redefined. While in most countries old-age care was perceived as a private family issue until quite recently, in other countries it became recognized as a public issue and as a new social risk for which new formal solutions should be sought, most notably long-term care insurance and support to home-based services for frail elderly persons.

Insofar as the traditional welfare state, developed in the post-war period, cannot compensate for emerging new social risks, one view is that a new post-industrial welfare state with a particular focus on services is needed (Armingeon and Bonoli, 2006; Huber and Stephens, 2006). Regarding the development of old-age care systems in the European Union (EU), a goal is to foster a sustainable mix of public and private means of financing; for services in addition to residential care, home-based and community services have been prioritized (Pickard et al., 2007; OECD, 2011; EC, 2012). Empirical studies, however, reveal a considerable difference between the 'service-rich' Nordic countries and the 'service-poor' Southern European countries, where only very few services are available for frail older persons (Sarasa and Billingsley, 2008; Saraceno, 2010).

A further dimension of welfare of older people in a context of ageing societies concerns changing living arrangements. A particular characteristic of older people's living arrangements is that they live in smaller households than other age groups; principally single-person households. There are, however, large cross-country variations. In their examination of living arrangements of older people based on the EU Statistics on Income and Living Conditions (2007), Iacovou and Skew (2010, p. 22) reported that single-adult households among older people are most common in the Nordic group of countries and least common in the Southern group. Of women aged 65 years and over, 56.0 per cent lived alone in Denmark but only 25.5 per cent in Spain. Further, co-residence between older people and their adult children was relatively unusual for older people in the Nordic group of countries and more common in the Southern countries. According to SHARE (collected in 2004), the rates of such co-residence varied from 29 per cent in Greece to 4 per cent in Denmark (Isengard and Szydlik, 2012, p. 16). Given that co-residence between older persons and their adult children is very high in Southern Europe, it is understandable that it has also been more often discussed in relation to family patterns and familialism in welfare provision. According to Esping-Andersen (2009, p. 150), cohabitation with children is an indicator of strong familialism.

Iacovou and Skew (2011) discussed the factors that lead to co-residence in Southern European countries and found that co-residence may at least partly occur because adult children have not yet left home, rather than because of any active preference. Moreover, cohabitation between generations is not simply a case of receiving care and support from the younger generation; it also entails helping the younger generations, particularly with child care. Poggio (2008) examined the relationship between family help with housing for younger family members and further mutual support between parents and adult children in Italy, and found evidence for the continuing importance of a 'care-for-inheritance generational contract' (although less common than in the past). Co-residence is therefore a crucial element of the analysis of the intergenerational flow of resources (also see Albertini et al., 2007, p. 326).

OLD-AGE WELFARE IN POST-SOCIALIST COUNTRIES AFTER THE TRANSITIONAL PERIOD

Having reviewed some of the main dimensions of the changing context of care for older people, we now consider the present configuration of old-age welfare in post-socialist societies and how this is linked to the wider phenomenon generally referred to as the 'transition' caused by the fall of socialist political regimes. In contrast to this vague term, here and where appropriate, the more specific term 'transformation' is used.[1]

In post-socialist countries, the present-day level of welfare – including old-age care – cannot be fully understood without taking account of the overwhelming impact of the transition and the shock it presented to most social domains. While the nature and aim of this transition were quite clearly defined in the market economy and political democracy areas, they were quite ambiguous and controversial in the welfare domain. In the overview of general developments provided shortly, we show that the present situation in the welfare system – especially in old-age care – can largely be seen as collateral damage of the transition, which was largely oriented towards welfare state retrenchment. With the fall of socialism, the widespread opinion emerged that the retreat of the (once socialist) welfare state was urgent and unavoidable. Kornai (1997), for example, argued that the socialist welfare system with its universal social entitle-ments had simply become unsustainable. In the face of the drastic fall in Gross Domestic Product (GDP), many international institutional advisers also advised retrenchment (cf. Ferge, 2001). The huge 'social cost' of the economic reforms and privatization was incurred through retrenchment of the welfare state (Stark and Bruszt, 1998).

These political and economic transformations had far-reaching and unprecedented social consequences. Most notably, economic restructur-ing generated a drastic and sudden drop in production, as many state-sponsored companies and even whole industrial branches were laid off. The building industry, for example, experienced tremendous cuts in invest-ment and in housing production so that, according to Struyk (1996, p. 3), housing served as a 'shock absorber'. It is perhaps insufficiently recognized that during the 1990s, Central and Eastern European (CEE) countries experienced a dramatic decline in GDP and did not manage to restore GDP to its 1989 level until 2000, or even later (Philipov and Dorbritz, 2004). This was therefore a lost decade with huge, adverse social conse-quences. The European Commission (2005) provided a detailed account of the rise of unemployment, decreased wage levels, and other newly emerg-ing social risks, which were not sufficiently addressed by the diminishing state-provided transfers and services. As a consequence, poverty increased and large segments of the population, such as older people and the disabled, became even more vulnerable. Poverty-related policies in CEE countries were devised relatively late, prompted by EU accession (Ferge, 2001; Offe and Fuchs, 2007).

In addition to the dramatic decrease in GDP leading to cuts in welfare expenditure and welfare programmes (see Guardiancich, 2004), the welfare systems in CEE countries were also undergoing other changes such as modernization, pluralization, and Europeanization (Ferge, 2001; Juhasz, 2006). However, the actual course and outcomes of those changes, as well as the issue of similarity between countries, are still open to examination and discussion. A number of instances of both convergence and divergence with the old EU Member States have been identified (see Deacon, 2000; Manning, 2004). In their study of social protection systems in the region, Offe and Fuchs (2007) found that, during the 1990s, a Bismarckian type of social insurance system was established in all new Member States while none of these countries turned to a predominately market-liberal model. This development and the declining social expendi-ture (as a percentage of GDP) were the only two features common to all CEE countries. They could not identify any other pattern of change dis-tinguishing post-socialist welfare states from other European countries. Rather, what dominated were 'eclectic attempts to balance given internal and external pressures' and an 'ideologically faceless, and economically and politically unstable potpourri of policies' (Offe and Fuchs, 2007, p. 32). As Hacker (2009) and Kazepov (2008) also argued, post-socialist systems are not (yet) converging.

With regard to the nature of changes in the welfare system, several analysts have shown how these were dominated by current interests, overshadowing long-term issues such as demographic ageing. Hacker (2009) argued that pension reforms in the region were not so much aimed at tackling future demographic challenges as a reaction to the economic conditions created by the transition. Offe and Fuchs (2007) refer to this as 'short-termism'. Velladics et al. (2006), in their analysis of mass media coverage of demographic ageing, found huge differences between European countries. While in Western European discussions the focus was on the challenges of future decades – such as the sustainability of protection systems – and on intergenerational solidarity, in transitional countries the discussion mostly concerned current problems, particularly the low pensions and poor living standard of the elderly. The changing welfare system following the end of socialism was furthermore marked by the growing significance of the informal sector, family, and kinship networks (Read and Thelen, 2007). According to Kovacs (2002), in transitional welfare states the principle of universalism was gradually replaced by the ambiguous notion of 'individual responsibility' and self-insurance. Velladics et al. (2006) found that in transitional countries, intergenerational solidarity is much stronger than in the EU at large, where formalized institutional solidarity is more supported.

With regard to changes in those welfare domains most relevant for the welfare of the older population, less seems to be known (Lendvai, 2004); however, changes in the housing and pension domain are documented relatively well. In most countries, the previous social housing was sold to tenants to such an extent that, from a European perspective, they became 'super-home ownership countries' (Stephens, 2003; Stephens et al., 2015). As a consequence, there are problems for poor home owners ('cash-poor' and 'asset-rich' households) and difficulties with the upkeep and management of the privatized housing stock, which is rapidly deteriorating (Hegedus et al., 2012; Mandič, 2012; Cirman et al., 2013). A crucial element of changing old-age welfare provision in post-socialist countries pertains to pension reforms. Through arrangements permitting non-standard early retirement of diverse categories of claimants (such as those of poor health or the older unemployed), the pension system – with its dominant mandatory public pension scheme – was used to conceal and tackle the massive unemployment arising from the economic shock during the early 1990s. This created fiscal imbalances between pension system inflows and outflows, which called for solutions in two directions: raising the statutory retirement age in the public pension system (the first pillar) and passing part of the financial responsibility for older people onto two other sources – occupational pensions and private savings (the second and third pillars, respectively) (Guardiancich, 2004; Stanovnik and Čok, 2009).

There is neither much data nor much literature on the changes in old-age care provision and their outcomes in post-socialist countries. Armingeon (2006) found that the proportion of public expenditure devoted to old-age care and other family services in new Member States is considerably smaller than in other European countries. Saraceno (2010) analysed the coverage of the elderly population by support services outside of the wider family and found that it is rising in transitional countries (yet still comparatively very low), with the family retaining a key role. Lethbridge (2011) observed old-age care in post-socialist countries and classified it as a 'family model of care'; that is, coverage of the elderly by the formal provision of care (both institutional and home-based) is low in comparison to other countries, so increasing pressures for modernization and public funding may be expected in the future.

From this overview, it might be concluded that old-age care in post-socialist countries was one of the welfare domains most adversely affected by the social cost of the transition. As a 'new social risk', it entered the policy agenda during the transition period, which was characterized by a reconfiguration of responsibilities between the public and private spheres. Current demands and distributive struggles between vested interests dominated over less acute long-term concerns, such as population ageing. With the delayed modernization of services and their inclusion into formal welfare systems, old-age care remained largely in the private sphere, dominated by the family. However, important cross-national differences exist.

Finally, there has been a growing interest in long-term care issues by the European Commission (EC) (2015), particularly the extent to which a country relies on formal versus informal care. Informal provision of long-term care services is provided by families, mainly children and spouses. Formal care is provided at home by care assistants or in an institution, most notably nursing homes and care centres. EU Member States' involvement in either the public provision and/or financing of long-term care services varies strongly across countries (EC, 2015). While some Member States rely heavily on the informal provision of long-term care and only have low expenditures on formal care, other Member States provide extensive public old-age care services. For recipients of home care and of institutional care combined,[2] for the 'old' Member States (EU–15) the average coverage rate of long-term care recipients (expressed as a percentage of the dependent population) is 33 per cent, substantially exceeding the average of 23 per cent in the new Member States. It is furthermore expected that the pressure for increased public provision and financing of long-term care services may grow substantially in coming decades, particularly in those Member States where most care is currently provided informally (EC, 2015, p. 146).

THE POTENTIAL OF HOME OWNERSHIP TO BRIDGE THE OLD-AGE GAP IN POST-SOCIALIST COUNTRIES: AN EMPIRICAL EXPLORATION

We now turn to an empirical exploration of the gap in old-age welfare provision, caused by the delay in adjustment to the needs of demographic ageing and in the modernization of related services. First, we examine the existence and forms of a structural old-age welfare gap in post-socialist countries, also considering possible between-country differences; second, we explore the potential of owned homes to help bridge this gap; and third, we establish how distinct post-socialist countries are when compared to countries in Southern Europe.

Data for our analysis were compiled from a number of sources: the Organisation for Economic Co-operation and Development (OECD) (2011), Eurobarometer (2007), and the fourth wave of the Survey of Health, Ageing and Retirement in Europe (SHARE), the major source of micro-data on the welfare of the older population.[3] We encountered some problems in obtaining relevant, comparable data for several countries, particularly for the post-socialist countries, which joined SHARE in a very limited number from the fourth wave onwards. We hence limit our analysis to the 16 countries in SHARE 2011, and group them according to the standard welfare regimes typology. The social-democratic group consists of Denmark, Sweden, and the Netherlands; the continental group consists of Austria, Belgium, France, and Germany; the Southern European group consists of Italy, Portugal, and Spain, and new EU Member States are Czech Republic, Estonia, Hungary, Poland, and Slovenia. It should be noted that no country representing the liberal welfare regime (the United Kingdom or Ireland) participated in SHARE, while, due to its unclear welfare regime classification, Switzerland was not used in our exploration.

Old-Age Care: Level, Responsibility, and Funding

In the previous sections, we argued that – as a response to the needs created by demographic ageing – the provision of services for old-age care and their funding have entered the public policy agenda. The recognition of care needs as a new social risk requires the traditional, family-based patterns of care to increasingly be complemented by new policy responses, such as long-term care insurance and home-based services for frail older persons.

Whereas Southern European countries still rely considerably on familialistic patterns, in post-socialist countries there has been a delay in upgrading this welfare domain due to the transitional shock and subsequent priorities. In making cross-national comparisons of old-age care, it is important to observe whether the phenomenon of ageing in post-socialist societies differs from other countries. The basic demographic data on ageing presented in Table 8.1 indicate that there are between-group differences. In the new Member States, the trend towards demographic ageing is slightly weaker: life expectancy is on average 77 years, which is 4 to 5 years less than other group averages. Notwithstanding differences within this group, it seems reasonable to conclude that the post-socialist countries display relatively weak – but nevertheless actual – pressures of demographic ageing, and are thus faced with concomitant societal challenges. Moreover, the latest estimates on the effects of population ageing in Europe show that new Member States are heavily affected. Whereas projected public expenditure on long-term care as a percentage of GDP significantly varies among the 28 EU countries, the average among the new Member States exceeds that for the EU–15 (EC, 2015, pp. 145–66).

Table 8.1 also offers some basic figures indicating the level and sources of old-age care. The percentage of long-term care recipients among the population aged 65 and over varies strongly across European countries, ranging from 2 per cent in the Southern European group to 17 per cent in the social-democratic group. The variation among post-socialist countries is especially large: from a low of 1 per cent in Poland to a high of 13 per cent in the Czech Republic. The group average of 7 per cent is considerably lower than for the social-democratic group and the continental group (17 per cent and 14 per cent respectively), but exceeds that of the three Southern European countries.

Furthermore, there are important differences in the extent of funding covered by the social security system or insurance, as opposed to private out-of-pocket expenditure. While there are large within- and between-group variations, it is apparent that private financing is prominent in Southern Europe, much more so than in the social-democratic group, with the new Member States falling in between these two groups. Within the latter group, however, private financing varies from as low as 0 per cent in the Czech Republic to as high as 24 per cent in Slovenia.

The observed patterns of within- and between-group variations can be complemented by opinions about old-age services (Table 8.2). The

Table 8.1 Indicators of population ageing and expenditure for long-term care by sources of funding

	Population ages 65+ (% of total)	Life expectancy at birth, total (years)	Long-term care (LTC) recipients as % of 65+ population	Long-term care (LTC) expenditures by sources of funding, 2007 (%)			
				Private households' out-of-pocket expenses	General government (excluding social security)	Social security funds	Private insurance and other
Total	18	80	10	12	45	40	2
Social-democratic group	18	81	17	4	66	30	0
Continental countries	19	81	14	12	42	42	3
Southern Europe	19	82	2	37	32	31	1
New EU members	*17*	*77*	*7*	*8*	*40*	*49*	*3*
Czech Republic	17	78	13	0	31	70	0
Estonia	18	76	/	12	48	39	0
Hungary	17	75	9	2	60	30	7
Poland	14	77	1	0	43	49	7
Slovenia	17	80	4	24	18	57	1

Notes:
Long-term care (LTC): long-term care services for home-based and institutionalized recipients.
Social-democratic group countries: Denmark, Sweden, The Netherlands; continental countries: Austria, Belgium, France, Germany; Southern Europe countries: Italy, Portugal, Spain; new EU Members countries: Czech Republic, Estonia, Hungary, Poland, Slovenia.

Sources: OECD (2010); World Bank (2013).

Table 8.2 Opinions and evaluation of old-age care with regard to its level, availability, responsibility for and sources of funding, 2007

	Opinions and the level			Responsibility for care		Sources of funding	
	1	2	3	4	5	6	7
	Should get service provider[a] (%)	Should go to nursing home[b] (%)	Home care is available[c] (%)	Public responsibility[d] (%)	Relatives, sacrificing career[e] (%)	Children should pay[f] (%)	Should consume housing[g] (%)
Total	28	13	36	94	36	47	27
Social-democratic group	57	17	56	97	13	16	19
Continental countries	35	12	42	95	26	40	29
Southern Europe	19	8	27	93	44	68	28
New EU members	13	14	26	93	52	56	29
Czech Republic	11	13	37	97	57	59	24
Estonia	19	12	19	98	49	62	24
Hungary	12	11	26	85	48	46	26
Poland	7	3	21	94	61	53	19
Slovenia	16	32	26	93	44	60	52

Notes:
Social-democratic group countries: Denmark, Sweden, The Netherlands; continental countries: Austria, Belgium, France, Germany; Southern Europe countries: Italy, Portugal, Spain, Greece; new EU members countries: Czech Republic, Estonia, Hungary, Poland, Slovenia.

Modalities chosen for a projective question: 'imagine an elderly father or mother who lives alone and can no longer manage to live without regular help because of her or his physical or mental health condition. In your opinion, what would be the best option for people in this situation?'

a. Public or private service providers should visit their home and provide them with appropriate help and care.
b. They should move to a nursing home.
c. 'Totally agree' and 'tend to agree' with the statement: 'professional care at home is available at an affordable cost.'
d. 'Totally agree' and 'tend to agree' with the statement: 'public authorities should provide appropriate home care and/or institutional care for elderly people in need.'
e. 'Totally agree' and 'tend to agree' with the statement: 'care should be provided by close relatives of the dependent person, even if that means that they have to sacrifice their career to some extent.'
f. 'Totally agree' and 'tend to agree' with the statement: 'children should pay for the care of their parents if their parents' income is not sufficient.'
g. 'Totally agree' and 'tend to agree' with the statement: 'if a person becomes dependent and cannot pay for care from their own income, their flat or house should be sold or borrowed against to pay for care.'

Source: Special EUROBAROMETER 283 (2007).

perceived availability of home care services to an older person in need in post-socialist countries is estimated as being only one-half of the level in social-democratic countries – somewhat lower than in the continental group and as low as in the Southern European group. The same ranking of groups can be observed with regard to the opinions that a hypothetical older parent, no longer able to live without regular help, should receive home-based services or move to a nursing home. One of these two options was selected by three out of four respondents in the social-democratic group, one out of two in the continental group, and only one out of four in the Southern European and post-socialist countries. However, the last two groups diverged somewhat with regard to the options selected; whereas Southern European countries prioritized home-based services, in post-socialist countries both options were selected to roughly the same extent.

With respect to opinions about the responsibility for financing old age care, two sources of payment – from selling the home and from the children – were tested for people in need of old-age care and without sufficient means of their own. Selling and consuming one's own flat or house was the least approved in the social-democratic group, and somewhat more in the three other groups, all with very similar results (close to 29 per cent). The option of the children paying was also the least supported in social-democratic countries, where only 16 per cent expressed it. In contrast, in the Southern European group this option was supported by a majority (68 per cent), closely followed by the post-socialist group.

Finally, the idea that public authorities are responsible for providing old-age care was given major support in all groups, ranging only between 93 per cent and 97 per cent. However, when it comes to close relatives' responsibility for such care, implying possible negative consequences for their career, there was a large divergence between the groups. Though afforded only minor support (13 per cent) in the social-democratic group, 26 per cent in the continental group supported this idea, even more supported it in the Southern European group (44 per cent), and in the post-socialist group more than one-half of the respondents (52 per cent) supported this view. To summarize, the data presented document a substantial difference in the availability of old-age care services in the post-socialist countries in comparison to the continental and especially the social-democratic countries, but a similar situation to that in the Southern European countries. The role of the family in providing and paying for care was distinctively considered the least important in the social-democratic group and was much more significant in the Southern European and post-socialist groups. However, these two groups differ in that the post-socialist group leads with regard to the preferred frequency of care given by relatives, while in the Southern European countries children's payment for care is the preferred option.

We conclude that the defamilialization of old-age care in the post-socialist group is lagging behind the Southern European 'familialistic' group, in which children's funding preferences indicate the commercialization of services. The opinion that an individual should bridge the void in the system's funding of old-age care by selling and consuming their housing asset is supported to a similar extent (about 30 per cent) in the post-socialist countries as in the Southern European and continental groups.

The Potential of Housing as a Resource to Meet Old-Age Needs

In this section, the characteristics of housing are examined with the aim of evaluating its potential to help meet the needs of the older population. In principle, housing can make a number of contributions. Housing assets represent a wealth reservoir and through their exchange value may be consumed to pay for old-age care (for instance). Houses also have physical attributes that impact on the quality of later life and on the chances of good, active, home-based ageing. In addition, the home may be the site of specific familial old-age care in the case of co-residence of older parents and adult children – a household arrangement that is prominent in familialistic societies. Indicators of these housing characteristics can be identified in the SHARE data and are presented in Table 8.3.

The rate of home ownership varies across groups of countries, both for the population at large and for the population aged 50 and over. Older people in the Southern European countries have the highest rates of home ownership – around 80 per cent – closely followed by those in the post-socialist group. Housing in special complexes with services for the elderly, as well as accommodation adapted for people with physical impairments, are most frequent in the social-democratic group followed by the continental group, but lower in Southern Europe and even lower in the post-socialist group. In the latter two groups, such accommodation is enjoyed by less than 5 per cent of the older population. In these two groups, older persons also have a lower mobility rate, represented by the number of years in their present accommodation. In terms of the average size of a dwelling, older persons in post-socialist countries are confronted with the lowest space standards. Co-residence with adult children – the key indicator of familialism, according to Esping-Andersen – is highest in Southern Europe, followed closely by the post-socialist group, roughly relating to half of the over-50 population. This is also supported by the last indicator in Table 8.3 regarding the role of the family, which refers to support in housing provision.

What does this tell us about the potential role of housing in supporting older people in the post-socialist countries? The high rates of home

Table 8.3 Housing of the population 50+ according to selected indicators

	Home owners[a] (%)	In a complex with services for the elderly[b] (%)	In a dwelling, adapted for people with physical impairments or health problems[c] (%)	No. of years in present accommodation (median)[d] (%)	Rooms per person[e] (%)	Co-residing with adult child[f] (%)	Bought or built by means of family help or inheritance[g] (%)
Total	73	4	7	24	2	38	19
Social-democratic group	62	10	14	15	2	18	4
Continental countries	66	4	7	24	2	30	20
Southern Europe	82	2	4	24	2	53	24
New EU members	78	1	4	29	2	45	22
Czech Republic	63	1	6	29	2	35	28
Estonia	85	0	3	25	2	29	21
Hungary	87	0	7	30	2	38	14
Poland	68	4	1	30	1	63	19
Slovenia	87	0	3	32	2	58	30

Notes:

Social-democratic group countries: Denmark, Sweden, The Netherlands; continental countries: Austria, Belgium, France, Germany; Southern Europe countries: Italy, Portugal, Spain, Greece; new EU members countries: Czech Republic, Estonia, Hungary, Poland, Slovenia.

a. Your household is occupying this dwelling as: Owner.

b. What type of building does your household live in?: A housing complex with services for the elderly.

c. Does your home have special features that assist persons who have physical impairments or health problems? (e.g. widened doorways, ramps, automatic doors, chair lifts, alerting devices (button alarms), kitchen or bathroom modifications): Yes.

d. How many years have you been living in your present accommodation?

e. How many rooms do you have for your household members' personal use, including bedrooms but excluding kitchen, bathrooms, and hallways [and any rooms you may let or sublet]? / Household size.

f. At least one adult child lives in household/building.

g. How did you acquire this property?: Purchased or build it with help from family or received it as a bequest.

Source: SHARE (2013).

ownership suggest a significant role, but in fact the high home-ownership rate in these countries is accompanied by a relatively high incidence of unfit housing (Cirman et al., 2013). This indicates a limited capacity to serve as a potential wealth reservoir that could be used to finance old-age care needs (Mandič, 2010). In addition, the relatively small housing space – specifically, the fact that supported housing for older people is lagging behind in terms of adaptation to their needs, including physical impairment – indicates relatively low potential for ageing at home. However, what was also highlighted is the high rate of older people co-residing with their adult children. This implies a specific situation in terms of both a support need (where co-residing children might play a supporting role) and a limitation for the option of consuming the asset (as it involves the children's home and housing wealth).

How Similar are the Post-Socialist Group and the Southern European Countries?

The indicators provided in Table 8.3 point to similarity across the post-socialist and Southern European groups. In this section, we consider whether or not this similarity is statistically significant. For this purpose, a hierarchical cluster analysis was performed. All variables included in Tables 8.1, 8.2, and 8.3 were standardized (z-scores) for this purpose, and squared Euclidian distances were used along with Ward's criterion. The results are presented in the form of a dendrogram (Figure 8.1).

In line with existing welfare regime typologies, the social-democratic countries formed a distinctive group. In the second step, two other distinctive groups emerged. The first was the continental group, in line with existing welfare regime typologies, with the exception of the inclusion of the Czech Republic. The second cluster consists of a mix of Southern European and post-socialist countries.

To test the statistical significance of these differences, a one-way analysis of variance (ANOVA) was conducted, comparing the average scores on indicators for the three resulting clusters. The second group of countries in the dendrogram served as a reference for comparison. Statistically significant differences between the second group on the one hand and the first and third groups on the other are marked in a darker shade. As an illustration, the mean percentage of home owners is 66 per cent in the second group, 61 per cent in the first group (the difference is not statistically significant), and 81 per cent in the third group (this is statistically significant and marked in a darker shade). We conclude from the cluster analysis that, regarding the capacity of older persons' housing to serve their needs and help solve the structural old-age welfare gap, there is no

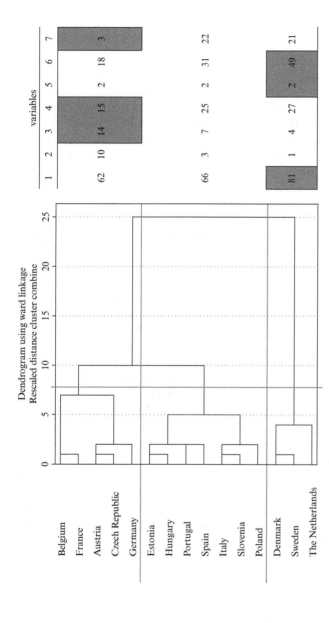

Note: Variables used: 1. % home owners; 2. % living in a housing complex with services for the elderly; 3. % accommodation adaptations for people with physical impairments or health problems; 4. number of years in present accommodation (median); 5. rooms per person; 6. % co-residing with adult child; 7. % bought or built by means of family help or inheritance. Group means for each variable; the difference in relation to the second group is marked where statistically significant.

Source: SHARE (2011).

Figure 8.1 Results from hierarchical cluster analysis

statistically significant difference between the Southern European and post-socialist groups.

CONCLUSION

In examining old-age care in post-socialist countries and observing the possible compensatory role of owned homes with regard to the structural old-age welfare gap, this chapter has identified a number of general developments and potentials. The existing literature indicates that the diverse structural factors in post-socialist countries – primarily linked to the social costs of the transition – affected their old-age care systems, hindering their modernization. As a 'new' social risk, old-age care has entered the policy agenda in extremely unfavourable times. The welfare state was not only unable to recognize and attend to the new ageing-related needs, but was also retrenched as part of the social cost of the transition. In the post-transitional welfare reforms – which tended to transfer some welfare costs and responsibilities to individuals and the private welfare pillar – development ran in the opposite direction from 'defamilialization', thus leaving a substantial share of care to the informal, family domain. Pensions and long-term care policies have been specifically affected by the distinctive demands of the transitional period and have been transformed to support these demands. On the one hand, pension systems were transformed to serve as a shock absorber during the transition, absorbing the unemployed and leading to unsustainability. On the other hand, the transformation of old-age care to adjust to the needs of the ageing society was delayed and overshadowed by other political priorities. However, it should be noted that, although some differences exist in the trend of demographic ageing between post-socialist and other countries, there are basic similarities in the ageing-related challenges, which are recognized by the European Commission (2015).

Empirical analysis has enabled exploration of the outcomes of this policy delay in terms of the old-age welfare gap and its manifestation in various domains, such as availability of formal care services, its funding, reliance on informal family support, and availability of housing that has been adapted to the needs of the elderly population. The results show a significant gap in the availability of old-age services in post-socialist countries compared to many other countries, but not to the 'familialistic' Southern European group. The significance of the family for old-age care – in terms of both providing care and helping to pay for it – was found to be roughly similar between these two groups, and quite different from other groups of countries. In comparison to the others, these two country groups have experienced a delay in providing new forms of care services and in integrating the cost of them into the formal system.

This analysis has also shed some light on the potential role of housing for different country groups in meeting the needs of older people. The potential of housing to compensate for the delay in old-age welfare policies in the post-socialist group of countries is mixed. Our empirical evidence indicates similarity with the Southern European group in a number of areas. Familialism, prominent in Southern Europe, was also found to be important in the post-socialist countries. Our cluster analysis also confirmed that the potential of owned homes to bridge the old-age welfare gap is very similar in the post-socialist countries and Southern Europe. In both groups, the choices and decisions on options for old-age care are not only an individual issue but also quite often a family issue. Where adult children co-reside with ageing parents, earnings, outlays, care, and assets are to some extent managed within the wider framework of the family. The Southern European arrangements of grandparents providing child care and the later 'care for inheritance' are also often present in the post-socialist countries.

However, some differences between post-socialist countries were also highlighted. While only five countries had data available for the analysis, an indicative divergence between them emerged in statistical terms. Most notably, the Czech Republic revealed greater similarity with the continental group than with the rest of the post-socialist group. Combined with the similarities between some of the post-socialist countries and the Southern European countries, our findings seem to call for further, more specific observations.

NOTES

* This paper uses data from SHARE Wave 4 release 1.1.1, as of 28 March 2013 (DOI: 10.6103/SHARE.w4.111). The SHARE data collection has primarily been funded by the European Commission through the 5th Framework Programme (project QLK6–CT–2001–00360 in the thematic programme Quality of Life), through the 6th Framework Programme (projects SHARE–I3, RII–CT–2006–062193; COMPARE, CIT5–CT–2005–028857; SHARELIFE, CIT4–CT–2006–028812), and through the 7th Framework Programme (SHARE–PREP, No. 211909; SHARE–LEAP, No. 227822; SHARE M4, No. 261982). Additional funding from the US National Institute on Aging (U01 AG09740–13S2; P01 AG005842; P01 AG08291; P30 AG12815; R21 AG025169; Y1–AG–4553–01; IAG BSR06–11; OGHA 04–064) and the German Ministry of Education and Research, as well as from various national sources, is gratefully acknowledged (see www.share-project.org for a full list of funding institutions).
1. We use the term 'transition' as a conventionally and widely used name for the abrupt and very complex social changes caused by the fall of socialist political regimes in Central and Eastern Europe. The nature, intensity, and direction of these changes are still far

from being fully identified. This is also manifested in the ongoing debate about the terms 'transition' and 'transformation'. Burawoy (2002, p. 270), for instance, claims that 'there has indeed been a market transition but without the anticipated economic, social and political transformation', thus arguing for 'transition without transformation'. In contrast, Stephens et al. (2015, p. 1) state that what occurred in post-socialist housing systems was 'a path-dependent "transformation" rather than a "transition".'

2. Because the cited source presents data in the form of bars, not figures, the respective figures have been estimated from the bars.

3. SHARE (Survey of Health, Ageing and Retirement in Europe) is a panel survey covering various topics (health, socioeconomic status, and social and family networks) conducted on approximately 110,000 individuals aged 50 or older and their partners. The first wave was in 2004/05, the second in 2006/07, the third (SHARELIFE) in 2008/09, the fourth mainly in 2011, and the fifth wave in 2013. So far, 20 European countries (plus Israel) have participated in SHARE (http://www.share-project.org/).

REFERENCES

Albertini, M., M. Kohli, and C. Vogel (2007), 'Intergenerational transfers of time and money in European families: common patterns – different regimes?', Journal of European Social Policy, 17 (4), 319–334.

Allen, J., J. Barlow, J. Leal, T. Maloutas, and L. Padovani (2004), Housing and Welfare in Southern Europe, Oxford: Blackwell Publishing Ltd.

Armingeon, K. (2006), 'Reconciling competing claims of the welfare state clientele', in K. Armingeon, and G. Bonoli (eds), The Politics of Post-Industrial Welfare States, London and New York: Routledge, pp. 100–122.

Armingeon, K., and G. Bonoli (eds) (2006), The Politics of Post-Industrial Welfare States, London and New York: Routledge.

Bonoli, G. (2006), 'New social risks and the politics of post-industrial social policies', in K. Armingeon, and G. Bonoli (eds), The Politics of Post-Industrial Welfare States, London and New York: Routledge, pp. 3–26.

Burawoy, M. (2002), 'Transition without transformation: Russia's involutionary road to capitalism', in D. Nugent (ed.), Locating Capitalism in Time and Space: Global Restructurings, Politics and Identity, Stanford: Stanford University Press, pp. 290–310.

Cirman, A., S. Mandič, and J. Zorić (2013), 'Decisions to renovate: identifying key determinants in Central and Eastern European post-socialist countries', Urban Studies, 50 (16), 3378–3393.

Deacon, B. (2000), 'Eastern European welfare states: the impact of the politics of globalisation', Journal of European Social Policy, 10 (2), 146–161.

Doling, J., and M. Elsinga (eds) (2013), Demographic Change and Housing Wealth: Homeowners, Pensions and Asset-Based Welfare in Europe, Dordrecht, Heidelberg, New York, and London: Springer.

Doling, J., and R. Ronald (2010), 'Property-based welfare and European home-owners: How would housing perform as a pension?', Journal of Housing and the Built Environment, 25, 227–241.

Doling, J., J. Ford and N. Horsewood (2003), 'Globalisation and home ownership', in J. Doling, and J. Ford (eds), Globalisation and Home Ownership. Experiences in Eight Member States of the European Union. Housing and Urban Policy Studies 21, Delft: Delft University Press, pp. 1–20.

EC (European Commission) (2005), Report on Social Inclusion 2005, SEC (2005) 256, Luxembourg: Office for Official Publications of the European Communities.

EC (European Commission) (2007), Europe's Demographic Future: Facts and Figures on Challenges and Opportunities, Brussels: European Commission, accessed 18 November 2008 at ec.europa.eu/employment_social/spsi/docs/social_situation/demo_report_2007_en.pdf.

EC (European Commission) (2012), Long Term Care, Brussels: European Commission, accessed 18 April 2012 at ec.europa.eu/social/main.jsp?catId=792&langId=en.

EC (European Commission) (2015), The 2015 Ageing Report, Brussels: European Commission, accessed 20 June 2015 at ec.europa.eu/economy_finance/public ations/european_economy/2015/pdf/ee3_en.pdf.

Esping-Andersen, G. (1999), Social Foundations of Postindustrial Economies, Oxford: Oxford University Press.

Esping-Andersen, G. (2009), The Incomplete Revolution, Cambridge: Polity Press.

Eurobarometer (2007), Eurobarometer 67.3 (May–June), TNS Opinion & Social, Brussels: European Commission, Eurostat.

Ferge, Z. (2001), 'European integration and the reform of social security in the accession countries', European Journal of Social Quality, 3 (1–2), 9–25.

Guardiancich, I. (2004), 'Welfare state retrenchment in Central and Eastern Europe: the case of pension reforms in Poland and Slovenia', Managing Global Transitions, 2 (1), 41–64.

Hacker, B. (2009), 'Hybridization instead of clustering: transformation processes of welfare policies in Central and Eastern Europe', Social Policy & Administration, 43 (2), 152–169.

Hegedus, J., N. Teller, and M. Lux (eds) (2012), Social Housing in Transition Countries, London and New York: Routledge.

Huber, E., and J. Stephens (2006), 'Combating old and new social risks', in K. Armingeon, and G. Bonoli (eds), The Politics of Postindustrial Welfare States, London: Routledge, pp. 143–168.

Iacovou, M., and A. Skew (2010), 'Household structure in the EU', ISER Working Paper Series No. 2010, 10, Essex: University of Essex.

Iacovou, M., and A. Skew (2011), 'Household composition across the new Europe: where do the new member states fit in?', Demographic Research, 25 (5), 465–490.

Isengard, B., and M. Szydlik (2012), 'Living apart (or) together? Coresidence of elderly parents and their adult children in Europe', Research on Aging, 34 (4), 449–474.

Juhasz, G. (2006), 'Exporting or pulling down? The European Social Model and Eastern enlargement of the EU', European Journal of Social Quality, 6 (1), 82–108.

Kazepov, Y. (2008), 'The subsidarization of social policies: actors, processes and impacts', European Societies, 10 (2), 247–273.

Kornai, J. (1997), 'The reform of the welfare state and public opinion', The American Economic Review, 87 (2), 339–343.

Kovacs, J. M. (2002), 'Approaching the EU and reaching the US? Rival narratives on transforming welfare regimes in East-Central Europe', West European Politics, 25 (2), 175–204.

Lendvai, N. (2004), 'The weakest link? EU accession and enlargement: dialoguing EU and post-communist social policy', Journal of European Social Policy, 14 (3), 319–333.

Lethbridge, J. (2011), 'Care services for older people in Europe: challenges for labour', London: PSIRU, accessed 18 April 2012 at www.epsu.org/IMG/pdf/Care_Services_Older_People_Europe_report_final.pdf.

Mandič, S. (2010), 'The changing role of housing assets in post-socialist countries', Journal of Housing and the Built Environment, 25 (2), 213–226.

Mandič, S. (2012), 'Home ownership in post-socialist countries: between macro economy and micro structures of welfare provision', in R. Ronald, and M. Elsinga (eds), Beyond Home Ownership: Housing, Welfare and Society, London and New York: Routledge, pp. 68–88.

Manning, N. (2004), 'Diversity and change in pre-accession Central and Eastern Europe since 1989', Journal of European Social Policy, 14 (3), 211–232.

Morel, N. (2006), 'Providing coverage against new social risks in Bismarckian welfare states: the case of long term care', in K. Armingeon, and G. Bonoli (eds), The Politics of Post-Industrial Welfare States, London and New York: Routledge, pp. 227–247.

OECD (Organisation for Economic Co-operation and Development) (2000) Public Long-Term Care Financing Arrangements in OECD Countries, accessed 28 July 2015 at http://dx.doi.org/10.1787/888932401577, http://dx.doi.org/10.1787/888932401615.

OECD (2011), Help Wanted? Providing and Paying for Long-Term Care, Paris: OECD, accessed February 2016 at http://ec.europa.eu/health/reports/docs/oecd_helpwanted_en.pdf.

Offe, C., and S. Fuchs (2007), 'Welfare state formation in the enlarged European Union: patterns of reform in the post-communist new member states', Discussion Paper SP IV 2007–306, Berlin: Wissenschaftszentrum Berlin für Sozialforschung.

Philipov, D., and J. Dorbritz (2004), Demographic Consequences of Economic Transition in Countries of Central and Eastern Europe, Council of Europe Population Studies No. 23, Strasbourg: Council of Europe.

Pickard, L., A. Comas-Herrera, J. Costa-Font, C. Gori, A. di Maio, C. Patxot, A. Pozzi, H. Rothgang, and R. Wittenberg (2007), 'Modelling an entitlement to long-term care services for older people in Europe: projections for long-term care expenditure to 2050', Journal of European Social Policy, 17 (1), 33–48.

Poggio, T. (2008), 'The intergenerational transmission of home ownership and the reproduction of the familialistic welfare regime', in C. Saraceno (ed.), Families, Ageing and Social Policy, Cheltenham, UK and Northampton, MA, USA: Edward Elgar Publishing, pp. 59–87.

Read, R., and T. Thelen (2007), 'Introduction: social security and care after socialism: reconfigurations of public and private', Focaal: European Journal of Anthropology, 50, 3–18.

Ronald, R., and M. Elsinga (eds) (2012), Beyond Home Ownership: Housing, Welfare and Society, London and New York: Routledge.

Saraceno, C. (2008), 'Patterns of family living in the enlarged EU', in J. Alber, T. Fahey, and C. Saraceno (eds), Handbook of Quality of Life in the Enlarged European Union, London and New York: Routledge, pp. 47–72.

Saraceno, C. (2010), 'Social inequalities in facing old-age dependency: a bi-generational perspective', Journal of European Social Policy, 20 (1), 32–44.

Sarasa, S., and S. Billingsley (2008), 'Personal and household caregiving from adult children to parents and social stratification', in C. Saraceno (ed.), Families, Ageing and Social Policy, Cheltenham, UK and Northampton, MA, USA: Edward Elgar Publishing, pp. 123–146.

SHARE (2011), 'Survey of Health, Ageing and Retirement in Europe (SHARE) Wave 4', Munich: SHARE–ERIC.

SHARE (2013), Survey of Health, Ageing and Retirement in Europe, accessed 20 March 2014 at http://www.share-project.org.

Special EUROBAROMETER 283 (2007), Health and Long-Term Care, accessed 10 April 2014 at http://ec.europa.eu/public_opinion/archives/ebs/ebs_283_en.pdf.

Stanovnik, T., and M. Čok (2009), 'The transition process and changes in income, income inequality and poverty: the case of Slovenia', in M. S. Stanculescu, and T. Stanovnik (eds), Activity, Incomes and Social Welfare, Burlington: Ashgate Publishing, pp. 231–268.

Stark, D., and L. Bruszt (1998), Postsocialist Pathways, Cambridge: Cambridge University Press.

Stephens, M. (2003), 'Globalisation and housing finance systems in advanced and transition economies', Urban Studies, 40 (5–6), 1011–1026.

Stephens, M., M. Lux, and P. Sunega (2015), 'Post-socialist housing systems in Europe: housing welfare regimes by default?', Housing Studies, 30 (8), 1210–1234.

Struyk, R. J. (1996), Economic Restructuring of the Former Soviet Bloc: The Case of Housing, Washington, DC: Urban Institute Press.

Velladics, K., K. Henkens, and H. P. Van Dalen (2006), 'Do different welfare states engender different policy preferences? Opinions on pension reforms in Eastern and Western Europe', Ageing and Society, 26 (3), 475–496.

World Bank (2013), Population Ages 65 and Above and Life Expectancy at Birth, accessed 28 July 2015 at http://data.worldbank.org/indicator/SP.POP.65UP. TO.ZS, http://data.worldbank.org/indicator/SP.DYN.LE00.IN.

9. Experiences of home ownership and housing mobility after privatization in Russia

Jane R. Zavisca and Theodore P. Gerber

INTRODUCTION

When the Soviet Union collapsed and Russia became an independent country in 1992, the new government initiated mass, free privatization of property rights to the occupants of socialist housing, creating the chief source of household wealth in the new economy. At the same time, the state drastically reduced its role in producing and distributing housing. Today, the vast majority of Russians live in private housing – nearly 85 per cent of households as of 2012 – and a housing market has emerged (EMF, 2013). Comparative studies report that Russia has one of the highest home-ownership rates among developed countries, mostly without mortgages (Mandič, 2010; Schwartz and Seabrooke, 2008; Stephens et al., 2015).

This high rate of home ownership, coupled with deep retrenchment of public housing provision and other social protections, means that private ownership is essential to welfare in Russia. Free privatization was intended to produce a physical safety net, protecting against income shocks during the transition to capitalism (Kosareva and Struyk, 1993). Unencumbered ownership, by reducing housing costs to families, has acted as a buffer against unemployment, currency fluctuations, and repeated economic crises in the post-Soviet era. The architects of Russia's housing reform further hoped that privatized housing would capitalize new markets and operate as a form of liquid wealth, which households could extract – for example, by selling a privatized home to use as a down payment on a bigger house, or as an income supplement via annuity contracts in old age (Buckley et al., 2003). The aspiration was to create the foundation for an 'asset-based' welfare regime in which housing wealth becomes a basis for welfare over the life course (Doling and Ronald, 2010). However, a financialized housing market has failed to emerge; the market is restricted mainly to the direct purchase and sale of housing, while mortgage finance and equity loans remain underdeveloped. Thus, the Russian case resembles less an asset-based welfare system than a pre-commodified family-based one, such as is characteristic of much of Southern Europe and post-socialist Eastern Europe (Delfani et al., 2014; Mandič, 2010).

Family-based housing systems, in which homes are seen less as financial investments than as transferable familial resources, create intergenerational dependencies and potential for intra-familial inequality. Few housing studies focus on intra-family property relations, perhaps due to the common assumption that ownership is a household- or family-level asset, the benefits of which accrue equally to all members. In Russia, this is often not the case, de jure or de facto. Not all adult household members necessarily share title, and title may be shared with non-resident family. This is not necessarily a problem if formal title arrangements either match or are irrelevant to de facto property rights. However, in Russia, the dispersion of title across extended families does not match local norms regarding meaningful ownership. To achieve the full cultural status of an owner in Russia requires having a place 'of one's own' (*svoi*), based on both owning and dwelling as a nuclear family (Zavisca, 2012).

The standard measure of owner-occupation as a household-level variable, then, presents a misleading picture of the extent and distribution of home ownership in Russia. Housing scholars have proposed alternative definitions of home ownership tenure that can be adapted to heterogeneous contexts. For example, Ronald (2008) derives a cross-cultural typology of home ownership based on the meanings ascribed to it and its valuation as investment, asset, or use. Others emphasize the gradient of security in property rights, for both owner and rental tenures (Cheng et al., 2014; Hulse and Milligan, 2014). For our purposes, we find most useful the perspective from the law and society literature on ownership as a 'bundle' of property rights. This bundle includes rights to exchange, use, and autonomy, which can be more or less secure and may or may not be concentrated in a single owner (Penner, 1996; Elliott and Wadley, 2013). These rights typically hang together in advanced housing markets but are frequently uncoupled in Russia, as exchange rights (title) and usage rights (residence) are often dispersed across extended families.

This chapter draws on an original survey to construct alternative measures of ownership consistent with local meanings. Our survey design permits us to measure the structure of familial property rights from 1992 to 2013. We find that, two decades after the onset of privatization, fewer than one-half of middle-aged urban adults had achieved full ownership for their nuclear families, although most were living in privately owned homes. Fragmentation of property rights creates inequalities across generations and even among spouses. Status characteristics such as education, occupation, and wages account for little of the variation in ownership, suggesting that familial reciprocity, not market exchange, still predominates in determining who becomes an owner and how.

We also explore paths to mobility in property rights. In established housing markets in which extended family households are uncommon, young adults' transitions to residential independence and ownership are usually coterminous with a move to a new home. However, property rights can change without ever moving; for example, when a home is privatized or when ownership shares are inherited. Such 'in-place adjustments' are common in post-socialist societies (Mandič, 2001). Conversely, leaving the parental home does not necessarily lead to residential independence, as young adults may move into the homes of other relatives, including in laws. A social rather than geographic conception of mobility reveals extensive transitions in tenure and independence in Russia, but these are achieved mainly via redistribution and reciprocity, not markets.

THE MEANING OF OWNERSHIP IN THE POST-SOVIET HOUSING REGIME[1]

In the late Soviet period, most urban Russians lived in state-owned housing. This was a result of the largest public housing initiative in history, launched in 1957 by Nikita Khrushchev. His goal was to house every Soviet nuclear family in a separate, state-owned apartment within twenty years. This ambitious plan was not fully realized, as waiting lists for apartments stretched for years. Nevertheless, mass construction of modest apartments led to radical improvements in housing conditions for millions of Soviet families. Between 1950 and 1970, the housing stock tripled, and half of the Soviet population moved; a similar mobility rate was obtained between 1970 and 1990. Although the state retained legal ownership over the apartments it built and allocated, it encouraged residents to think of these gifts of the state as 'their own'. People had the right to lifelong tenure and they could transfer these rights to their descendants, or swap them at will with anyone else who wanted to trade apartments. The logic of allocation, which prioritized couples with minor children, reinforced the nuclear family ideal. A separate apartment for the nuclear family thus transformed from a novelty to the centerpiece of what Russians call a 'normal life', and remains an aspiration and expectation today.

When Russia became an independent country in 1992, the new government tried to transform the socialist housing sector into a market, modeled on the American system. To jumpstart the market, residents were allowed to privatize for free the housing where they were registered as living in

1992. Millions of low-income households became home owners, and housing was more equitably distributed than other privatized assets such as factories and oil fields (Buckley and Gurenko, 1997). But this had little mitigating effect on overall economic inequality, while privatization itself exacerbated Soviet-era housing inequality (Yemtsov, 2007). People who occupied substandard housing – who were disproportionately young – lost out when market transition began, while those who occupied better units benefited from a large and unexpected transfer of wealth. Nothing was done for the 20 per cent of families who were still on waiting lists for free housing as of 1992, or the additional 25 per cent who were dissatisfied with their housing conditions and had hoped to join the now-defunct queues (Kosareva and Struyk, 1993).

The architects of housing reform expected a private sector of builders and lenders would arise to meet the housing demands of those left out of privatization. Elements of a market did emerge: mass privatization of socialist housing created a nation of home owners, and the legal and financial infrastructure for market transactions and mortgage lending exists. However, privatization was much more successful than marketization. Underdeveloped mortgage and rental markets limited liquidity of housing wealth and affordability, making it difficult to convert earnings at work into better conditions at home. Similar patterns emerged in other former Soviet territories that prioritized privatization in housing reform (Buckley and Tsenkova, 2001; Lux et al., 2013; Sharipova, 2015) as well as in China and Viet Nam (Tran and Dalholm, 2005; Walder and He, 2014).

After over a decade of retrenchment, the state has been reinvesting in the housing sector since 2006, through subsidies intended to stimulate mortgage markets as well as the birthrate. The centerpiece of these policies is 'Maternity Capital': vouchers worth approximately $10,000 that can be applied toward mortgages for Russian women who give birth to a second child. Related policies include down-payment assistance for young families, mortgage lending by state-controlled banks, and subsidies for construction of economy housing. Yet when the fledgling market peaked in 2008, Russian mortgage debt stood at just 3 per cent of Gross Domestic Product (GDP), compared to 50 per cent in the European Union and 80 per cent in the United States. The tiny market crashed during the international financial crisis and recovered from 2010–13, only to crash again in 2014 due to a currency crisis precipitated by international sanctions and falling revenue from oil and gas.

As a result, most housing wealth today is either directly or indirectly a result of privatization, as much of the starting capital for housing market transactions derives from the sale of privatized Soviet property. This creates particular challenges and dependence on family for people who transitioned to adulthood in the post-Soviet period. Privatized shares of socialist housing were allocated in equal measure to all registered occupants, often creating multiple owners across generations. This made post-Soviet housing a case of the 'tragedy of the anti-commons', in which transition regimes 'failed to endow any individual with a bundle of rights that represents full ownership' (Heller, 1997, p. 623). As our data show, title is still broadly dispersed across extended families, and immediate family members – even spouses – often do not share title.

Lack of affordable housing for young families also leads to extensive intergenerational households. Like young people in asset-based welfare societies, young Russians have difficulty transitioning to home owner-ship (McKee, 2012). However, rather than renting, which is unafford-able and insecure, most young Russians live with extended family well into adulthood. Some comparative studies classify post socialist housing regimes as resembling Southern European countries that have high home-ownership rates but delayed departure from the parental home (Saraneco and Olagnero, 2004; Schwartz and Seabrooke, 2008). These patterns are attributed to traditional family values, combined with constrained housing markets and minimal state assistance (Iacovou, 2001; Rossi, 1997). Although young Russians face similar constraints, traditional values are not keeping them in the parental home. Most respondents in public opinion polls agree in surveys that it is best for young families to live separately from parents (for example, Gudkov et al., 2011, pp. 37–38); we also found strong consensus on this matter in focus groups. Zavisca (2013) documents qualitatively the experience of young adult Russians living with extended family. In describing their aspirations for 'normal' housing, they portray their housing circumstances as pathological. They strive to carve out zones of autonomy in homes that they do not see as truly theirs, even if they share title. In the remainder of this chapter, we analyse trends in the dispersion of property rights, which attenuates the experience of full ownership.

DATA: THE SURVEY OF HOUSING EXPERIENCES IN RUSSIA (SHER)*

The SHER is a multistage probability sample of 1,000 residents of Russian cities with populations over 500,000, who are aged between 33 and 56 years old. We also separately interviewed respondents' current partners when available (N=318). The survey was conducted in late 2013, but captures changes in housing and family structure since 1992 via a retrospective design. Interviews were conducted face to face. The survey was carried out by the Levada Analytic Center, Russia's leading independent survey research organization. A chief concern was to verify respondents' capacity to retrospectively recall variables of interest over the previous two decades. Prior to the survey, we conducted two focus groups in Moscow and two in Yaroslavl, a provincial capital, on the topics covered by the survey. We also verified recall ability through analysis of 130 qualitative interviews on housing and family life collected in 2009 (see Zavisca, 2012). We then conducted two rounds of pretests before finalizing the questionnaire.

We restricted the study to urban areas, both due to cost considerations and because rural and urban housing dynamics are so different as to warrant separate study. Also due to cost considerations, we restricted the age range to 33–56-year-olds in 2013, our core retrospective cohorts of interest. This generation was aged 11–34 at the time of the Soviet collapse (January 1992), and thus passed through crucial transitions to young and middle adulthood during the two-decade period of study. The response rate was 34 per cent, which is typical for surveys conducted on national samples in Russia (the response rate for partner interviews was about 57 per cent). The cohort and city size restrictions of our sample prevent us from comparing our data to available census tables to assess its representativeness. However, the distributions of key variables in the SHER – including sex, age, education, and housing tenure – are similar to those in the Russian Longitudinal Monitoring Survey, a much larger dataset from which we can extract a comparable sample.

The survey collected housing histories of respondents since January 1992. Respondents were asked to describe their place of residence in 1992 and to indicate all the places where they had lived for at least six months since then. Detailed questions were asked about up to three residences that were apartments or homes: the first, current, and most recent, if applicable.[2] For each privately owned residence, we assessed whether the owners included the focal respondent, his or her partner, or anyone else other than his or her children. We also measured how each change in ownership status and/or residence was accomplished. Household structure was also retrospectively measured such that, in any given year, we know whether the respondent was living with their extended family (that is, anyone other than the respondent's partner or own children). Timing of other life-course transitions such as marriage, divorce, birth of a child, and death of a parent are also measured. The survey includes a broad range of measures of socioeconomic status, including education, occupation, and employment history of both respondents and partners. We transformed these data into a person–year file suitable for dynamic analysis, and used it to produce figures and tables showing trends over time.

In interpreting these data, it is important to bear in mind that the sample ages over the years of the study, raising challenges for interpreting change as a function of aging versus time period. The SHER provides no information about young adults in recent years, as the focal cohorts were ages 33 or older by 2013. We therefore supplement our discussion with descriptive statistics on younger adults from a cross-sectional survey of 18–49-year-olds we collected in 2015, the Comparative Housing Experience and Societal Stability (CHESS) survey. Data were collected from 2,401 Russian adults, 1,206 of whom live in medium to large cities, and are comparable to the SHER sample (other than in age). Survey protocols are similar across the two surveys; however, the CHESS does not provide retrospective histories. Due to space limitations, we do not describe the CHESS further here; details are available from the authors.

TRENDS AND INEQUALITIES IN HOME OWNERSHIP

How have home-ownership rates changed for our focal cohorts? Figure 9.1 shows trends between 1992 and 2013, using different definitions of ownership and independence. The trend line labeled 'respondent's family are owners' shows the increase in ownership as conventionally defined; that is, based on household-level owner-occupation. By this definition, home-ownership rates expanded from about 20 per cent in 1992 to nearly 80 per cent in 2013. Although our focal cohort is not a representative cross-section of the population in each year, these figures track statistics about the urban housing stock, 15 per cent of which was owned by private citizens in 1990, versus 86 per cent in 2013 (Rosstat, 2014).

Almost all of the change in overall rates of ownership among our sample is due to conversion of public or communal housing to private ownership; very few respondents transitioned from renters to owners. In 1992, 60 per cent were living in state housing; 15 per cent were living in communal settings, such as dormitories, barracks, and communal apartments; 22 per cent were living in privately owned housing, and only 3 per cent were living in private rentals. By 2013, 76 per cent were living in privately owned housing; just 14 per cent in state housing; 6 per cent in communal housing, and only 4 per cent in rentals.

As expected, the conventional measure indicates a remarkable transformation to an 'ownership society'. However, this picture of extraordinarily high rates of ownership is diminished when we examine property relations within families. The trend line labeled 'respondent is an owner' shows the proportion of respondents who held at least a share of ownership. The trend parallels that for familial ownership, but about 10–15 per cent of

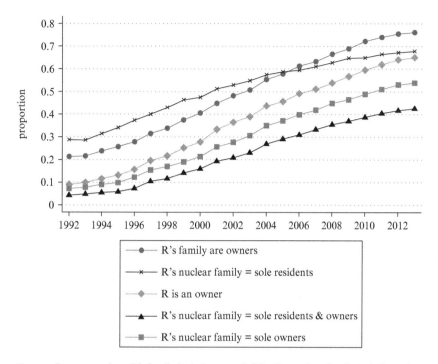

Notes: R = respondent; R's family includes extended family; nuclear family includes only R, R's partner, and R's own children.

Figure 9.1 Trends in ownership and household structure

residents of owner-occupied households were not owners themselves; this gap is consistent over time. As the overall rate of home ownership rises, the relative gap between respondents and their families decreases; by 2013, 85 per cent of all respondents living in owner-occupied households were owners themselves.

The third trend line further restricts the definition to exclusive ownership by the respondent's nuclear family: only the respondent and/or the respondent's partner are owners, with no one else on the title (other than the respondent's children). The gap between this line and the line for respondent owners indicates cases in which someone else is also an owner. By 2013, when respondents were ages 33–56, only about one-half of them had achieved independent ownership for the nuclear family; one-quarter were living in housing owned as well or instead by extended family.

Finally, we look at residential independence and how this intersects with property rights. The line labeled 'respondent's nuclear family are sole residents' indicates the overall proportion of respondents who are living with no one other than spouse/partner and/or children, and in non-communal housing.[3] The proportion more than doubled over the course of the period of the study, with the rate of change slowing over time. As of 2013, about two-thirds of respondents were living with nuclear family, while one-third lacked residential independence.

The lowest line shows the intersection of nuclear family ownership and nuclear family residence, both of which are required to consider a place truly one's own, based on local norms. According to this definition, fewer than one-half of Russians had achieved full and independent ownership after twenty years of housing market transition. The gap between this restrictive definition of full ownership and the conventional measure of familial ownership is very large, demonstrating that the measure matters for assessing home-ownership rates.

How much of the change we observe over the years of the study is a function of time period versus age? The panel nature of our data means that the trends in Figure 9.1 could reflect the aging of our sample rather than societal-level change over time. If in 1992 our respondents were ages 11–34 and some were still children, by 2013 they were ages 33–56. To visualize the extent to which changes in ownership and/or household structure are due to time period versus aging, Figure 9.2 compares trends over time for adults grouped by age (with restrictions to reflect data availability).[4]

The left panel of the graph shows trends in nuclear family ownership by couples (that is, respondents and/or their spouses). In 1992, we observe very low ownership rates for all age groups, followed by sharp increases over time for all but the youngest group. The change is steepest during the peak years of privatization between 1995 and 2000. The trend flattens for younger age groups after 2000, at about 20 per cent for ages 23–27 and 35 per cent for ages 28–32. Rates for elder groups track each other closely, and appear to stabilize after 2008 at between 50 and 60 per cent. SHER data are not available for younger age groups in later years. However, a comparable sample from the CHESS data in 2015 indicates that the rate of nuclear family ownership remains very low for the youngest group (6 per cent). Rates for 23–27- and 28–32-year-olds were 30 per cent and 42 per cent respectively, both somewhat higher than comparable age groups in earlier years. Taken together, this data is consistent with both increasing ownership rates and increasing age differentiation, particularly among younger groups, during the post-Soviet period.

The right panel shows analogous data on sole residence. Here we see a story of stability since the Soviet period; the consistency over time within age groups is striking, especially when compared to the panel on ownership. Despite increasing opportunities for sole ownership, there is little

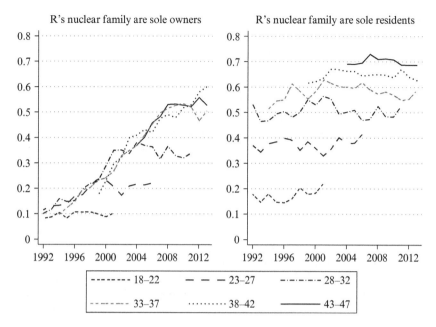

R's nuclear family are sole owners   R's nuclear family are sole residents

| ------- 18–22 | — — — 23–27 | –·–·–·– 28–32 |
| ------- 33–37 | ·········· 38–42 | ———— 43–47 |

Notes: R = respondent; R's nuclear family includes only R, R's partner, and R's own children.

Figure 9.2   Trends in ownership and household structure by age group

change in propensity to live separately from extended family. This sheds a different light on Figure 9.1, which includes the entire sample. The rise in sole residence over time is mainly a function of aging of our sample, rather than a general change in propensity to live separately from extended family. By contrast, the propensity toward increased ownership is largely a period effect, but with older respondents being more likely to have sole ownership. However, our 2015 CHESS data do suggest that there could be some change in young people's propensity to live independently. Although rates of independent housing for the youngest group remained at a low 19 per cent, nearly 60 per cent of those aged 23–27 and 28–32 were living on their own – significantly more than in previous years. Nevertheless, a significant proportion of young adults clearly still lives with extended family well into adulthood today – about 40 per cent through age 30.

Intra-Familial Inequality

The high degree of both co-ownership and co-residence with extended family in Russia (represented in Figure 9.1 by the gap between familial ownership and 'full' nuclear family ownership) produces intra-family inequalities. Many of our respondents were living with their parents or other relatives when privatization began, and many still share property rights with extended family – both resident and non-resident – including parents and siblings. As of 2013, when the SHER respondents were aged 33–56, one-half of those who were living in owner-occupied dwellings shared ownership and/or residence with someone other than their partners or children. According to the CHESS survey, younger generations of owners have not caught up in this regard – 70 per cent of owner-occupiers aged 18–32 in 2013 shared either ownership or residence with extended family.

This dispersion of property rights within families is a result of Russia's approach to privatization, compounded by weak market development. Privatization created joint ownership across generations by design, as housing was privatized in equal shares to all registered occupants of state-owned dwellings. It is possible that such arrangements reflect preferences rather than constraint. Yet extended family households conflict with normative definitions of ownership and often lead to a sense of subordinate and insecure property rights. Despite de jure equality of ownership shares, younger generations tend to perceive elders as the main owners (see Zavisca, 2012, chapters 5 and 6). This 'logic of the family estate' with respect to subjective sense of property rights has also been observed in China (Davis, 2004). Even those who live independently may still face insecurity when ownership shares are dispersed, as the property cannot be sold without consensus from non-resident owners. Unequal sense of ownership also has implications for everyday experience; when living and/or owning together with extended family, younger generations often lack a sense of ability to make the place their own by using and transforming the space to their liking (Zavisca, 2013).

Asymmetric Spousal Ownership

The earlier analysis defines independent ownership and residence in terms of the nuclear family. This approach overlooks possible differences in property rights between spouses. Among the subset of cases in which at least one member of a couple was an owner, about one-third had asymmetric ownership, where only one of the spouses holds title (36 per cent across all person–years, and 34 per cent for couples in 2013). We are aware of only two other surveys that measure individual-level ownership among couples. In the United Kingdom, the rate is estimated at 13 per cent of unions in owner-occupancy (Lersch and Vidal, 2015), whereas in China, the rate is 70–80 per cent, mostly male sole owners (Chen, 2015). We expect that such arrangements will vary across other national contexts, depending on gender norms, divorce law, and familial roles.

Asymmetric ownership can create insecurity and vulnerability for the non-owning partner. Our data do not tell us directly whether asymmetry is due to trust (trusting spouses may feel no need to formalize shared property rights) or distrust (advantaged spouses may refuse to share property and risk losing control). However, our knowledge of the Russian context leads us to suspect the latter. Russia has one of the highest divorce rates in the world, which means that many couples will face the problem of who gets the house. Keeping title in one spouse's name advantages that spouse after divorce, as family law stipulates that property that was owned solely prior to marriage or bequeathed to only one spouse belongs only to that individual. As we shall see in the next section, the majority of couples acquire their housing (directly or indirectly) with assistance from extended family. Qualitative evidence indicates that extended family, aware of this, try to prevent familial property from falling into the hands of children-in-law by denying title to them (Zavisca, 2012, Chapter 6).

Our survey data allow us to test for subjective asymmetries in perceived ownership, and also to assess the consequences of asymmetric ownership for relationship stability. Both respondents and their current partners were asked whether they perceive their housing as belonging only to themselves, shared with other members of the family, or not belonging to them. Among non-owning spouses in asymmetric relationships, one-half said they did not share a sense of ownership, whereas two-thirds of their title-holding partners said ownership is shared. Although N is relatively small (there are only 112 couples with asymmetric ownership for whom partner interviews are available), this suggests that unequal formal rights are often accompanied by unequal perceptions of ownership. Couples with asymmetric ownership are also less stable, particularly when the wife is the sole owner – in a separate analysis of partnership histories, we found that such couples are more likely to divorce than both joint owning and non-owning couples (Gerber and Zavisca, 2015). This suggests that women are more likely to leave unhappy marriages when they have autonomous rights to the family home.

Notably, women were equally as likely as men to be sole owner within an asymmetric couple at the onset of the relationship (our retrospective data measures ownership at beginning of cohabitation and any changes thereafter). This suggests that, in the aggregate, dispersed property rights in Russia do not exacerbate gender inequality, and might even mitigate it. In a related qualitative study in Ukraine, Anderson (2015) finds that asymmetric home ownership within couples influences negotiations over pooling and control of income, and gives female owners a source of bargaining power over household finances. When men are unwilling to bargain, the result of women's independent resources may be divorce (Cooke, 2006).

Demographic and Socioeconomic Stratification of Home Ownership

How is home ownership distributed across social strata in Russia? Table 9.1 uses various indicators of socioeconomic status to compare our measures of ownership at the time of the interview in 2013. Our three focal age cohorts (who were 11–18, 19–26, and 27–34 in 1992) have similar rates of familial ownership (column 1; the conventional measure). However, there are differences in rate of sole ownership, and especially sole residence, resulting in large differences by age in full ownership – one-half of those who were ages 48–55 lived and owned as a nuclear family, versus just one-third of those ages 32–39. Marital status also matters: never-married respondents are much less likely than married respondents to own or reside independently. Divorced respondents are nearly as likely to live in family-owned housing as married respondents, but less likely to own or reside independently. This likely reflects the tendency for Russians, especially women, to move back in with extended family after divorce.

Turning to measures of socioeconomic status, we find no major differences by education level; for each measure of ownership, rates are virtually identical for those with a higher education and those with only a secondary education. For occupation, we do see some differences, especially in sole ownership. Familial ownership is around 80 per cent for all occupation groups, except for the very lowest-status occupational groups (semi/unskilled manual) and those who are not working – who still own at a remarkable 70 per cent. This is the legacy of privatization, as Soviet people across the occupational structure were given state-owned housing, and all were eligible to privatize. The measure of sole ownership by the nuclear family exhibits more signs of occupational stratification; rates are higher for professionals and skilled workers than for either routine or less skilled manual workers. Finally, there is relatively little difference in ownership rates by household income (equivalized for household size) among the top four income quintiles. Only the poorest quintile has lower ownership rates, across all measures.

Taken together, these findings indicate that the main determinants of home ownership in post-Soviet Russia are demographic, with socioeconomic status playing a secondary role. We cannot draw strong conclusions

Table 9.1 Ownership rates (%) by socioeconomic characteristics, 2013

	R's family are owners	Sole owners (nuclear family)	Sole residents (nuclear family)	Sole owners and residents
Age				
48–55	79	59	75	49
40–47	76	53	70	43
32–39	76	52	55	35
Marital Status				
married/cohabitating	79	59	71	47
divorced/widowed	76	49	61	37
never married	62	40	59	32
Gender				
Male	82	59	68	47
Female	72	51	66	38
Education				
higher	81	59	70	45
specialized secondary	72	51	66	39
secondary or less	81	56	65	45
Occupation				
professional, higher	83	64	68	46
professional, lower	84	63	73	51
routine non-manual, higher	79	52	69	47
routine non-manual, lower	78	48	64	34
manual, skilled	79	57	69	48
manual, semi/unskilled	72	52	67	44
not working	68	50	62	34
Household Income Quintile				
81–100 (richest)	81	58	75	51
61–80	77	52	61	35
41–60	83	60	65	42
21–40	81	60	69	49
10–20 (poorest)	71	48	61	39

Note: N=882 (118 cases are missing valid data for 2013).

from bivariate correlations, however, as variables could be confounded and associations spurious. In a separate multivariate analysis (not shown; results available from authors), we found that this general conclusion is still supported – demographic factors explain more variation in owner-ship rates across the entire time period of the study than do education or occupation.[5] Other studies likewise find only a weak association between income, occupation, and housing status in Russia and other post-Soviet countries (Dewilde and Lancee, 2013, p.1198; Lux et al., 2013; Mandič, 2010; Zavisca, 2012, Chapter 4).

The evidence presented is consistent with the argument that, while ownership is widespread, its attainment depends more on life course and familial assets than on human capital or occupational attainment. We can more directly test this hypothesis by examining the mechanisms for mobility – how are transitions to ownership achieved, and what is the role of markets versus state and family in such transitions? The next section turns to this question.

MOBILITY MECHANISMS: PATHS TO OWNERSHIP AND INDEPENDENCE

Since the Russian Government instituted privatization, the foundations of a housing market have emerged. The state now permits the private owner-ship and construction of most housing, and housing can be bought and sold at will for a profit. This creates an opening for market-based mobility – particularly of younger generations, who were too young to have received a home of their own from the state prior to the Soviet collapse. However, the heavy weight of privatization, coupled with weak development of either rental or mortgage markets, calls into question the degree to which markets have been driving housing mobility in Russia. We follow Polanyi (1944) in classifying mobility on the basis of three different forms of exchange: market transactions, state redistribution, and familial reciproc-ity. Our data enable us to distinguish these three mechanisms, both for residential mobility (change in address) and for transitions to ownership (not necessarily involving a change in address).

Residential Mobility

A first impression can be gained by looking at how respondents acquired the housing they were living in at the time of the interview in 2013 (see Table 9.2). Notably, nearly one-half of our respondents had been living in the same place since 1992 (and 20 per cent had been living there since

Table 9.2   How acquired current residence (as of 2013)

	All	Birth cohort		
		1957–64	1965–72	1973–80
State (given home/voucher)	9	13	7	9
Family (moved in with/inheritance)	19	14	20	23
Market (purchase/rental)	24	14	24	33
Other	1	1	1	2
No change (living there since 1992)	46	58	47	34

birth). About one-quarter of our sample are 'market movers', having acquired their current residence through a market transaction since 1992. Among these, the vast majority purchased a home (only about 4 per cent were in private rentals). Another 19 per cent moved with help from their family – by moving into a place that other family members already occupied, or via gift or inheritance. Finally, 9 per cent reported that they were allocated their current housing directly by the state since 1992, as there is a residual although small sector of government redistribution. However, these figures are only for moves since 1992. Of the half of respondents who have not moved since 1992, most received their current housing from the Soviet State.

To further understand market moves, we asked those who purchased their homes what their primary source of finance was. Just over one-half reported that market income (resources from work, savings, or mortgages) was the main source. The remainder relied upon the sale of previous (mainly privatized) housing, help from family and friends, or government subsidies. In short, only about 15 per cent of our sample acquired their current housing via market transactions, using market income (other than capital from sale of privatized homes). The rest acquired their housing, directly or indirectly, from the state or their family.

Our evidence does suggest that market moving is on the rise for younger cohorts. Two-thirds of the youngest cohort had ever moved since 1992, versus only about 40 per cent of the older cohort. And, among those who had ever moved, the younger cohort was more than twice as likely to have purchased a home on the market (33 per cent versus 14 per cent). We expect this trend will continue, as the lack of state support will push young families onto the market. Analysis of all moves observed over the twenty-year period of the study (not shown here due to space considerations) also indicates that market moves are on the rise, particularly among younger cohorts. Nevertheless, moving via the market is still far from a predominant housing experience, even for our youngest respondents;

although they transitioned to adulthood during the post-Soviet period, one-third have yet to move, and another one-third live in homes acquired from state or family.

Mobility Into Ownership

Residential mobility is neither necessary nor sufficient for change in property rights – either in transitions to formal ownership or in transitions to residential independence. Many property rights transitions occur 'in place', primarily due to privatization and changes in household structure (cf. Mandič, 2001). Table 9.3 shows the proportion of transitions to various forms of ownership that happened in place versus through a move. In our sample we observed 624 transitions to private ownership at the household level, 63 per cent of these were achieved without moving, through privatization. In-place moves also predominate for transitions to individual and nuclear family ownership. By contrast, transitions to nuclear family residence mainly involve a move; only one in four of such changes occurs in place (that is, when extended family move out or die). The last row shows the transition to full ownership (exclusive title and residence for nuclear family); three out of four such events happened in place.

In sum, the majority of changes in property rights over the past two decades happened without moving house. This pattern was persistent over time; we did not find significant differences in these trends over the twenty years of the study. As with moves, we can compare the relative weight of state, family, and market in transitions to ownership. We find that state privatization is the primary driver of transitions to ownership, whether measured in terms of ownership by anyone in the respondent's family, by the respondent individually, or by the respondent's nuclear family. Familial reciprocity, by contrast, is the primary driver of transitions to residential

Table 9.3   Mechanisms of property rights transitions

Changes in property rights	Type of transition (row %)		N
	Residential move	In place	
	move	(no move)	
R's family became owners	36.6	63.4	624
R became an owner	32.6	67.4	579
R's nuclear family became sole owners	39.8	60.2	469
R's nuclear family became sole residents	73.2	26.8	462

independence, either through in-place changes in household structure, or through moves to housing already in possession of someone in the extended family. Across all measures of ownership, the market plays only a secondary role in mobility.

CONCLUSION

Despite two decades of market reform, the housing experiences of Russians who entered adulthood just before or after the collapse of the Soviet Union are predominantly a function of state redistribution (privatization) and familial reciprocity (mainly transfer of property rights to privatized homes). Although market transactions occur, access to markets is still more a function of familial support and privatized assets than of typical markers of market position, such as occupation, education, and income. In our previous work, we have described Russia's regime as one of 'property without markets', in which housing is privately owned but only partially commodified (Zavisca, 2008). Markets do matter, but, as long as the mortgage and rental sectors remain underdeveloped, the main determinants of access to markets will be familial support and recirculation of assets from sale of privatized property. Labor market income has limited value in such a system, except for the highest paid workers.

Subjective data bear this out. We asked our respondents how likely they think it is that they will acquire housing in the next three years via help from family, versus via their own means. About 20 per cent think it is at least somewhat likely that they will receive a gift or inheritance of housing from family, and this does not vary by either wages or household income. By contrast, there is a large difference by income in expectations for obtaining housing through the market. The highest quintile of wage earners was twice as likely (30 per cent) as the fourth quintile (16 per cent) and about three times as likely as the bottom three quintiles (ranging from 6 per cent to 10 per cent) to expect to obtain housing via their own means (similar patterns obtain for household income).

We did not ask about expectations of acquiring housing with help of the state, as we assumed that few would have such an expectation, given how drastically the state has scaled back its involvement in the housing sector. However, focus groups we conducted in 2014 for the CHESS study yielded a surprising amount of discussion of strategies for obtaining state assistance with housing, either via waiting lists for direct purchase or allocation of housing from the state, or through subsidized mortgage loans that can be used to purchase homes on the private market. Zavisca (2012, Chapter 3) describes resurgent state attempts to shape the market since 2006, primarily through demonstration programs and associated discourse. Although our survey suggests that very few Russians have received state housing assistance, talk about these programs reaches a broad audience and reinforces expectations that the state can and should provide housing – even as (and perhaps especially because) the Russian economy has entered a new stage of crisis.

The result is a home-ownership regime in which the institutions supporting home ownership conflict with local understandings (Ronald, 2004). The high rate of private ownership does not necessarily provide a meaningful place of one's own; that is, a secure and separate home for the nuclear family. Here we have focused only on property rights in relation to the local meaning of ownership. However, a home is more than property; it is also a locus of family, lifestyle, and stored value (financial and symbolic). Quality and affordability concerns make it difficult for many Russian home owners to carry out practices of place-making that make a dwelling 'homey'. Post-socialist home ownership regimes transferred responsibilities for, as well as rights to, an aging Soviet housing stock. This has created a class of impoverished home owners without the means to maintain their homes in decent condition or to accrue wealth through ownership (Mandič, 2010). All of this calls into question the degree to which, even if property rights are bundled and secure, ownership per se is sufficient to fulfill the broader meaning of having a place of one's own.

Based on our findings for the Russian case, comparative housing scholars should test rather than assume concentration of property rights at the household level. Scholars have identified intra-household inequalities across indicators ranging from consumption to leisure time to subjective wellbeing. Yet surprisingly few consider sub-household variation in ownership of housing assets, particularly in industrialized societies (there is a more work on developing countries; see, for example, Jacobs and Kes, 2015). The extent and consequences of dispersed property rights are likely especially strong in cases like Russia, in which formal titling programs were rapidly overlaid onto existing property relations; policies to formalize title in developing countries have likewise failed to 'unlock' the capital presumed to be inherent in familial housing and land and thus improve welfare (Campbell, 2013; Payne et al., 2009). Better understanding familial property relations could also be useful for understanding the consequences of asset-based housing regimes. Inequalities in asset wealth, particularly across generations, are recognized as a major limitation of such welfare systems (Searle and McCollum, 2014). How wealth is divided, transferred, and extracted within families – across generations, among siblings, and even among couples – matters for inequality in such housing systems.

NOTES

*   The SHER survey was supported by the U.S. National Science Foundation (award no. 1124009). The CHESS survey was supported by the U.S. Army Research Laboratory and the U.S. Army Research Office via the Minerva Research Initiative program (grant no. W911NF1310303). The views reported here do not represent those of the U.S. Army or the U.S. Government.
1.   This section is based on Zavisca's (2012) prior historical and qualitative research.
2.   Only 4 per cent of cases lived in more than three apartments or homes and so had missing data; residential spells in dormitories, barracks, or transient housing are assumed to be of substandard quality and non-private tenure.
3.   Residents of dormitories and barracks are not considered residentially independent, even if they have a room of their own, as they typically share kitchens, bathrooms, and hallways with others. Such situations do not qualify as truly independent housing according to Russian norms. Note that living with roommates in rentals remains rare in Russia; only 3 per cent of CHESS respondents ages 18–30 did so in 2015. See Zavisca (2012) for further discussion of aversion to rentals or roommates.
4.   Not all age groups are observed at all time periods due to the retrospective panel design. We exclude minors under the age of 18, as they had not yet entered adulthood, and also those over the age of 47, because insufficient respondents reached older ages during the course of the study to observe trends over time.
5.   These findings are also consistent with Zavisca's (2012, Chapter 4) analysis of correlates of familial ownership and residential independence based on the Russian Longitudinal Monitoring Survey, which has more limited measures of ownership but draws from a much larger sample.

REFERENCES

Anderson, N. (2015), 'The push for normalcy: financial stress and gender roles in Ukraine', Working Paper, Tucson: University of Arizona.

Buckley, R.M., and E.N. Gurenko (1997), 'Housing and income distribution in Russia: Zhivago's Legacy', World Bank Research Observer, **12** (1), 19–32.

Buckley, R.M., and S. Tsenkova (2001), 'Housing market systems in reforming socialist economies: comparative indicators of performance and policy', European Journal of Housing Policy, **1** (2), 257–289.

Buckley, R.M., K. Cartwright, R. Struyk, and E. Szymanoski (2003), 'Integrating housing wealth into the social safety net for the Moscow elderly: an empirical essay', Journal of Housing Economics, **12** (3), 202–223.

Campbell, P. (2013), 'Collateral damage? Transforming subprime slum dwellers into homeowners', Housing Studies, **28** (3), 453–472.

Chen, W. (2015), 'Gender inequality in wealth: determinants of wife's house ownership in urban China', Working Paper for the Meetings of the RC–28 Research Committee for Social Stratification and Mobility, Philadelphia: University of Pennsylvania.

Cheng, Z., S.P. King, R. Smyth, and H. Wang (2014), 'Housing property rights and subjective wellbeing in urban China', Monash Economics Working Paper 44–14, Melbourne: Monash University.

Cooke, L.P. (2006), '"Doing" gender in context: household bargaining and risk of divorce in Germany and the United States', American Journal of Sociology, **112** (2), 442–472.

Davis, D. (2004), 'Talking about property in the new Chinese domestic property regime', in F. Dobbin (ed.), The Sociology of the Economy, New York: Russell Sage Foundation, pp. 288–307.

Delfani, N., J. De Deken, and C. Dewilde (2014), 'Home-ownership and pensions: negative correlation, but no trade-off', Housing Studies, **29** (5), 657–676.

Dewilde, C., and B. Lancee (2013), 'Income inequality and access to housing in Europe', European Sociological Review, **29** (6), 1189–1200.

Doling, J., and R. Ronald (2010), 'Home ownership and asset-based welfare', Journal of Housing and the Built Environment, **25** (2), 165–173.

Elliott, P., and D. Wadley (2013), 'Residents speak out: re-appraising home ownership, property rights and place attachment in a risk society', Housing, Theory and Society, **30** (2), 131–155.

EMF (European Mortgage Federation) (2013), Hypostat 2013: A Review of Europe's Mortgage and Housing Markets, Brussels: EMF.

Gerber, T.P., and J.R. Zavisca (2015), 'Housing and divorce in Russia, 1992–2013', Conference Paper, Population Association of America Annual Meeting, San Diego, May 2015.

Gudkov, L.D., B.V. Dubin, and N.A. Zorkaia (2011), Molodezh' Rossii. Moscow: Moskovskaia shkola politicheskikh issledovanii.

Heller, M.A. (1997), 'The tragedy of the Anticommons: property in the transition from Marx to Markets', Harvard Law Review, **111** (3), 621–688.

Hulse, K., and V. Milligan (2014), 'Secure occupancy: a new framework for analysing security in rental housing', Housing Studies, **29** (5), 638–656.

Iacovou, M. (2001), 'Leaving home in the European Union', ISER Working Paper Series 2001–18, Colchester: University of Essex Institute for Social and Economic Research.

Jacobs, K., and A. Kes (2015), 'The ambiguity of joint asset ownership: cautionary tales from Uganda and South Africa', Feminist Economics, **21** (3), 23–55.

Kosareva, N., and R. Struyk (1993), 'Housing privatization in the Russian Federation', Housing Policy Debate, **4** (1), 81–100.

Lersch, P., and S. Vidal (2015), 'My house or our home? Entry into sole homeownership in British couples', DemoSoc Working Paper No. 2015–57, Barcelona: Universitat Pompeu Fabra.

Lux, M., P. Sunega, and T. Katrňák (2013), 'Classes and castles: impact of social stratification on housing inequality in post-socialist states', European Sociological Review, **29** (2), 274–288.

Mandič, S. (2001), 'Residential mobility versus "in-place" adjustments in Slovenia: viewpoint from a society "in transition"', Housing Studies, **16** (1), 53–73.

Mandič, S. (2010), 'The changing role of housing assets in post-socialist countries', Journal of Housing and the Built Environment, **25** (2), 213–226.

McKee, K. (2012), 'Young people, homeownership and future welfare', Housing Studies, **27** (6), 853–862.

Payne, G., A. Durand-Lasserve, and C. Rakodi (2009), 'The limits of land titling and home ownership', Environment and Urbanization, **21** (2), 443–462.

Penner, J.E. (1996), 'The bundle of rights picture of property', UCLA Law Review, **43** (3), 711–820.

Polanyi, K. (1944), The Great Transformation: The Political and Economic Origins of Our Time, Boston: Beacon Press.

Ronald, R. (2004), 'Home ownership, ideology and diversity: re-evaluating concepts of housing ideology in the case of Japan', Housing, Theory and Society, **21** (2), 49–64.

Ronald, R. (2008), 'Between investment, asset and use consumption: the meanings of homeownership in Japan', Housing Studies, **23** (2), 233–251.

Rossi, G. (1997), 'The nestlings. Why young adults stay at home longer: the Italian case', Journal of Family Issues, **18** (6), 627–644.

Rosstat (2014), Statistical Yearbook of Russia, Moscow: Statistics of Russia Information and Publishing Centre.

Saraneco, C., and M. Olagnero (2004), 'Quality of life in Europe: first results of a new pan-European survey', Dublin: European Foundation for the Improvement of Living and Working Conditions.

Schwartz, H., and L. Seabrooke (2008), 'Varieties of residential capitalism in the international political economy: old welfare states and the new politics of housing', Comparative European Politics, **6** (3), 237–261.

Searle, B.A., and D. McCollum (2014), 'Property-based welfare and the search for generational equality', International Journal of Housing Policy, **14** (4), 325–343.

Sharipova, D. (2015), 'Who gets what, when and how? Housing and informal institutions in the Soviet Union and Post-Soviet Kazakhstan', Central Asian Affairs, **2** (2), 140–167.

Stephens, M., M. Lux, and P. Sunega (2015), 'Post-socialist housing systems in Europe: housing welfare regimes by default?', Housing Studies, **30** (8), 1210–1234.

Tran, H.A., and E. Dalholm (2005), 'Favoured owners, neglected tenants: privatisation of state owned housing in Hanoi', Housing Studies, **20** (6), 897–929.

Walder, A., and X. He (2014), 'Public housing into private assets: wealth creation in urban China', Social Science Research, **46**, 85–99.

Yemtsov, R. (2007), 'Housing privatization and household wealth in transition', United Nations University World Institute for Development Economics Research (UNU–WIDER), accessed 12 October 2015 at http://www.wider.unu.edu/sites/default/files/rp2007-02.pdf.

Zavisca, J.R. (2008), 'Property without markets: housing policy and politics in post-Soviet Russia, 1992–2007', Comparative European Politics, **6** (3), 365–386.

Zavisca, J.R. (2012), Housing the New Russia, Ithaca and London: Cornell University Press.

Zavisca, J.R. (2013), 'A home not one's own: how young Russians living with extended family navigate and negotiate space', in M. Kusenbach, K. Paulsen, and M. Milligan (eds), Home–Place–Community: International Sociological Perspectives, New York: Peter Lang, pp. 153–174.

10. The changing nature of outright home ownership in Romania: housing wealth and housing inequality

Adriana Mihaela Soaita

INTRODUCTION

This chapter takes a long-term perspective in order to trace the historical construction and persistence of almost universal, outright owner-occupation of housing in Romania. This long-term view assists understanding of the historic centrality of home ownership to household subsistence and welfare in this context. It also helps trace the enduring legacies of historic forms of housing provision to the current characteristics of the housing system that restrict the potential to draw upon this mortgage-free housing wealth as a resource for family welfare in twenty-first-century Romania. The chapter specifically addresses the ways that housing availability and quality, mobility practices and affordability render the outright owner-occupied home as a form of wealth that can be mobilized to provide for family welfare.

The analysis draws on secondary data sources and employs Burawoy's (2015) distinction between the two faces of inequality: *exclusion* and *unequal inclusion*. Regarding the financial possibilities facilitated by home ownership, *exclusion* distinguishes home owners from non-home-owners; while non-home-owners are generally taken to be renters, some institutionalized persons and the homeless, they also include the many individuals living rent-free in complex, family-related households in Romania. *Unequal inclusion* highlights inequalities among owner-occupiers; not only in terms of housing quality and suitability to house-hold characteristics, but also in terms of single- or multiple-dwelling ownership. Theoretically, the more widely home ownership is spread across a society, the higher the inequalities that can be expected among owner-occupiers and the stronger the link between housing and socio-economic inequality.

The history of housing and tenure development in Romania is quite specific, even among the super-home-ownership societies of Eastern Europe (see Clapham et al., 1996). Prior to 1945, Romania was an agrarian state whose deprived peasantry tended to own their homes and small parcels of land. Only 23 per cent of the population was urban (Ronnas, 1984). After the Second World War, Communist governments had embarked on a political project of industrialization resulting in severe everyday consumption shortages, including in housing. Over the Communist period, the urbanization rate increased to 54 per cent and 65 per cent of the population owned their own homes, mostly outright.

After the fall of Communism in 1989, Romania entered another deep, decade-long economic crisis. Gross Domestic Product (GDP) fell drastically in the early 1990s; by 1999, it remained at 75 per cent of its 1989 level. Real wages meanwhile declined by 46 per cent and inflation peaked at 260 per cent (Åslund, 2007). Consequently, about 71 per cent of the population found it difficult to meet their basic needs during this period (Ellman, 2000; UNECE, 2001). In this context of economic upheaval, home ownership and housing privatization took on a particular salience. State-rented housing stock established during Communism was sold to sitting tenants from 1990, increasing home ownership rates from 65 to 95 per cent over the decade (Eurostat, 2016). Additionally, high inflation undermined the burden of these fixed-rate privatization loans and debt to equity ratio, facilitating full repayment in a matter of months. Romania increasingly became a nation of outright home owners. Home ownership functioned as a critical 'shock absorber' in a volatile era of transition that undermined the socioeconomic position of most citizens (Hegedüs and Struyk, 2005).

In contrast to the 1990s, Romanian economic growth in the 2000s was spectacular. Between 2001 and 2008, GDP per capita increased by an average of 7.7 per cent annually; by 2013, it had risen from one-quarter to just over one-half of the European Union (EU) average (NIS, 2014). Macroeconomic growth was followed by an economic recession – when GDP fell by 6 per cent after the Global Financial Crisis (GFC) – but by a relatively good recovery after 2010 (ibid.). In housing, Romania registered its first boom-and-bust housing cycle: values initially increased eleven-fold but later plunged by 54 per cent in real terms (EPS, 2014; Renderman, 2014). Overall, Romania now faces important social challenges, not least income inequality (one of the highest in the EU: Eurostat, 2016). Moreover, the welfare system is far from able to address the extent of poverty. According to EU data, one-quarter of the total population is still poor[1] even after taking social transfers into account (EC, 2015). In this context, inclusion in outright home ownership is critical to household welfare, whereas exclusion drives inequality and impoverishment.

In exploring the emerging role of housing wealth in Romanian socioeconomic and welfare development, this chapter continues in four sections. The first section highlights the two big trade-offs of outright home ownership in Romania, namely pension provision and the working-age benefit system. It also concisely reflects on other possible strategies of mobilizing housing wealth besides the benefits of imputed rents. The second section presents the historic construction of (almost) universal home ownership in Romania since the early 1900s, its persistence during Communism in a decommodified form, and its recommodification after the fall of Communism. In context of these historic outcomes, the third section analyses the ways in which housing availability and quality, mobility practices and housing affordability now render home ownership and housing wealth a possible resource for family welfare. The chapter concludes by arguing that the nature of home ownership in Romania affords passive and reactive approaches, rather than proactive strategies, for mobilizing housing wealth as a source of family welfare.

THE TWO REALLY BIG TRADE-OFFS OF OUTRIGHT HOME OWNERSHIP

Neoliberal policies and fiscal austerity have increased the importance of home ownership as a key compensatory element of shrinking welfare states in many countries, including the post-Communist states (Doling and Elsinga, 2013; Doling and Ronald, 2010a). Certainly home ownership has long been promoted and subsidized by many governments. Given that outright home ownership is generally achieved by the age of retirement in the advanced economies of highly urbanized societies, Kemeny (2005) has emphasized the 'really big trade-off' between home ownership and pension provision, which has been partially confirmed by empirical studies (for example, Delfani et al., 2014). Indeed, the benefit of imputed rents has been an essential financial complement for retirement in Romania.

The Communist pay-as-you-go pension system was maintained during the 1990s transition period. However, given the depressed state of the economy and policies promoting early retirement, pensions decreased in real terms despite a two-and-a-half-fold increase in contributions. By 2000, pensions had more than halved in real value compared to the inadequate 1989 levels, which required family support for most in order to make ends meet. Subsequent pension reforms between 2002 and 2007 increased the value of 3.7 million pensions, particularly those in the bottom 6 percentiles (Mihart and Garoschy, 2009). Only by 2008 did the share of people aged over 65 who were in poverty become similar to that of people aged under 65, at 26 versus 22 per cent respectively (Eurostat, 2016). Critically, however, most households in Romania have benefited from outright home ownership during much of their working-age lives, given that home owner-ship was rarely sourced through mortgages. Although estimates vary, currently only 1 per cent of the total population (and around 2.5 per cent of households) are mortgagees, which is the lowest figure in the EU (Eurostat, 2016). As Romania has devoted some of the lowest shares of GDP to working-age benefits during Communism and after (Eurostat, 2016; Ronnas, 1984; Sillince, 1990), it could be argued that – besides home ownership's 'really big trade-off' with pension provision – there has been a similar trade-off with the social security system. Hegedüs and Struyk (2005) refer to this particular function of home ownership in post-Communist countries as a 'shock absorber': one that has been particularly important in the context of the upheaval of macroeconomic restructuring.

Imputed rents have clearly helped working-age households make ends meet during the post-2008 economic crisis. The 2010 austerity programme, which entailed a 25 and 15 per cent cut across public salaries and social benefits (except pensions) respectively, resulted in poverty patterns being reversed. According to Eurostat (2016), by 2014, 17 per cent of people aged over 65 lived in poverty versus 27 per cent of under 65s (only Spain showed similar trends). Imputed rents obviously help lower the cost of living. However, economists estimated the median of imputed rents in 2010 at €100 to €150 per month in the Czech Republic, Poland, Estonia and Hungary – and, perhaps surprisingly, at only €8 per month in Romania (EC, 2013). This does not mean that rents in Romania's small private rental sector (housing just 1 per cent of the total population) were trivial or that the running costs of housing in the owner-occupied sector were not significant, as we will see later in this chapter.

Besides the passive benefit of imputed rents, long-term growth in house values has intensified academic debates regarding the possibilities for households to draw upon their housing wealth as a resource for welfare (Elsinga et al., 2007; Ronald and Elsinga, 2012). House values increased around eleven-fold between 2000 and 2008 in Romania and, despite subse-quent falls of more than 50 per cent, this mortgage-free wealth remains sig-nificant relative to income (EPS, 2014; Renderman, 2014). As specialized mortgages for equity withdrawal are not available in Romania, housing wealth can be liquidated through downsizing or by renting out a room or additional property. Any of these routes for extracting wealth, however, necessitates higher-than-minimum space standards, location rent, low transaction costs, active housing markets and social norms surrounding active residential mobility. Variation in these complex factors means that the realization of housing wealth is a country-specific practice (Doling and

Elsinga, 2013; Doling and Ronald, 2010a, b; Elsinga et al., 2007; Smith and Searle, 2010; Toussaint and Elsinga, 2009).

For instance, strategic financial planning through practices of upsizing or downsizing have been found to be high in the UK, low in France and Germany and non-existent in Portugal and Hungary. Other proactive strategies, such as low-income owners taking in lodgers, has been a common strategy in Norway but also practised in Sofia and Budapest (Lowe and Tsenkova, 2003). Engaging in landlordism has historically been encouraged in Germany and has also become popular in the UK and Australia in recent decades. However, the private rental sector has always been minute in Eastern Europe, particularly in Romania.

In order to understand the path-dependent ways in which households may access their housing wealth, it is necessary to examine the historic construction of (almost) universally outright home ownership in twenty-first-century Romania, which is the focus of the following section. The section after that considers the implications of these legacies for the ways in which current housing availability and quality, mobility practices and affordability restrict the potential for housing wealth to serve as a resource for family welfare.

THE HISTORIC CONSTRUCTION OF UNIVERSAL OUTRIGHT HOME OWNERSHIP

Pre-1945: An Agrarian Nation of Deprived Smallholders

The idea that asset ownership enables citizens to build up family prosperity, as well as national wealth more broadly, underpinned Abraham Lincoln's 1862 Homestead Act in the US and inspired substantial land reforms elsewhere, including Romania. In 1864, 1921 and 1945, Romanian parliaments enacted the most radical land reforms in Europe in order to tackle poverty among peasantry and thus to enable them to provide for and take care of their families (Cartwright, 1999). The legacies of these historic land reforms are vital to the understanding of the nature of home ownership in Romania during and after Communism.

The 1864, 1921 and 1945 land reforms redistributed (at a cost) about 2 million, 5 million and 1.5 million hectares of arable land, respectively, from the Church, the gentry and the Crown, transforming an impoverished peasantry into smallholders. By 1927, there were 3.8 million holdings in a 17.9-million population, while only 11 per cent of agricultural land was still owned by the gentry (Ronnas, 1984). Strong norms of equal inheritance further widened land ownership among peasantry but also triggered extreme fragmentation. One-half of all smallholdings became too small to facilitate prosperity. The 1948 agricultural census recorded almost universal freehold home ownership in villages. Among 3.15 million households, only 1.3 per cent was landless. Overall, 5.5 million adult peasants – that is, one-half of the adult rural population – were landowners (Ronnas, 1984). Nationalized during Communism (except the housing plots), land parcels were returned in kind to their owners or their heirs after 1990.

The urbanization rate barely reached 23 per cent by 1948, with urban networks consisting of small agricultural and commercial towns where owner-occupation of detached houses predominated (Golopenția and Georgescu, 1948). Even in the capital Bucharest, for instance, Communist authorities only confiscated around 17 per cent of the housing stock on grounds that it was being rented out privately or was 'under-occupied' (Chelcea, 2012). Across rural and urban areas, data thus show almost universal owner-occupation, along with a strong association between an owned home, land ownership and basic subsistence. Anthropological studies have further evidenced that this essential link between home ownership and family subsistence underpinned a strong resistance to paying rent (Bernea, 1997; Cartwright, 1999; Golopenția and Georgescu, 1948; Ronnas, 1984).

1946–1989: Decommodified Home Ownership Under Communism

After the Second World War, Western Europe witnessed a period of economic prosperity and social solidarity, which allowed for the creation of welfare states as redistributive institutions for income and services (Esping-Andersen, 1990). Conversely, beyond the Iron Curtain the quest for industrialization produced economies of shortages that permeated everyday life (Kornai, 1992). Hegedüs and Struyk (2005) have argued that the Communist states of the Eastern Bloc could be conceptualized factually, rather than just ideologically, as a type of welfare regime. However, the idea of welfare Communism is at odds with the hardline Stalinist variant practised in Romania (Kornai, 1992).

The quest for housing decommodification meant that new housing tenures were established; namely, personal ownership and public renting. Unlike private property, personal ownership represented a limited bundle of rights, particularly prohibiting the use of home as an asset. For instance, personal ownership was restricted to one unit of a size matching household characteristics. This could only be inherited by eligible family members; otherwise, it was expropriated and allocated to eligible applicants. Taking in lodgers was intermediated by state institutions and nominal rents applied. Moreover, property could be expropriated by the state at any

Table 10.1   Historic housing provision by source of finance (000s)

	1951– 1960	1961– 1970	1971– 1980	1981– 1985	1986– 1990	1991– 2000	2001– 2010
State	150.3	553.1	1267.7	655.7	no data	79.9	44.6
Households	1143.4	1000.2	324.8	51.3	no data	222.0	367.2
Total	1293.7	1553.3	1592.5	707.0	no data	301.9	411.8

Sources: Soaita (2010); NIS (2016b).

time. Likewise, public renting was restricted to one appropriately sized unit. It offered lifetime secure tenure (which could be inherited) at minimal rent levels, although tenants had to organize and finance maintenance and repairs themselves. Consequently, it can be argued that both tenures offered a quasi-owned home but not an asset (Ronnas, 1984; Soaita, 2010; Turnock, 1990).

The existing owner-occupied housing stock (and their plots) remained in personal ownership, apart from large homes, which were nationalized (Chelcea, 2012). Besides this initial redistribution, access to new housing was decommodified in two different ways: self-building and public supply and allocation. During the 1950s and 1960s, about 80 per cent of all new housing was self-built, particularly in villages (Table 10.1). Self-building was rarely assisted by the state, unlike in neighbouring Hungary and Yugoslavia. Moreover, construction materials were in short supply and finding a plot of land for construction was difficult unless land was already owned by the family (Cartwright, 1999). During this period, Romania produced the highest number of dwellings per 1,000 inhabitants within the Eastern Bloc, despite having the second lowest total capital investment in housing after Albania. Prodigious output under conditions of low investment, however, promoted widespread poor housing quality in terms of the large number of small dwellings produced, the use of substandard materials and poor utility provision. Currently, over 2.1 million houses and 600,000 flats in the Romanian housing stock date from this period (Soaita, 2014). Housing inequality decreased, but mostly at the expense of those who lost (parts of) their homes and the many who, by struggling to self-build, produced a large stock of small homes. The first generation of urbanites able to rent newly built, centrally located flats were, on the other hand, clearly privileged.

Conversely, during the 1970s and 1980s, state-supplied rental flats dominated housing provision when Ceausescu's systematization programme aimed 'to more powerfully homogenize our socialist society' (Lowe, 1992,

p. 224). This meant large reconstruction programmes that involved massive demolitions and an absolute ban on self-building (Sillince, 1990). Housing inequality decreased in cities due to growing stock homogeneity – although flats in the developed city centres were more prestigious – but became more acute between urban and the less provided rural areas. However, rural homes regained their centrality to household subsistence during the 1980s, given that small-scale agricultural production helped compensate for widespread food shortages during the excessive austerity imposed to reimburse the national debt (Ronnas, 1984). Currently, about 800,000 houses and 2.1 million flats date from this period (Soaita, 2014).

In the Yugoslavian context, Mandič and Clapham (1996) showed that, given widespread housing shortages, accessing independent housing was the key concern of most households under Communism. The primacy of getting housed was even more acute in the USSR and Romania, where shortages were higher and alternatives were fewer (Attwood, 2012; Lowe, 1992). Despite more than 5 million homes being built in Romania during Communism, these were inadequate in both number and quality standards. For instance, more than one-third were built of substandard materials (of adobe and wattle-and-daub), only about one-half were provided with sewerage and only about one-third had a gas connection. Occupancy per room remained high, though it fell from 3.6 to 2 persons during the 1970s and 1980s. Thus, while housing conditions did improve, Romania's performance remained one of the poorest in the Eastern Bloc, leaving enduring legacies of poor housing conditions in subsequent decades (Sillince, 1990; Soaita, 2010). Recent Romanian governments have officially recognized housing policy as one of the crimes of Communism, specifically in terms of illegal confiscations and the demolition of thousands of homes, the system of residential visas which tied people to places and the corrupt allocation of state flats (Tismăneanu, 2006).

Post-1990: The Recommodification of Housing

Post-Communist housing reforms have by now been well documented and there is an increasing understanding of the path-dependent similarities and differences between countries (Åslund, 2007; Clapham et al., 1996; Hegedüs and Struyk, 2005; Soaita, 2010). Romanian post-Communist governments embarked on large-scale (re)privatization programmes, which have redistributed industrial, land and housing assets to citizens. The privatization of industry was pursued by distributing free coupons to every citizen over the age of 17, which could be exchanged for shares (Åslund, 2007). The 1991 Land Act enacted the reprivatization of land via in-kind restitution to prior owners of 1949 (or their heirs). This has recreated a fragmented land market, which has nonetheless facilitated the revival of self-building and suburbanization. The privatization of state housing proceeded according to Decree 61/1990, which provided for the unit-by-unit privatization at discounted prices, typically involving down payments and fixed-interest loans administrated by local municipalities. Home ownership increased from 64 per cent in 1989 to 92 per cent by 1994 (and to 98 per cent currently: Eurostat, 2016). Finally, Law 10/2001 provided for the restitution of housing that had been confiscated during the 1945–89 period.

In total, about 15 million adults received privatization coupons. Overall, 14 million land parcels changed ownership into private hands; about 2.2 million state flats were privatized (representing 27 per cent of the housing stock) and about 200,000 claims for housing restitution were recognized for in kind transfer or financial compensation (Stan, 2006; Van Meurs, 1999). In terms of national wealth, it can be appreciated that public-to-private transfers were massive in coupon privatization, followed by land restitution and state housing (re)privatization. However, there were marked capital inequalities within each asset category, which further increased once markets matured (Åslund, 2007).

Subsequent capital appreciation resulted in significant gains for those households who were eligible for land restitution or housing privatization. Housing and land value augmentation was substantial, particularly from the late 1990s to 2008. Even though values have since significantly fallen, they are still impressive. For instance, the real-estate-specialized media agency Imobiliare (2016) reported that agricultural land values outside localities have on average increased three-fold since 2008, with current asking prices ranging from €3,000 to €7,000 per hectare. Comparatively, land values in the suburbs of large cities are only one-half of their 2008 peak, with current asking prices ranging from €25 to €110 per square metre. Likewise, the value of privatized Communist flats was less than one-half of the 2008 peak (EPS, 2014), with current asking prices in large cities ranging from €400 to €1,000 per square metre. Nonetheless, given the typical size of these asset categories, these valuation figures are not trivial – particularly in comparison to the national gross average income of €500 per month (but below €100 for the bottom quartile: NIS, 2016a).

While many homes have thus been turned into assets – and some arguably into liabilities, given the recognized poor quality of much of the housing stock (Mandič and Cirman, 2011) – Table 10.1 shows that few have been built since 1990. The decline in new construction has been dramatic, falling from an annual average of 80,000–100,000 units during the Communist period to around 30,000 during the 1990s. Notwithstanding the economic crisis, yearly output increased to 40,000 after 2008 (EC, 2015). Disregarding the completion of unfinished Communist-period flats, private housing provision represented well over 80 per cent of all new housing, with most being financed with cash. High inflation and land availability have reactivated traditional strategies of self-building. By cutting down construction costs and using incremental financing – sometimes by liquidating privatized assets, often by using remittances and exceptionally by significant 'sweat equity' – households were able to access independent or better housing when affordability in terms of price-to-income ratio was estimated at 4–20 (Hegedüs and Struyk, 2005; Soaita, 2013). After 2000, for-profit developers started to engage in the provision of middle-market condominiums, but (unlike self-building) activity in this submarket plunged after 2008.

Overall, the post-Communist addition to the housing stock now accounts for 11 per cent of total housing, whereas the built legacy of Communism remains dominant, accounting for 75 per cent of stock (Soaita, 2014). Given that Romania entered its post-Communist transformation with acute housing shortages and widespread poor housing quality, and that few new dwellings have been built since, interesting questions arise regarding the extent to which current housing availability and quality, mobility practices and affordability may render homes as wealth generators and housing wealth as a potential resource for family welfare. The following section turns to this.

INEQUALITIES WITHIN AND BETWEEN HOUSING INSIDERS AND OUTSIDERS

Given the universal expansion of outright home ownership – only 1 per cent of the total population are mortgagees (around 2.5 per cent of housholds) – few individuals are overtly excluded from its likely benefits. According to the 2011 Census, those explicitly excluded from home ownership included 96,300 long-term institutionalized persons, 268,000 persons renting in social and some forms of cooperative/religious housing and around 385,000 persons renting privately, with an additional 627,000 persons renting free of charge (NIS, 2016b). Together with an estimated 14,000 homeless individuals, non-owner-occupiers constitute almost 6 per cent of the total population. Conversely, around 93 per cent of the population theoretically benefits from living rent-free as well as mortgage-free in their outright owned homes. Nonetheless, given low GDP per capita and high levels of socioeconomic inequality, such widespread inclusion is necessarily patterned. The most important differentials, which may render homes into assets that can actively be drawn upon, are examined here (see also Figure 10.1).

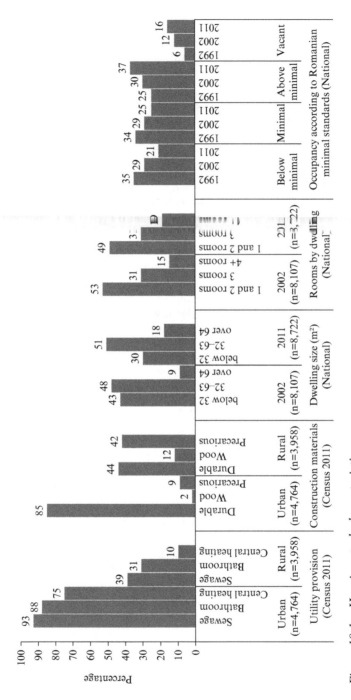

Figure 10.1 Housing stock characteristics

Housing Quality and Availability

Recent improvements in, and diversification of, the housing stock have paradoxically increased both average housing quality and inequality by adding a small top-quality segment, improving conditions for some in the middle section but keeping the bottom sector largely unaltered. Progress in utility development has been evident but slow. For instance, between 2002 and 2011 (NIS, 2016b), the share of all dwellings without an indoor bathroom and sewage disposal fell from 49 to 38 per cent and 47 to 32 per cent, respectively. The share of dwellings without central heating also fell from 64 to 54 per cent (Figure 10.1). In terms of the quality of construction materials, improvement was much slower; for instance, the share of dwellings of wattle-and-daub or adobe only fell by 5 percentage points between 1992 and 2011, still accounting for 20 per cent of all dwellings (37 and 7 per cent in rural and urban areas, respectively). This is not only a rural phenomenon, but rather one characteristic of detached housing in Romania being maintained through new construction. The contrast between the new, large 'villas' of middle- and upper-income households and the 27 per cent of new dwellings built with substandard materials illustrates sharp housing inequality. Remittances and capital gains helped finance much of the former; in this particular sense, (re)privatized land and flats have been actively used as assets for a few to move up the housing ladder (Soaita, 2013). Conversely, the disadvantaged Roma population have financed much of the latter with 'sweat equity' (Fleck and Rughiniș, 2008). Overall, Figure 10.1 clearly shows that the inherited urban–rural divide regarding poor utility provision and construction materials still endures.

As the provision of infrastructure improved (albeit slowly), so too did the availability of habitable space (NIS, 2016b; Soaita, 2014). Through the combined effects of new construction, extensions and demolitions, the share of small-area dwellings fell from 43 to 30 per cent between 2002 and 2011, whereas that of larger ones doubled. However, in terms of number of rooms, improvements in the structure of the stock seem somewhat less significant (Figure 10.1). Notwithstanding the question of housing quality, given the combined effect of the 14 per cent increase in the number of dwellings and 14 per cent population fall between 1992 and 2011, the three censuses recorded an increasing surplus of dwellings compared to the number of households at every administrative level (although the number of households has meanwhile increased by 2 per cent). Nationally, this surplus was 380,000 units in 1992, 701,000 units in 2002 and 1.25 million units in 2011 (NIS, 2016b).[2] However, as Figure 10.1 shows, the number of vacant dwellings increased significantly over each census period, reaching an astonishing 1.4 million units in 2011. This reflected a steady increase in second/holiday home ownership, with only 1 per cent being permanent vacancy. Obviously, increasing second-home ownership indicates that housing space is more unequally distributed. If we ignore this large number of vacant dwellings, however, then there was a corresponding shortage of housing by 95,000 units in 1992, 150,000 units in 2002 and 174,000 units in 2011. While at the 2010s average rate of construction this would only take 5 years to complete, the replacement of the 1.8 million dwellings built of adobe and wattle-and-daub would require an additional 51 years.

Despite this unequal distribution, occupancy levels have improved (NIS, 2016b). Figure 10.1 shows that the share of dwellings occupied below and equal to Romanian Minimal Space and Occupancy Standards – which are experienced as extreme overcrowding and as shortage of space, respectively (Soaita, 2014) – fell for the first time to just below one-half of the housing stock. In 2002, 6 million people consumed less than 8 m^2 of habitable rooms; this fell to 4 million by 2011 (but still represents 20 per cent of the whole population). Moreover, a further 40 per cent of population consumed between 8 m^2 and 15 m^2. The structure of the housing stock, family cycle and income have been key determinants of overcrowding. For instance, in 2011, 49 per cent of all dwellings had only one or two rooms, in which the overcrowding rate was still 66 per cent. Likewise, 51 per cent of all three-roomed homes were overcrowded. Not surprisingly, overcrowding rates were much higher for families with children than for childless households (70 versus 30 per cent, respectively). Comparatively, the effects of income were lower: 66 per cent of the bottom income quintiles versus 40 per cent of the top income quintiles lived in overcrowded homes (Eurostat, 2016).

This widespread shortage of space within owner-occupation – even among the top income quartile – and the poor quality of many homes restricts the potential to liquidate housing wealth for welfare purposes via downsizing without jeopardizing wellbeing, rendering downsizing an option of last resort. Conversely, it can be argued that the 1.5 million dwellings that are 'underoccupied' (generally by one room; that is, having a spare bedroom) and the 1.4 million vacant units may eventually constitute an accessible wealth resource for their owners through lodging, renting out, downsizing or selling off. However, there are several caveats to this apparent reserve of fungible housing wealth, which relate to subjective needs and actual space distribution.

First, qualitative research has shown that the small floor area of most dwellings means that households need at least one room above the Bedroom Standard in order to feel comfortable (Soaita, 2014). Second, the extent to which the quality and location of vacant dwellings enable their use as permanent homes is unclear. Third, there is an underexamined relationship between temporary migration – in terms of underoccupation or 'vacant' housing – and either part of or the whole household working temporarily outside Romania. The high number of vacant dwellings evidenced by the 2011 Census may indeed represent containers of personal belongings and homes to which owners plan to return after periods of temporary migration, rather than an idle, easily accesible source of wealth. Finally, the extent to which those owning vacant or 'underoccupied' homes also have higher financial resources (being therefore less dependent on the liquidation of housing wealth) is also unclear. For instance, out of the 1.4 million vacant dwellings recorded by the 2011 Census, 33,700 were deemed for demolition and 51,000 were permanent homes. Further research is required to illuminate these aspects.

Housing and Mobility

A healthy vacancy rate of around 5 per cent is often considered a necessary condition to facilitate housing mobility, whereas higher levels can indicate imbalances (Hegedüs and Struyk, 2005). The 2011 Census recorded that only 1 per cent of the housing stock consisted of vacant dwellings that were up for rent or sale. Conversely, the existence of 900,000 second homes (10 per cent of the housing stock) points to a cultural preference for intertwining an urban and a rural residence in Romania (Soaita, 2015). While inheritances may have contributed to the growth in second homes, their increasing share in the housing stock draws particular attention to the strengthening of the link between economic and housing inequalities. Indeed, while some individuals can maintain ownership of multiple dwellings, others have no option but to share with their (extended) family. The share of complex non-nuclear family households, including multigenerational ones (with or without unrelated others), has not changed between the last two censuses, accounting for 20 per cent of all households (1.6 million). While this may be a cultural preference or a temporary family strategy for a few, for most individuals it reflects the lack of affordability of individual housing (Soaita, 2012, 2014, 2015). The fact that half of all these complex households lived in overcrowded dwellings is a statement about lack of choice and evidences a concealed form of exclusion from home ownership; that is, from a home of one's own.

Urban-to-rural residential mobility has been symptomatic of the economic difficulties of those unemployed or forced into early retirement. Many of these migrants could no longer afford the high running costs of their privatized flats and instead looked for basic subsistence in increasingly pauperized villages (Mihalache and Croitoru, 2011). Some urban-to-rural migrants sold their privatized flats, but many more moved into parental homes – typically in the countryside – while their children have continued to occupy the former city flats. Residential mobility was also theoretically facilitated by a revival in self-building. Again, many vacated homes were retained as residences for self-builders' children. While self-building may permit later disinvestment, this has not yet materialized. Investment motives have been shown to be non-existent for most self-builders, who aim to build a comfortable family home and, perhaps, a social symbol of distinction (Soaita, 2013).

Overall, residential mobility remained low between 1990 and 2012, with annual rates averaging 15 per 1,000 inhabitants. This means, in crude terms, that one-third of the population changed residence over this period. Eurostat (2016) data show that Romania has had the lowest rate of residential mobility within the EU. Only 1.8 per cent of the population changed residence between 2006 and 2011, which was four and ten times less than the average in Eastern Europe and the EU, respectively. While home ownership was recognized as inducing low residential mobility rates, this view can be disputed, as high Romanian owner-occupancy rates have failed to undermine international migration towards better economic opportunities.

Housing Affordability

Besides a low supply of new dwellings, mobility has clearly been challenged by a lack of affordability. As housing conditions have improved since the Communist period, so have social expectations of owning a home of one's own. Arguably, aspirations have increased at a faster pace than household capabilities of financing them. Indeed, except for those earning high incomes, young people's likelihood of accessing independent housing if not assisted by family has been almost nil over the two decades.[3] Living with parents has been the only option for many young people and families during and after Communism (Mandič, 2008; Sillince, 1990). This resulted in many adult children inheriting in-place home ownership upon their parents' passing (Soaita, 2012).

In order to estimate movements in affordability levels since 1990, I will use the measure of house-price-by-income ratio and focus on the housing type more likely to attract low- to middle-income entrants to home ownership: that is, privatized Communist flats. Little is known either about the 'affordability' conditions during the 1990s privatization (given the highly volatile macroeconomic environment) or subsequent movements. House price indexes are recent in Romania; the EPS (2014) index reports national values since 2005, the Renderman (2014) index reports asking prices in Bucharest since 1996 and the Institute of National Statistics

Table 10.2   Average affordability in a typical Communist estate in the city of Pitesti

Year	Studio (average)	1-bed flat (average)	2-bed flat (average)	Gross national annual income	Affordability ratios
2000	€2,700	€5,500	€7,000	€1,350	2.0 – 4.1
2008	€30,000	€60,000	€80,000	€5,600	5.4 – 10.7
2014	€21,400	€33,200	€44,000	€6,300	2.6 – 5.3

Sources: House values: Imobiliare (2016), Soaita (2010); income: NIS (2016a). Exchange rate: €/RON 5 4.44 (2014) and 3.68 (2008); $/€/leu 5 21,700 leu (2000) by BNR.

index was not initiated until 2010. However, my own research in a typical Communist estate in a second-tiered, economically successful city offers some interesting insights (Soaita, 2010, 2015).

State housing was privatized at nationally set prices ranging from 57,000 to 400,000 leu, depending on flat size and construction period.[4] Based on the minimal Romanian occupancy standards,[5] price-to-income ratios were between 2.5 to 4 in 1990 and 1991 (but state loans at fixed-interest rates were provided). High inflation improved affordability to between 1 to 3 between 1992 and 1993 and later super-inflation watered down the debt. Subsequent house price movements in the emerging markets were not documented but by 2000 were relatively similar to those in 1990/91 (Table 10.2). In the 2008 peak, however, average house-price-to-income ratios ranged from 5 to 11, given that values increased eleven-fold in the 2000–08 period. Table 10.2 shows the housing crash improved affordability as prices continued to fall year on year to a cumulative 54 per cent and income increased on average by 12 per cent (EC, 2015). In Bucharest, the house-price-to-income ratios for the two-roomed flat market (rather than within the submarket of Communist period flats; Renderman, 2014) ranged from 3.7 to 7 in 2000, peaked at between 9 to 17 in 2008 and fell to between 4.5 to 9 by 2014. Such constrained affordability levels indicate that overcrowding is likely to continue as a strategy of financing entrance to home ownership. However, to a large extent these affordability ratios remain theoretical in the case of Romania – not only because of unavailable or uncompetitive mortgage markets, but also (and chiefly) because little disposable household income remains available after paying for basic goods and utilities charges (Eurostat, 2016; UNECE, 2001).

Indeed, between 2008 and 2014, the share of households that paid more than 40 per cent of their disposable income on housing costs fell from 18 to 14 per cent among outright owner-occupiers and from 73 to 32 per cent among private tenants (one per cent of total population); conversely, the share increased from 15 to 31 per cent among mortgagees (1 per cent of total population) (Eurostat, 2016). While these figures may not seem particularly dramatic in comparison with those in other EU countries, it should be remembered that they are reported for a housing stock owned outright, almost one-half of which is overcrowded. Unsurprisingly, income is the most significant determinant of very high housing costs (taking more than 40 per cent of household disposable income). Indeed, in 2014, 43 versus 3 per cent in the bottom and top income quintiles respectively faced difficulties in paying housing costs. Meanwhile, 34 per cent of single-person households were affected. Overall, 30 per cent of the whole population were in arrears for housing costs (utility bills, rents or mortgages), which situates Romania among the top five within the EU in this respect (Eurostat, 2016). High housing running costs and pressure from long-deferred maintenance may thus cast the owned home as a liability rather than an asset, just as it may increasingly become an hazardous place to live in for many owner-occupiers (Mandič and Cirman, 2011).

Market-price differentials now capture divisions in real or perceived housing quality. For instance, Communist flats built before the 1977 earthquake face a price penalty of about 10 per cent compared to those built after standards improved. Likewise, centrally located flats can be twice as expensive as those located in peripheral estates. Conversely, the newly built flats face a price premium of about 10 to 20 per cent compared to Communist-era flats (Imobiliare, 2016). Improvements in the housing stock have become a testimony to the social standing of their residents. For instance, the conspicuous difference between a few totally thermal-retrofitted blocks and the many mosaic-patched or timeworn façades tell a tale of economic differentiation between home owners while also signalling out economically depressed towns, neighbourhoods, blocks or flats whose residents can hardly afford to run their homes.

CONCLUSIONS

This chapter has taken a long-term perspective in order to examine the implications of historic forms of housing provision for the current characteristics of the housing stock – and, correspondingly, for the potential of home ownership to form a base for household welfare. It has particularly focused on the ways in which housing availability and quality, mobility practices and housing affordability may render the owner-occupied home as a form of wealth that could be used passively (imputed rents) or mobilized reactively (sharing; overcrowding), proactively (letting; lodging) or strategically (upsizing; downsizing; self-building) in order to provide for family welfare.

First, I argued that successive and extensive land reforms had transformed the agrarian country of Romania into a nation of smallholders prior to the imposition of Communism, when the owned house, together with its plot, formed a core base for household welfare. This reactive role of rural home ownership persisted during Communism. Personal ownership of a rural home was central to basic subsistence, with small-scale agricultural production helping to compensate for widespread food shortages, particularly during the 1980s. Housing was further decommodified and rationed in order to eradicate its usage as an asset. Widespread quasi-owner-occupation not only persisted but also – paradoxically – was strengthened, given the large numbers of self-built homes constructed during the first two decades of Communism and the secure public tenancies in the many urban flats built in the last two decades of Communism (the 1970s and 1980s). Nonetheless, and despite prodigious output, severe housing shortages persisted, leading to extensive and acute overcrowding. Housing served as a place of home, the urban or rural location of which could (or could not) connect households to services and opportunities, which were exclusive to cities. Owned or rented, housing costs were nominal. However, using Burawoy's (2015) distinction, this universal inclusion into quasi-home-ownership was achieved at the cost of significant insider inequalities; these include the struggle to get housed by self-building, poor housing quality, widespread overcrowding and rural isolation.

Second, these enduring legacies of Communism have remained broadly unchallenged in twenty-first-century Romania, as have the commonly passive ways in which home ownership contributes to household welfare. Upon the legal reinstatement of private property rights, which have formalized existing occupancy norms, the mortgage-free home played the passive role of a 'shock absorber' for those who lost their jobs, were forced into early retirement or whose income just covered basic subsistence during the prolonged 1990s crisis. Notwithstanding the poor condition of many dwellings, outright home ownership (and other redistributed assets) helped to compensate households' welfare shortfalls, commonly by staying put rather than changing residence. This also meant that markets have been slow to emerge.

Third, post-2000 economic growth has energized emerging housing markets. Home values increased eleven-fold between 2000 and 2008, but subsequently fell by more than 50 per cent to 2015. Given low residential mobility and almost universal outright home ownership, for most home owners these house price movements represented merely virtual gains and losses. Notwithstanding the fall in house values, significant wealth is now required in order to access independent or adequate housing, which precludes many socioeconomic groups from obtaining adequate space, let alone a space of their own – despite the fact that population decline has reduced housing pressures during the last two decades. A lack of affordability precluded household mobility, but so did a historic housing stock of very small dwellings, an increasing share of second homes and – the latter excluded – persistent shortages.

Finally, the analysis evidenced that the benefits of imputed rents in outright home ownership have remained central to household subsistence for many – particularly for individuals in the bottom income quintile and single-person households. For a majority of these people, despite living mortgage- or rent-free, housing running costs account for more than 30 per cent of income. The passive benefit of home ownership as a complement to income through rent-free living was also used reactively (sometimes perhaps also strategically) by engaging in complex household formation and overcrowding (or both). It could be argued that the owner-occupied home was used reactively by one in every five households, which have resorted to complex multigenerational arrangements within the extended family, likely because of lack of affordability or viable alternatives. Likewise, the owned home was often used reactively by those home owners living in overcrowded conditions, in homes of substandard construction materials and with poor utility provisions. For these, liquidating housing wealth by downsizing may represent an option of last resort that would likely lead them into material depravation.

Nonetheless, lack of affordability for young people has intensified prolonged stays in the parental home as well as active family-based housing strategies. Besides sharing, there has been a purposeful engagement in self-building in order to accommodate extended families or gift children the vacated home (or both), deeper engagement in practices of parental urban-to-rural residential mobility and international migration as a means of financing new homes. While these active strategies focus on providing a family home, they also (indirectly) create assets, the future mobilization of which remains to be seen.

While income correlates somewhat with the ways in which a home is occupied, the prevalence of poor-quality housing and significant levels of overcrowding do not yet afford the proactive exploitation of the owner-occupied house for most Romanians. Nonetheless, for some, housing assets have provided more than just a means to get by. More proactive strategies included becoming a landlord in the very small Romanian private rental sector (of which little is known), self-developing large houses or buying a second home. While more research is needed to understand the particular features of these phenomena, it can be argued that housing is not *driving* but rather increasingly *mirroring* economic inequality in Romania. Moreover, given robust legacies of decommodified access to outright owner-occupation and its transmission down family generations, it could be argued that outright home ownership still moderates broader economic inequalities – even though it commonly does so at the expense of poor, sometimes hazardous housing conditions.

NOTES

1. Based on the EU poverty threshold of below 60 per cent of median equivalized income.
2. There are methodological differences between the 2011 Census and previous censuses, including that Romanian citizens living abroad for longer than twelve months were no longer recorded.
3. Governmental programmes also helped; for example, 139,000 loans were guaranteed during 2009–2015 (with an average loan of €38,000).
4. 1990/1993 change: annual inflation rates rose from 5 to 256 per cent, net average monthly income from 1,800 to 61,000 leu and US$/leu exchange course from 22 to 760 (Soaita, 2010).
5. One-roomed flat/one income; two-roomed flat/one income; two- or three-roomed flat/ two incomes.

REFERENCES

Åslund, A. (2007), How Capitalism Was Built: The Transformation of Central and Eastern Europe, Russia and Central Asia, Cambridge: Cambridge University Press.

Attwood, L. (2012), 'Privatisation of housing in post-soviet Russia: a new understanding of home?', Europe–Asia Studies, 64 (5), 903–28.

Bernea, E. (1997), Spatiu, Timp si Cauzalitate la Poporul Roman, Bucuresti: Humanitas.

BNR (Banca Națională a României) (2016), Cursul de schimb: Serii zilnice, medii lunare și anuale [Exchange rate: daily, monthly and annual series], accessed 1 February 2016 at http://www.bnr.ro/Cursul-de-schimb-3544.aspx.

Burawoy, M. (2015), 'Facing an unequal world: 2014 presidential address', Current Sociology, 63 (1), 5–34.

Cartwright, L.A. (1999), 'Implementing land reform in post-communist Romania', PhD thesis, Warwick: University of Warwick.

Chelcea, L. (2012), 'The "housing question" and the state–socialist answer: city, class and state remaking in 1950s Bucharest', International Journal of Urban and Regional Research, 36 (2), 281–96.

Clapham, D., Hegedüs, J., Kindrea, K., Tosics, I. and Kay, H. (eds) (1996), Housing Privatization in Eastern Europe, London: Greenwood Press.

Delfani, N., De Deken, J. and Dewilde, C. (2014), 'Home-ownership and pensions: negative correlation, but no trade-off', Housing Studies, 29 (5), 657–76.

Doling, J. and Elsinga, M. (2013), Demographic Change and Housing Wealth: Home-owners, Pensions and Asset-based Welfare in Europe, London: Springer.

Doling, J. and Ronald, R. (2010a), 'Home ownership and asset-based welfare', Journal of Housing and the Built Environment, 25 (2), 165–73.

Doling, J. and Ronald, R. (2010b), 'Property-based welfare and European homeowners: how would housing perform as a pension?' Journal of Housing and the Built Environment, 25, 227–41.

EC (European Commission) (2013), 'The distributional impact of imputed rent in EU–SILC 2007–2010', Methodologies and Working Papers, Luxembourg: European Commission.

EC (European Commission) (2015), 'Macroeconomic imbalances, country report: Romania 2015', European Economy, Brussels: European Commission.

Ellman, M. (2000), 'The social costs and consequences of the transformation process', Economic Survey of Europe, 2/3, 125–44.

Elsinga, M., deDecker, P., Teller, N. and Toussaint, J. (eds) (2007), Home Ownership Beyond Asset and Security: Perceptions of Housing Related Security and Insecurity in Eight European Countries, Delft: IOS Press BV.

EPS (Eurobank Property Services) (2014), 'Indicele Rezidential, Trimestrul 2, 2014 Romania', Bucharest: EPS.

Esping-Andersen, G. (1990), The Three Worlds of Welfare Capitalism, Cambridge: Polity Press.

Eurostat (2016), 'Income and Living Conditions', accessed 1 February 2016 at http://ec.europa.eu/eurostat/web/income-and-living-conditions/data/database.

Fleck, G. and Rughiniş, C. (eds) (2008), Come Closer: Inclusion and Exclusion of Roma in Present Day Romanian Society, Bucharest: Human Dynamics.

Golopenția, A. and Georgescu, D.C. (1948), 'Populatia Republicii Populare Romane la 25 Ianuarie 1948', Bucuresti: Institutul National de Statistica.

Hegedüs, J. and Struyk, J.R. (eds) (2005), Housing Finance: New and Old Models in Central Europe, Russia and Kazakhstan, Budapest: Open Society Institute.

Imobiliare (2016), 'Real Estate News', accessed 1 February 2016 at http://www.imobiliare.ro/info/.

Kemeny, J. (2005), '"The really big trade-off" between home ownership and welfare: Castles' evaluation of the 1980 thesis, and a reformulation 25 years on', Housing, Theory and Society, 22 (2), 59–75.

Kornai, J. (1992), The Socialist System: The Political Economy of Communism, Oxford: Oxford University Press.

Lowe, S. (1992), 'Romania: an introduction', in B. Turner, J. Hegedüs and I. Tosics (eds), The Reform of Housing in Eastern Europe and Soviet Union, London: Routledge, pp. 218–29.

Lowe, S. and Tsenkova, S. (eds) (2003), Housing Change in East and Central Europe: Integration or Fragmentation?, Aldershot: Ashgate.

Mandič, S. (2008), 'Home-leaving and its structural determinants in western and eastern Europe: an exploratory study', Housing Studies, 23 (4), 615–37.

Mandič, S. and Cirman, A. (2011), 'Housing conditions and their structural determinants: comparisons within the enlarged EU', Urban Studies, 49 (4), 777–93.

Mandič, S. and Clapham, D. (1996), 'The meaning of home ownership in the transition from socialism: the example of Slovenia', Urban Studies, 33 (1), 83–98.

Mihalache, F. and Croitoru, A. (2011), Mediul Rural Românesc: Evolutii si Involutii, Bucuresti: Expert.

Mihart, O. and Garoschy, D. (2009), Evolutia Sistemului National de Pensii, Bucuresti: CNPV.

NIS (National Institute of Statistics) (2014), 'Indicatori statistici de dezvoltare durabila', Institutul National de Statistica Bucuresti, accessed 1 February 2016 at http://www.insse.ro/cms/files/Web_IDD_BD_ro/index.htm.

NIS (National Institute of Statistics) (2016a), 'Castiguri salariale din 1991', Institutul National de Statistica Bucuresti, accessed 1 February 2016 at http://www.insse.ro/cms/ro/content/castiguri-salariale-din-1991-serie-lunara.

NIS (National Institute of Statistics) (2016b), 'Census of population and dwellings: RPL 1992, 2002 and 2011', Institutul National de Statistica Bucuresti, accessed 1 February 2016 at http://colectaredate.insse.ro/phc/public.do?siteLang=ro.

Renderman (2014), 'Index Imobiliar', accessed 1 February 2016 at http://index imobiliar.blogspot.ro/p/evolutie-1996-prezent.html.

Ronald, R. and Elsinga, M. (eds) (2012), Beyond Home Ownership: Housing, Welfare and Society, Abingdon: Routledge.

Ronnas, P. (1984), 'Urbanization in Romania: a geography of economic and social change since independence', PhD thesis, Stockholm: Stockholm School of Economics.

Sillince, J. (ed.) (1990), Housing Policies in Eastern Europe and Soviet Union, London: Routledge.

Smith, J. Susan and Searle, A.B. (eds) (2010), The Blackwell Companion to the Economics of Housing: The Housing Wealth of Nations, New York: Blackwell.

Soaita, A.M. (2010), 'Unregulated housing privatism', PhD thesis, London: King's College London.

Soaita, A.M. (2012), 'Strategies for in-situ home improvement in Romanian large housing estates', Housing Studies, 27 (7), 1008–30.

Soaita, A.M. (2013), 'Romanian suburban housing: home improvement through owner-building', Urban Studies, 50 (10), 2084–101.

Soaita, A.M. (2014), 'Overcrowding and "under-occupancy" in Romania: a case study of housing inequality', Environment and Planning A, 46 (1), 203–21.

Soaita, A.M. (2015), 'The meaning of home in Romania: views from urban owner-occupiers', Journal of Housing and the Built Environment, 30 (1), 69–85.

Stan, L. (2006), 'The roof over our heads: property restitution in Romania', Journal of Communist Studies and Transition Politics, 22 (2), 180–205.

Tismăneanu, V. (2006), 'Raport final', Bucuresti: Comisia prezidentiala pentru analiza dictaturii comuniste din Romania.

Toussaint, J. and Elsinga, M. (2009), 'Exploring "housing asset-based welfare": can the UK be held up as an example for Europe?', Housing Studies, 24 (5), 669–92.

Turnock, D. (1990), 'Housing policy in Romania', in J.A.A. Sillince (ed.), Housing Policies in Eastern Europe and Soviet Union, London: Routledge, pp. 135–69.

UNECE (United Nations Economic Commission for Europe) (2001), Countries Profiles on the Housing Sector: Romania, Geneva: UNECE.

Van Meurs, W. (1999), 'Land reform in Romania: a never-ending story', South-East Europe Review, 2 (99), 109–22.

Epilogue   Housing wealth and welfare: spatially and temporally contingent

John Doling

INTRODUCTION

As the authors of one of the chapters in this volume remind us (Bengtsson, Ruonavaara and Sørvoll), almost 40 years ago Jim Kemeny argued that there was a conventional model – engendered in western, English-speaking countries – that espoused the virtues of home ownership. During the decade or so that followed there was an active debate in the housing studies literature about the usefulness of tenure, and specifically the term 'home ownership', as a basis for comparative study (see, for example, Ruonavaara, 1993). Central to the debate was a criticism that, whereas most studies implicitly assumed an 'elision between taxonomic and substantive collectives' (Barlow and Duncan, 1988, p. 221), home ownership was actually temporally and spatially contingent.

Notwithstanding the now increased orientation toward explicit comparative research and publications, similar criticisms could be levelled against the recent literature concerning the linking of housing wealth and welfare, especially through the label 'asset-based welfare'. A conventional model – one might say 'stylized fact' – has also developed here, based largely on developments in western, English-speaking countries. This sees asset-based welfare in the context of first a growth of home ownership – to around 70 per cent of households – and second a neoliberal-driven individualization of societies and welfare restructuring that together place more emphasis on those with housing wealth to literally draw on their own assets to meet their welfare needs. Further, the conventional view incorporates the significance of a growth in housing finance to facilitate activity in the four stages, identified by Köppe and Searle (in this volume), of acquiring, managing, using and transferring housing wealth. Arguably, this model is also temporally and spatially contingent.

The chapters of the present volume collectively challenge the conventional model to submit, as Norris (in this volume, p. 55) demands, to the need for a 'more nuanced reading' of housing and asset-based welfare. Because it is a collection of independently conceived and written chapters, it is impossible for this edited volume to provide a comprehensive account, but it does offer selective illustrations of the experiences of a sample of individual countries. These illustrations are organized under three headings: the growth and development of national home-ownership sectors; the intended links between housing wealth and welfare; and the actuality of property asset-based welfare.

THE DEVELOPMENT OF HOME-OWNERSHIP SECTORS

The nuances begin with the very different sizes, characters and roles of home ownership as an asset. In the cases of Russia and many of the post-socialist countries of Eastern Europe, the last decade of the twentieth century was characterized by one-off, rapid and large-scale transformations of their housing systems as former state-owned housing, often in the form of large apartment blocks, was privatized (Zavisca and Gerber; Mandič and Mrzel; and Soaita, in this volume). The resulting so-called 'super home ownership' societies contain large proportions of asset-rich, income-poor households – although relative to households in most Western European countries, both assets and incomes are on average low. Moreover, because the incomes of younger people are often low, and with a dearth of housing for sale within their means, many young people are effectively forced to live with their parents. In contrast, the home ownership rate in the former East Germany – also, of course, one of the post-socialist societies – increased from just under 30 per cent in 1990 to only about 42 per cent by 2012 (Kolb and Buchholz, in this volume). This increase has been especially located among younger cohorts. Home ownership in Western European countries also varies widely. For example, the rate in the former West Germany has crept up in recent decades, but remains at only about 50 per cent and is disproportionately the preserve of higher-income groups (Kolb and Buchholz, in this volume).

THE INTENDED LINKS BETWEEN HOUSING WEALTH AND WELFARE

Actually, even before the popularity in the housing studies literature of the concept of asset-based welfare, it was common for a link to be seen between home ownership as an asset and the protection of citizens; in other words, housing wealth as an element of welfare. In the case of the post-socialist countries, the post-socialist transition generally involved the dismantling of the pre-existing systems of welfare with their universal entitlements, invoking greater reliance on non-state solutions, especially solutions involving the extended family. In these circumstances, the housing reforms were commonly and explicitly viewed as a means of providing a buffer against unemployment and meeting the needs of older people. As Zavisca and Gerber argued in their chapter on Russia, the 'aspiration was to create the foundation for an "asset-based" welfare regime in which housing wealth becomes a basis for welfare over the life course' (p. 214).

In the case of Ireland, the linking of home ownership to welfare happened even earlier. In much of the literature, there is an assumption that Ireland developed similarly to other English-speaking countries, and thus conforms to the conventional model. But rather than a neoliberal project, the growth of home ownership through the twentieth century was fuelled by deep state interventions and redistribution. The result was a high home-ownership rate across all income groups, that was based on rather socialist foundations that promoted home ownership as part of the assurance of people's welfare. This progressive form of redistribution of land and property rights was seen as a way of protecting low-income families (Norris, in this volume).

In contrast to both some of the post-socialist countries and Ireland, among the Nordic countries of Norway and Finland, asset-based welfare has only recently – since the onset of the Great Financial Crisis (GFC) – entered the policy vocabulary; not so much in the form of significant policy developments, but more in terms of recognitions that home owners have a major asset. In Sweden, the debate has not yet reached this level (Bengtsson, Ruonavaara and Sørvoll, in this volume).

THE ACTUALITY OF PROPERTY ASSET-BASED WELFARE

Whatever the apparent intentions of national policy makers, many of the chapters in this volume present examples of countries in which their models of asset-based welfare have not involved large-scale equity release by, for example, moving down market or reverse mortgage products. In Russia, the architects of the housing reforms did actually intend something like this, hoping that privatized housing would act as a form of wealth that households would extract in order to use as a deposit on a more expensive house, or as income. In practice, a financialized housing market has not emerged; the housing finance sector remains small and most house purchases are cash-driven. In part, this is also the consequence of the way in which housing was privatized, with ownership being transferred in equal shares to all registered occupants, which in many cases resulted in houses being owned as 'family estate'. One result is that homes may not necessarily be sold or refinanced without the permission of all owners, whether currently occupying or not. Likewise, in many other post-socialist countries housing is occupied by parents and adult children with ownership passed through the generations; this appropriately enables people to live with low housing costs, but housing equity is not mobilized in order to fund welfare.

Northern Ireland provides another, but quite different, example. Here, the emphasis on the home as a family resource was not as marked, resembling more the situation in the United Kingdom (UK). But the large decline in house prices after 2007 brought to an end any notion of the home as a liquid asset; rather, it reinforced the importance of the use value of housing, protecting from economic downturns by virtue of access to cheap housing (Wallace, in this volume).

SOME CONCLUSIONS

So, what general conclusions can be gleaned from these illustrations about home ownership as the foundation of asset-based welfare? First, as a policy objective as well as a real-world outcome, home ownership has contributed to asset-based welfare in many countries represented in this volume. Indeed, in many cases, it is clear that its origins actually predate much of the literature. Accordingly, it seems reasonable to conclude that – notwithstanding the limited range of the country-origin and country-orientation of the bulk of the literature on which the conventional model is located – property asset-based welfare does indeed have general relevance to the point of becoming a corollary or general attribute of home ownership.

Second, notwithstanding the general relevance, it is also clear from the country cases in this volume that the way in which the asset in home ownership is used – and with it the welfare gain – is often limited. The literature has identified two contributions derivable from home ownership: income in kind (in the form of rent-free or cheap housing that may protect owners from unemployment or limited pensions) and income in cash (if some or all of the equity is released in order to contribute to household expenditure). In many of the countries represented in this volume, the former has dominated.

One view is that this orientation can be attributed to two, arguably linked, factors. With the exception of Northern Ireland, these countries have – by the standards of the economies in which the conventional model fits – small housing finance sectors. One consequence is that households have limited access to financial products that would facilitate equity release. Whereas this is not the only way in which equity may be released, it is a significant cornerstone of the conventional model. In addition, their welfare models are built around the family; home ownership is a family resource, often to be passed through the generations rather than being realized to meet the needs of one generation. This is largely consistent with Lennartz's chapter (in this volume) and the evidence that the liberal European welfare regimes, plus some other northern European countries, have adopted explicitly asset-based welfare policies as part of strategies to restructure their welfare systems toward a more productive and employment-oriented social policy approach. In contrast, those countries (many in Eastern and Southern Europe) that have continued with more traditional protective functions have also continued with a more traditional, less financialized approach to home ownership.

THE FUTURE OF HOUSING WEALTH AND WELFARE

Given that much of the recognition – in both policy discourse and academic studies – of links between housing wealth and welfare in the form of asset-based welfare has been fairly recent, what of the future? Will home-ownership asset-based welfare become more or less significant?

The first dimension of this issue pertains to housing wealth. Over countries as a whole and over the long run – from the second half of the twentieth century on – house prices have tended to increase (see, for example, Piketty, 2014; Scatigna et al., 2014). As a long-term asset, housing therefore has tended to provide a positive return. Extrapolating from the evidence of the past, there are strong reasons for concluding that house prices in the developed economies will continue to grow. The growth of populations fuelled by net in-migration, the concentration of increasing numbers of people on the finite supply of land in large cities and the growth of economies all point in this direction. As in the past, this does not mean that there will not be downturns in market prices nor that housing wealth will be shared equally across regions and cities, but in general there seems likely to be more, not less, total housing wealth in most developed countries.

But it is by no means certain that housing wealth will continue to be widely devolved through the populations of advanced economies. In many, since at least the start of the present millennium, the average age of first-time entry into home ownership has been increasing, indicating a relative reduction of the flow of households into the sector. The combination of this with the constraints of the GFC means that since 2007, the previous growth trajectory of home ownership has faltered. In some countries, notably the United States (US) and the UK, this has been markedly so; but throughout all the Western European Member States, with the main exception of France, the trajectory has been downward or just about static (Bouyon, 2015). Home-ownership sectors are not only tending to decrease in size; since 2007, they have also become more concentrated at the upper end of national income distributions (Bouyon, 2015), so that there is a general shift towards the ownership of housing wealth, achieved through home ownership, being more limited to those who tend also to have higher levels of non-housing wealth.

A corollary of any reduction in the size of home-ownership sectors has been an increase in the numbers of households that own more than one house. In turn, this can be viewed as a consequence of processes in many advanced economies leading to increasing inequality of wealth and income (see, for example, Piketty, 2014). Increasing inequality has not only affected access to home ownership – dampening demand and reducing the growth toward mass home ownership and the devolution of housing wealth – but also stimulated alternative avenues into housing wealth. The reduction in home-ownership sectors has tended to be matched by increases in private rental housing, again notably in the US and the UK (Lennartz et al., 2015). In a series of related publications (for instance, Paris, 2010), Chris Paris has identified a number of types of second-home owning; for example, as *pied-à-terre* and as holiday homes. There has also been a substantial increase – mostly confined to large, especially capital, cities – in the use of residential property as an overseas investment (Anderlini, 2015; Knight Frank, 2013).

It may therefore be reasonably conjectured that the future in developed economies will be a tendency toward greater concentrations of housing wealth. The more that housing wealth is concentrated in the portfolios of those who are already asset-rich, as opposed to being widely devolved throughout national populations, the less that asset-based welfare can be a viable substitute for state-provided welfare systems.

Finally, there are, of course, national politics and policies supporting – or not – the development of asset-based welfare. As Lennartz's chapter indicates, asset-based welfare developed especially in those countries that were attempting to restructure their welfare policies in a certain direction. In many of these same countries, increases in house prices – which contribute to the attractiveness of housing as the foundation of asset-based welfare – were deliberately fuelled as part of their economic growth models

(Crouch, 2009). Yet, in the aftermath of the Great Financial Crisis and continued concerns in the Eurozone, as well as wider fears of global recession, the future of the sustainability of the neoliberal model that underpinned asset-based welfare is uncertain (see, for example, Mason, 2015; Ostry et al., 2016). The future could conceivably involve less privatization, greater state roles and more redistribution, all resulting in less space for individualized solutions through asset-based welfare.

The future, then, may not be simply more of the same. The present volume highlights a continuing challenge to explore the developing variations in not only home ownership and not only the relationships between home ownership and welfare, but also wider changes in the models of capitalism in which they are located.

REFERENCES

Anderlini, J. (2015), 'Surge in Chinese housebuying spurs global backlash', Financial Times, 25 February, accessed on 8 July 2015 at http://www.ft.com/cms/s/0/fcc2d346-bcd3-11e4-9902-00144feab7de.html#axzz3fEKV3lFv.

Barlow, J. and Duncan, S. (1988), 'The use and abuse of tenure', Housing Studies, **3** (4), 219–231.

Bouyon, S. (2015), Recent Trends in European Home Ownership, Brussels: European Credit Research Institute, accessed 6 July 2015 at http://www.ecri.eu.

Crouch, C. (2009), 'Privatized Keynesianism: an unacknowledged policy regime', The British Journal of Politics and Internationals Relations, **11** (3), 382–399.

Knight Frank (2013), International Buyers in London, London: Knight Frank.

Lennartz C., Arundel, R. and Ronald, R. (2015), 'Younger adults and homeownership in Europe through the global financial crisis', Population, Place and Space. Early view. DOI: 10.1002/psp.1961.

Mason, P. (2015), Postcapitalism: A Guide to our Future, London: Penguin Books.

Ostry, J., Loungani, P. and Furceri, D. (2016), 'Neoliberalism: oversold?', Finance and Development, **53** (2), 38–41.

Paris, C. (2010), Affluence, Mobility and Second Home Ownership, London: Taylor and Francis.

Piketty, T. (2014), Capital in the Twenty-First Century, Cambridge, MA: Harvard University Press.

Ruonavaara, H. (1993), 'Types and forms of housing tenure: towards solving the comparison/translation problem', Housing Studies, **10** (1), 3–20.

Scatigna, M., Szemere, R. and Tsatsaronis, K. (2014), Residential Property Price Statistics across the Globe, Bank of International Settlements Quarterly Review, **September**.

Index